The ABCs of Self-Care

Your Guide to Creating a Happy,
Healthy & More Peaceful Life

SHERI E. BETTS

BALBOA.PRESS
A DIVISION OF HAY HOUSE

Balboa Press books may be ordered through booksellers or by contacting:

Balboa Press
A Division of Hay House
1663 Liberty Drive
Bloomington, IN 47403
www.balboapress.com
844-682-1282

Because of the dynamic nature of the Internet, any web addresses or links contained in this book may have changed since publication and may no longer be valid. The views expressed in this work are solely those of the author and do not necessarily reflect the views of the publisher, and the publisher hereby disclaims any responsibility for them.

The author of this book does not dispense medical advice or prescribe the use of any technique as a form of treatment for physical, emotional, or medical problems without the advice of a physician, either directly or indirectly. The intent of the author is only to offer information of a general nature to help you in your quest for emotional and spiritual well-being. In the event you use any of the information in this book for yourself, which is your constitutional right, the author and the publisher assume no responsibility for your actions.

Any people depicted in stock imagery provided by Getty Images are models, and such images are being used for illustrative purposes only.
Certain stock imagery © Getty Images.

Print information available on the last page.

ISBN: 978-1-9822-7235-7 (sc)
ISBN: 978-1-9822-7236-4 (e)

Library of Congress Control Number: 2021915870

Balboa Press rev. date: 01/07/2022

For all my coaching clients, whose willingness to incorporate more self-care into their lives is an inspiration to everyone they encounter.

CONTENTS

FOREWORD

When Sheri first began talking about her idea for a book on self-care, I hadn't heard the phrase before and asked if this was a real movement or simply a concept used to encourage people to take better care of themselves. After she assured me that self-care was indeed a burgeoning cultural phenomenon, I started to see articles and media mentions about it pop up everywhere. I scoured each one to learn more about it because, like so many women, taking time to care for myself as well as I was taking care of everything and everyone else wasn't even on my radar. I didn't realize it at the time, but I *needed* to take steps to ensure better self-care – and I'll bet you do too.

Although both men and women will benefit from this book, the emergence of self-care comes at a particularly critical time for women. The advent of COVID has exacerbated the degree to which women put their own needs on the back burner. With increased work and home responsibilities, nearly half of the women in one survey reported that stress and worry over the pandemic has impacted their mental health. Yet only 16% of these women sought psychological assistance. Ironically, when you think you have the least time for self-care, that's the precise time when you need it most.

If you've ever felt like you've reached the end of your tether and wondered how you'll find the strength to go on, then this self-care guide can help you. If you stay in unhealthy relationships far too long, then self-care and this book is for you. And if you find yourself experiencing health issues that often have no physical genesis, then self-care and this book is definitely something to check out. But don't confuse self-care with selfishness or self-centeredness. It's neither of those things. Like the well that becomes dry if the pump isn't primed, your physical, emotional, and mental wells require replenishment. Sometimes that comes in the form of taking action to re-fuel yourself and other times it comes in the form of not giving others implicit or explicit permission to drain your well. This book will teach you how to do just that – and so much more.

Drawing on her depth and breadth of experience as an executive coach, Sheri does a masterful job of taking you on a journey of self-exploration where you will identify your own unique self-care challenges and, more importantly, develop a plan to take action to address them. For your sake, for the sake of your family and friends, and for the sake of those you love and who love you, use this book to take control of your life as you never have before. Give it a try. You have nothing to lose and happiness, health, and peace of mind to gain.

Lois P. Frankel, Ph.D.
Author of *Nice Girls Don't Get the Corner Office, Nice Girls Don't Get Rich* and *Nice Girls Don't Speak Up or Stand Out*

INTRODUCTION

Welcome! Are you ready to start living your best life? Okay, that was obviously a rhetorical question. The fact that you've got this book in your hands tells me that you're the type of person who is not content to slog your way toward life's finish line merely *existing*. Good! Me neither!

During my decades of coaching clients, whose reasons for seeking my help ranged from complicated personal challenges to professional leadership issues, the most common denominator in all their lives was a lack of attention to self-care. That's right – *self-care: the practice of taking an active role in protecting one's own well-being and happiness*. Put another way, self-care is *making deliberate choices to protect our mental, emotional, and physical health*. Practicing self-care consistently leads to living a life that is happy, healthy, and peaceful. Too often, we see the obvious signs that we need more self-care in our daily routines: burnout, insomnia, overwhelm, stress, anxiety, fatigue, irritability, lack of interest in activities we used to enjoy, or uncontrollable reactions to situations. And yet we often ignore those signs and keep pushing, striving, and surviving on a heavy diet of numbness and denial. Because denial keeps us safe until we are ready for the truth. It is only the truth that ultimately wakes us up to the better life that awaits us.

Perhaps the truth is that you do okay with self-care yet know deep down inside that your life could be better, so you're open to learning new self-care tools and information. In the coaching world, we call that *having a growth mindset*. People who have a growth mindset take more risks, set higher goals, perform better, and have better relationships. As a result, they also experience less stress, anxiety, and depression. Whether we evaluate our current state as numb or moderately satisfied, we can make different choices to create happier, healthier, and more peaceful lives. We must take better care of ourselves before we hit rock bottom, because it makes it an even tougher struggle to rise like a phoenix from the ashes. We must care enough to keep our cups full on a consistent basis.

My Journey to Self-Care

I've had to rise like a phoenix more than once. It happens to the best of us. Several decades ago, I went through a dark night of the soul that involved crippling depression and anxiety. I wasn't practicing what I was preaching, and it began to show. At the time, I was working as the executive director of a nonprofit, responsible for everything from managing a board of directors made up of high-powered corporate leaders, to replenishing the toilet paper supply. The majority of my work involved bettering the futures of promising young leaders, which added extra stress to my role because I wanted so badly to come through for these gifted up-and-comers. The depth of my own denial was astounding. Once, even during a bout of uncontrollable sobbing, I was unable to admit how much I had ignored self-care in my own life. I just thought I needed a new job! So, I took matters into my own hands and downsized my role. Not surprisingly, that didn't fix the problem. I was still outwardly strong and confident, while inside I was a sniveling mess.

My next avoidance tactic was to blame my geographic location. After all, a recent massive earthquake in Southern California had shaken my house – and my soul – to the core. Surely a change of scenery would fix the deep sense of despair I was keeping hidden within me. So, I moved to New York, leaving both Los Angeles and my nonprofit career behind me. Now on the east coast, I was in a relationship that could lead to marriage with a smart, handsome, athletic bachelor. You see, I had developed uterine fibroids that might ultimately necessitate a hysterectomy, so I felt as if I had a metaphorical countdown clock for reproduction hanging over my head. I wasn't even *close* to accepting the possibility of not having my own biological children one day. I looked to my new home, my new job, and – my new boyfriend to "fix" the deep sense of emotional angst within me. Despite all these big changes, I remained inwardly miserable, unable to recognize the flawed thinking behind my choices – the same flawed thinking, ironically, that I had been helping others to correct in their own lives.

Do you recognize the common thread running through each of the bold actions I took to, *allegedly*, improve my inner state of depression and anxiety? They were all *external* solutions to a deeply *internal* issue. And that issue had deep roots in a lack of commitment to my own self-care. I had spent years, decades even, dedicating my time and talents to caring for and improving the lives of others. Sadly, I put my own needs at the end of the line.

Did I love my new job, love my new state, and marry the love of my life? Ha!

As is often the case when we only address external circumstances while continuing to ignore internal needs, things didn't work out so well. Life, in her infinite wisdom, was going to make sure I learned the lessons of self-care once and for all. First, the executive who'd hired me left the firm and, as a result, I was unceremoniously "outplaced" – from an outplacement firm! Ironic, right? Second, the new relationship led to my spending six years with a man who wasn't ready for marriage. Can you say *bye-bye, childbearing years*? Third, the constant "buzz" of New York City took a toll on my California "Zen" vibe. Then the extreme cold – relative to Southern California – left me challenged with frequent colds and bronchitis. To make matters even worse, my job required being on-call 24/7 for customers and near-nonstop travel, all while under pressure from senior management to drive my team of 21 to stronger performance results. Even taking small breaks throughout my 10 - 12 hour workdays was frowned upon by my increasingly abusive supervisor. Throughout it all, I kept striving to ignore the many micro-aggressions I encountered and to live up to the unrealistic standards I was being held to. Severe migraines joined my still unresolved depression and anxiety, and finally – *finally!* – I hit my breaking point. I left the job, left the boyfriend, and took an entire year to myself to address the internal challenges I had been in denial about for too long. In addition to the depression and anxiety, I now added PTSD to my lineup of ailments – all of which, I believe, could've been avoided had I paid more attention to my needs through a stronger commitment to self-care.

I chose to relocate to San Francisco because I'd always thought it was a beautiful city and it satisfied my need for a warmer climate. (Well, except for the summers. As Mark Twain once joked: *The coldest winter I ever spent was a summer in San Francisco.*) I took another year to simply heal and work on myself, slowly beginning to incorporate some of the self-care habits in this book into my life. I grew a lot during that self-care sabbatical, and I'd love to tell you that I "lived happily ever after" without any further glitches. But we all know the truth of life; It's rarely a straight line of upward progress, is it? And clearly, I had more lessons to learn along my self-care journey.

Thinking I had put hardship behind me and healed my battered psyche, I moved to Philadelphia for a man I was sure was my soul mate and forever partner. Wrong again! And so, I endured yet another painful end to a relationship. Even though I had gained some valuable lessons about protecting myself and making better choices, setting boundaries, and voicing my needs, I obviously *still* had *more* to learn. I believe we keep getting the lesson until we learn it. But hey – that's how it goes with life, right? It's a lifelong process of stumbling, course-correcting, and growing...wash, rinse, and repeat.

Fortunately, with each new cycle of learning we encounter, we get to build upon what we've already learned, taking our challenges and solutions to the next level of evolving as both humans and souls. And I can honestly say, I have no regrets about all I went through because I learned one of the most valuable lessons through it all: the importance of loving myself, of being my own best friend. My deepest internal work had finally yielded the results I didn't realize I'd been looking for all along. I was finally living fully – with or without a partner or biological children. I returned to the geographic location that best suited me and my unique needs – Los Angeles. I made better self-care choices, not just occasionally or when I had time, I made them more of the time. As a result, I continue to create a better version of me, living a happier, healthier, and more peaceful existence.

The optimist in me looks back at those challenging and deeply painful years and believes that they happened for a reason. And that reason was for me to thoroughly understand, through direct experience, the dire importance of taking care of oneself – not just with food, shelter, and clothing, but *all* our needs: physical, emotional, psychological, intellectual, financial, and spiritual. A commitment to self-care can help us address and fulfill these needs as well as our heartfelt desires.

What Self-Care Looks Like

We will likely hear a lot of mentions of *self-love* in discussions of self-care. That's because loving ourselves enough to want what's best for us is the foundation on which self-care is built. In a sense, self-care takes self-love one step further because it's about loving ourselves enough *to treat ourselves better.* Many people mistakenly believe that self-love (and self-care) is the same as pampering – the occasional massage, facial or mani-pedi. Sure, self-care can include these activities. In fact, they are a great way to reward yourself, celebrate wins, or focus on grooming. Although temporary, they can be a way to self-soothe when we need it. However, in its truest form, self-care is about *demonstrating love for ourselves with consistent actions and choices. Choice* is a mainstay of self-care. Simone Biles, most decorated American gymnast, modeled this for us when she chose her own well-being over medals by pulling out of gymnastic competitions during the Tokyo Olympics held in 2021. She didn't let the chance at more external validation "win" over the need to protect her mental, emotional, and physical health. Making smart choices like this for ourselves will get easier the more we move beyond the behavior patterns and stories we've told ourselves for years. They keep us trapped in a victim role, and who wants to be the victim in their own life story? Not one person.

The kind of self-love I hope to help us each develop becomes a protective force field against disrespect, intimidation, prejudice, and other bad behaviors of others, while simultaneously strengthening the important relationships in our lives. This sort of self-love demands that those who wish to come into, or remain in, our lives treat us with respect, love, dignity, and support – all of which we will reciprocate. It also teaches us how to communicate in a way we'll be heard. Ultimately, however, we will each determine for ourselves what our current needs are and what self-care habits are most appropriate given our circumstances at any given time. Sounds good, right?

Committing to Self-Care

Committing to self-care isn't simply a matter of power-reading a book to hopefully absorb its concepts. Theory alone isn't enough. We must put theory into *practice*. Practice means engaging in new behaviors over and over to create a new and healthier behavior or habit. These new behaviors and habits should, in general, strive to eliminate major sources of stress, anxiety and worry (SAW) in our lives. This is the mantra of a dear friend. Self-care is more of an art than a science because what makes one person stressed, anxious or worried is not necessarily the same for another person. This is where the *art* of self-care comes into play: determining through reflection, and then trial and error, what the most suitable self-care tools and techniques are for your unique self. And because self-care, in all its many versions, boosts our mood and reduces stress, it's well worth the effort. A daily commitment to self-care can decrease illness and accidents, improve overall wellness, increase career satisfaction, remove toxic people from our lives, and even help us eat more healthfully. Given all these positive implications, shouldn't self-care be high, if not highest, on our list of daily priorities? Shouldn't we spend most of our waking hours with a self-care mindset? Absolutely! And yet...it doesn't usually work out that way.

Why? Because most of us need to work for a living, in addition to having other responsibilities that preclude us from focusing exclusively on self-care. Fair enough. We may also engage in self-sabotage that keeps us stuck in a holding pattern of suffering. Therefore, to develop a consistent self-care practice, we must make deliberate choices throughout each day – choices that protect us from the inevitable wear and tear of life and support us in making self-care improving decisions. And to do this, we must become aware of our needs.

Being aware of our needs isn't always easy, especially for women. We've been socialized to be a caretaker, often to the point of martyrdom. The belief that it is "noble" to take better care of others than we do of ourselves may have been instilled in us – even to the point of our own personal decline. I've had many clients over the years tell me that they get immense satisfaction from giving to others. In fact, most spiritual practices and religious tenets promote this idea. And that's great! But giving until our metaphorical cup is empty means there's nothing left to quench our *own* thirst. And that does no one any good. I admit, this was one of the toughest obstacles early in my own quest to develop a self-care mindset – namely, learning to overcome the shame or guilt I felt whenever I made a self-care choice. Trust me – it got easier! Don't be discouraged if you face some internal resistance as you embark on your self-care journey. You too can become more comfortable with making self-care choices – one healthy behavior at a time, one self-care ABC at a time – until it becomes second nature.

One common misperception about self-care is that it means being *selfish*, that committing to self-care means we're only focused on our own interests and needs, regardless of the needs of others.

Not true! However, many of us have the scales tipped so far on the side of putting others' needs and wants ahead of our own that we may have to be a bit more self-*focused* to develop a self-care routine. And that isn't selfish, it's prudent. Having no regard for our own needs means our own lives will suffer. Self-care depends on prioritizing our own needs to the same degree that we prioritize the needs of those we care about. This may require a bit of reprioritizing, schedule juggling or childcare renegotiating.

A former dentist of mine has a sign on the wall of his office that reads: *You don't have to floss all your teeth – only the ones you want to keep.* In the same spirit, we don't have to practice self-care every day – only on the days we want to keep our sanity and improve the quality of our lives. In other words, commit to self-care – and flossing – daily. Self-care is floss for the soul.

Happiness, Health and Peace of Mind

You're going to see that I use the phrase "happiness, health and peace of mind" throughout this book. After all, what's the point of all this self-care business – or anything we do for that matter – if it doesn't somehow lead us to greater levels of happiness, health and/or peace of mind? Take a few minutes right now, close your eyes, and imagine what your life would look like if you were happier, healthier, and more at peace. Really see it, feel it, play with it. Know that the gap between where you want to be (as you just imagined it) and where you are now gets closed by setting goals and taking action.

In my profession as an executive and life coach, we tend to ask clients questions to help them reflect on a particular situation or challenge to arrive at solutions or answers that are already within them. Throughout this book, I'll be asking questions for *you* to reflect on in the *Invitation to Reflect* section. These questions will help you uncover the barriers that keep you from better self-care, which are also, not surprisingly, barriers to greater levels of happiness, health, and peace of mind. Before we dive into each of the ABCs of self-care, let's take a minute to dig a bit deeper into the specifics of these three important concepts, shall we?

Happiness

Let's start with a few reflection questions:

- Am I happy most of the time, or am I often simply pretending to be happy?
- Am I taking enough time for the things that bring me joy?
- Do I even know what those things are?
- How much do I smile and laugh in a day?

We all intuitively understand that there are both physical and psychological benefits of happiness; we've felt them in our own lives. Happiness is such an important topic that there are even classes, degree programs and entire schools dedicated to Positive Psychology or Applied Happiness. Does this mean we, as a society, are over-focused on trying to achieve a state of eternal bliss? Absolutely not! But consider this: *unhappiness* is a warning that something needs to change; if recognized, it can propel us into action that can lead to greater happiness. Therefore, unhappiness is beneficial too – in small doses and only if acted upon. Happiness and unhappiness are both contagious. I suggest you focus on spreading happiness.

Health

More questions to reflect on:

- Do I have a consistent level of lethargy that I accept as normal, often relying on caffeinated beverages to get through the day?
- Do I typically eat for nutritional value or fuel? Or for emotional comfort?
- Am I eager to get to the end of the day when I can have that "doctor-approved" glass (or two or three) of wine?

Taken individually, none of these behaviors are *major* causes for concern. But they may be indicators that you could be much healthier if you'd begin to incorporate better habits around your physical health. So, the real question is: *Do you want to feel better physically?*

Peace of Mind

A few more questions to consider:

- Do I regularly rely on alcohol or drugs to achieve a sense of peace within?
- When was the last time I felt persistently peaceful?
- What are the common triggers that rob me of inner peace?

Peace of mind is basically a mental state of calmness or tranquility, a freedom from worry and anxiety. It can manifest in many ways: a drama-free day with a difficult coworker; the handling of a necessary confrontation without discomfort; simply knowing that your kids or other loved ones are safe; the easy acceptance of another's differing perspective or political leaning or remaining calm after missing a connecting flight. You needn't be a seasoned yogi to attain peace of mind. We simply need to develop it – with intention and discipline. It means we must choose loving thoughts over hateful ones, faith instead of fear, compassion, or patience instead of road rage. Ok wait…I had you up until the road rage part, right?

In fact, all three of these benefits of a good life can be developed using a variety of the self-care tools and techniques in this book. And when it comes to creating more happiness, health and peace of mind, the greatest resource you have is…(drumroll, please)…*yourself*. This is not a task that can be delegated. The work required and the responsibility for creating greater happiness, health and peace of mind falls squarely on your shoulders. So, the only question left to ask yourself is: how much do you want it?

The Importance of Self-Care, Now More Than Ever

The Covid 19 global pandemic has brought on a deluge of isolation, unemployment, and decimated businesses. Not to mention the heartache of losing loved ones to the virus, or the fear of dealing with long-term health challenges for those fortunate enough to recover from the virus. Mental health issues continue to skyrocket as therapists and other mental health providers struggle to keep pace with demand. Frontline workers – be they grocery store employees or nurses or schoolteachers – continue to tirelessly keep up with serving others, while they themselves have more exposure to the virus than many of us. I can think of no other period in my lifetime when the collective need for self-care was greater – and I've lived through a handful of unsettling times (e.g., the AIDS crisis, 9/11, the real estate and tech crashes, racial protests). We have a long way to go before we, as a global community, can settle into whatever the "new normal" will look like. I only hope that when we do, it is with a greater appreciation for how critical self-care is for our health and well-being – both as individuals and as a society. Self-care isn't just a "feel good" strategy. It's a critical tool for building resilience and more mental and emotional strength, which are essential in times such as the ones we're currently experiencing. And since nothing is constant but change, self-care arms you with the thriving skills needed for the future.

It is my sincere desire to help others become more adept at incorporating self-care into their lives, for themselves and for those they love. It all begins with the belief that we can make positive, supportive changes in our lives. Do you *believe* you can change? Do you *want* to change? If the answer to both these questions is a resounding *Yes!* then congratulations. You've already taken the first step to a better life. The next step is to make a personal commitment to yourself, right here, right now. It's not about perfection; it's about small steps in the right direction. We all have the inner strength or power to be better at self-care – the choice is yours.

Now, let's begin the self-care journey together…

HOW TO USE THIS BOOK

This is not an exhaustive book about self-care. Instead, the material is presented as an interactive guide. It is designed to help you make better *choices* and *actions* that support a self-care lifestyle, while also making the self-care habits and tools easier to remember – as easy as, say, remembering your ABCs!

In my own journey of self-care, I found that associating each concept with a letter of the alphabet helped me remember the many self-care options available to me. I hope this format will assist you as well in your self-care journey. Within each of the lettered chapters that follow, I will share with you not only the concept being presented, but also a variety of activities, mindsets, and action steps relevant to that concept.

As a coach, it is my responsibility to help my clients develop inner awareness around their mindset: attitude, thoughts, beliefs, assumptions, and feelings. I do my best to lovingly help others make the connection between their inner mindset and their outer performance, specifically as it pertains to the achievement (or lack thereof) of their goals and aspirations. Once that connection is made, I assist clients in shifting their mindsets to align with the results they want to achieve – and then holding them accountable to their planned actions. This book is designed with the important step of *accountability* in mind.

By incorporating action plans and reflection questions to monitor your individual progress, the book allows you the space to hold yourself accountable for the changes you wish to see in your life. It would be better, however, to make self-care a collaborative effort. I recommend finding an accountability partner or partners to work through this book with, simultaneously. A partner can help you stay committed to your self-care lifestyle, by providing support and encouragement. A few suggestions on how a partnership might work during your periodic check-ins:

- Share mutual progress or setbacks.
- Brainstorm how will you celebrate all the "wins" – small or large – along the journey. (e.g., pampering appointments, days off, social gatherings, alone time, etc.)
- Discuss the intention for a chapter or create your own.
- Discuss the story in each chapter and how you each might handle the situation.

Your "Accountability Partner" can be a close friend, a professional coach, your spouse, or partner, or even a small support group that is formed for the explicit purpose of committing to a self-care lifestyle. If you prefer to undertake the self-care journey on your own, that's fine too! It's all about what works best for you and your unique personality.

I recommend you take your time with this book, staying with and practicing each self-care letter until it's ingrained in your psyche, until each principle becomes second nature. By taking this approach, you will consciously make different choices over and over, until more positive, productive habits become the norm, and each self-care habit is naturally woven into your lifestyle. You may wish to commit to one self-care letter per week, making this a six-month program. Alternatively, you could focus on each letter for a two-week period, culminating in a year-long self-care journey. You can also skip around, selecting chapters based on which concepts in the Table of Contents you are most drawn to. The Quick Check questions at the beginning of each chapter can help you choose which chapters to work on. You can also take the Self-Care Questionnaire in Appendix A or online at www.abcsofselfcare.com to determine which elements of self-care you're currently the most in need of developing, and prioritizing those. There's no right or wrong way to dive in each concept; what's important is to do the diving that gets you into the metaphorical self-care pool.

Once you've read through and practiced each of the self-care habits, you'll want to maintain the new lifestyle you've worked so hard to develop. Maintenance is a lot easier if you *believe* you are worth the effort to sustain it. Upon waking each morning, or even at times throughout your day, you may find yourself feeling unmotivated to follow through on your self-care plans. If this happens, you'll need to immediately disrupt that complacency and take action – even if the action is something as simple as taking four deep breaths or going for a brief walk around the block. Similarly, you may find yourself in a state of resistance when you begin to take a self-care action. This too needs immediate disruption, even if it means giving yourself a gentle nudge out of your comfort zone. Think of a time when you may have begun a new workout routine, perhaps after not setting foot inside a gym for several years. Of course, you're going to feel resistance to going that first time. One surefire way to overcome the resistance is to set appointments with a personal trainer to help you through those early workouts. That trainer would then guide you through various exercises to strengthen your body, having you do a certain number of repetitions of each exercise. You do the exercises even if you "don't feel like it" because you're not about to argue with your trainer in the middle of a workout. This repetitive action is how you strengthen your body and resolve, as well as how you remember each exercise in the future when you're working out on your own. Think of this book as that personal trainer. Set an appointment with the book and commit to focusing on the material. When you get to one of the exercises or recommended actions, don't view it as optional. Don't try negotiating with the book. Don't try arguing with the book. (Because, come on, you'd look pretty silly anyway.) *Just do it.* The exercises and recommended actions are the very things that will build your self-care muscles, resulting in an attractive, admirable self-care lifestyle worthy of catcalls. (Am I carrying this analogy too far yet?)

Want to take your self-care "workouts" even deeper? Then check out the additional resource materials in Appendix B. And don't skip listening to the song recommendations offered with the reflection section of each chapter. These songs were carefully selected to enhance your reflections on each concept by providing an extra dose of inspiration. Not only can music lift your spirits as you do your reflecting, but each song can also assist in memory recall with the corresponding concept.

What you focus on in life expands and grows. To focus more on self-care *actions*, remember the Three Rs: **R**eminders, **R**ituals, and **R**epetition:

- **Reminders**: Set reminders in your smartphone or daily planner or write post-it notes to yourself and stick them in places you will easily notice them.
- **Rituals**: Create little rituals that incorporate some of the recommended actions in this book. They needn't be time-consuming, but they do need to be meaningful to you.
- **Repetition**: Repeat your rituals and the other recommended actions consistently until they become as second nature as brushing your teeth.

This book is not exhaustive, but it is comprehensive. It can be read a little at a time. Accept that self-care is an essential life skill that has to be learned. And *choose* to improve your happiness, health, and peace of mind today – even if it means taking only a tiny step. Just start.

A

ACT ON AWARENESS AND ACCEPTANCE

Every action you take is like a vote for the person you want to become...the true reason that habits matter so much.

– James Clear

❦

To get different results with self-care – or anything for that matter – we must take different actions. We know this instinctively. However, mustering the courage or motivation to *act* requires an *awareness* of the issue or problem, and then *acceptance* of what it is.

Let's look at an example of the opposite of acting on awareness and acceptance or AAA. While this story (and the others you'll find in the following chapters) is fictional, many of the circumstances and responses are based on a blend of real clients I've worked with over the years.

Alicia and AAA

Each morning, Alicia awakens with a sense of dread for the day that stretches out before her. She feels trapped in a relationship in which she feels undervalued and even, at times, verbally abused. Two years into her engagement to an overbearing and hyper-critical fiancé, Alicia has lost most of the confidence she possessed in college, where she felt supported by mentors who encouraged her growth and development as both a student and a person.

Alicia's fiancé joins her in the kitchen, where she hands him a fresh cup of coffee that he immediately criticizes as being too strong. Alicia apologizes and then reminds him that she will be meeting with friends after work and won't be home for dinner. His reaction is swift and cutting. *What about him? What about their time together? Is she even serious about their relationship? If so, she wouldn't be leaving him on his own tonight!* He turns his back on her and says he's hurt that she seems to prefer a couple of "losers from college" to him, the man who loves her more than anything.

Alicia instantly regrets having made plans with her friends, reminding herself that she knows her fiancé has abandonment issues from a rough childhood, so how could she be so insensitive? She believes that with enough love from her, he will feel more secure and not be so jealous of her friendships. She offers to cancel her plans, which results in an immediate smile and a bear hug from him – which feels a bit too tight, like a subtle show of domination. She reminds herself to be patient with him, that progress will come. She does not mention the fact that he goes out with his heavy-drinking buddies at least three times a week, sometimes canceling plans with her at the last minute.

She tells herself that he will improve over time, that their life together will improve over time. But will it? No, not one bit. Alicia is not only unaware of just how unhealthy her relationship is, but she is also actively working to stifle any awareness of the situation, ignoring troubling signs on a daily basis.

Quick Check - Select all that apply:

- ☐ I often stay busy and seldom take time to think about my life.
- ☐ I often beat myself up when I make a mistake.
- ☐ I want a different life, but I seem to keep doing the same things I've always done.

Commit to Awareness

First, let me state emphatically that *it's okay to not be or feel okay.* It's okay to not like where we are currently in our lives, to not have the level of happiness or health that we desire, or to not understand what is getting in the way of our peace of mind. It's okay to not know why we haven't yet changed any bad habits or negative thought patterns that we've been vowing to change for years. In fact, we may be having these feelings no matter how many accomplishments we've racked up over the years. And guess what? That's okay too. This is where awareness comes in.

Quite simply, awareness is about checking in with our feelings and emotions periodically to determine if we're feeling okay...or not. Awareness can help us understand where we are relative to our natural desire for a fulfilling life. For me, personally, a fulfilling life means having happiness, health, and peace of mind as much as possible (while also accepting that occasionally I'm going to be thrown off my game by unexpected challenges). Being comfortable in my own skin and living up to my potential is a big part of my definition of a fulfilling life. For you, a fulfilling life may mean something else – and that's okay too! The point is: if we aren't where we want to be in life, awareness of this fact and awareness of what's standing in our way is the first step to moving closer to the life we've envisioned for ourselves.

It's never too late to shift the trajectory of our lives. We are never too old to grow, learn, or change – three actions that require self-reflection. Self-reflection leads to awareness. The gap between where we are now and where we want to end up can be bridged by these three steps (AAA):

1. Define the problem or determine the obstacle (awareness)
2. Accept the current circumstances (acceptance)
3. Take action (act)

In other words, implement the power of AAA (No, I'm not talking about an auto service that comes to your home to jumpstart your awareness!). To get started, we'll want to cultivate, in the moment, awareness of *what* we're doing and *why* we're doing it – especially when it comes to building more self-care into our busy days. Are we constantly performing to get "props" and validation from others? Are we trying to prove something to ourselves because we don't feel we're enough? Are we habitually taking on more than we can realistically handle, thereby squeezing out any plans for self-care? Are we trying to be liked? Do we have a bad habit of saying *yes* when we'd prefer to say *no*? Are we busy because we're being productive and purposeful, or do we tend to stay busy as a means of avoiding the reality of our present circumstances that we'd rather not deal with? Ouch – if this last one really hits home, that means we're likely in denial about something in our lives. But that's okay too! Denial is a subconscious means of keeping ourselves safe until we're ready to deal with the truth; it's our mind's way of protecting us. So be gentle with yourself as you reflect on all these questions. The answers may not be easy or comfortable yet uncovering them is the path to awareness.

Reflecting on our past may help us discover how we got to where we are today. A major loss (e.g., death of a loved one) or major change (e.g., divorce) in our lives, if not properly dealt with, can lead us to developing behaviors that don't support us, such as consistently blowing off the need for self-care by telling ourselves we have "more important" things to do. What could be more important than our overall well-being? Being aware, at the root level, of why we don't practice self-care will help us move past this common obstacle to our health, happiness, and peace of mind. And doing a Root Cause Analysis (or 5 Whys System) begins with identifying challenges or obstacles that stand between us and our self-care habits. For example, let's assume one obstacle to self-care is that we overcommit to things others want us to do. You start the analysis by asking the question, *Why?* And then ask it *four* more times. Each answer to the *Why?* question before it is what you ask *Why?* about the next time. The idea is to get clearer as you question the previous answer. To get to the root of the issue, you may have to ask *Why?* 10 times or more. You could conceivably do a root cause analysis for any of the 26 Self-Care habits suggested in this book that create a challenge for you. However, let's start with a focus on saying "no" more. Be sure to keep the focus on *you* and not on others. The conversation might go something like this:

Me:	I always seem to be overcommitted, leaving no time for self-care.
Reflective Me:	Why?
Me:	Because I have a hard time saying "no" to others.
Reflective Me:	Why?
Me:	Because I hate disappointing other people.
Reflective Me:	Why?
Me:	Because growing up, it was obvious when my parents were disappointed in me and I *hated* that feeling.
Reflective Me:	Why?
Me:	Because it made me nervous that if I disappointed them too much, they wouldn't love me.
Reflective Me:	Why?
Me:	Because if my parents couldn't love me, how could I love myself? That would mean I'm unlovable. And who wants to be unlovable?

Now we're getting somewhere! We've identified the *symptom* of overcommitting, while the *root cause* is the fear of not being loved or lovable. Addressing the root cause with actions that specifically target it will help resolve your challenges. When you solve problems at the root of the issue, you will more than likely come up with a better solution.

Do you see how digging into and acknowledging our past is a powerful way to become aware of why we participate in some of the unhealthy, self-sabotaging habits or addictions we may have developed to numb our pain? Examples include:

- Staying in unhealthy relationships.
- Being in constant motion to avoid being alone with our thoughts.
- Letting our to-do lists control us instead of us controlling them.
- Over-eating, even when we're full.
- Over-eating, for comfort or to ignore strong emotions.
- Excessively drinking alcohol
- Shopping beyond our needs and budget
- Abusing drugs

According to research, addictions are often in service of avoidance. In other words, any bad habits or addictions we've developed may be, strangely, helping us compensate for past hurts and painful feelings we are trying to avoid. Sugar is my go-to addiction, and I recognize that I often prefer a donut over acknowledging emotional pain. Thankfully, my awareness of this bad habit has helped me get it under control. Mostly. I do happen to live near a gourmet donut shop. Wish me luck.

We may sometimes need professional help to get past these unhealthy habits and addictions. Admitting you need expert help is such an act of courage. I applaud you! Asking for professional help can do wonders for our self-confidence and self-worth. There are many resources available, starting with your general physician, who can refer you to a specialist. There are also counselors, coaches, support groups run by therapists, and alternative therapies, which can likely be found in your local area with just a little bit of research. Taking advantage of professional resources will also help get us one step closer to creating a better present and future through conscious commitment to better self-care.

Be Aware of Which Mind Is in Charge

We don't want our eight-year-old selves running our lives, do we? Yet research suggests that 88% percent of our brain activity comes from our subconscious mind, which was developed before we were eight years old, while only 12% of our brain activity comes from our conscious mind. That's a lot of brain control in the hands of a kid, wouldn't you say? This subconscious mind, which isn't as fully aware as the conscious mind, influences both our thoughts and behaviors, and is fueled by fears, doubts, and insecurities from our younger years. This explains why, at times, we behave in less mature ways. This is likely why, at times, we want to yell, "Will you just grow up?!" to ourselves...or others. The 12% of our brain function operated by the conscious mind is where we find logic, reasoning, analytical decision making, choices and willpower. So, one can see how the deck is already stacked against us when such a large majority of our thinking, and therefore our behaviors, are ruled by our "less aware" mind.

Hypnotherapy has been a tool that most helped me shift more of my brain function toward the conscious mind, freeing myself of the lingering impact of childhood trauma that lurked in my subconscious mind. The result is much less anxiety, less sensitivity, more patience, and fewer made-up stories about what is going on in my life.

Before working with hypnotherapists Ted Moreno and Emma Dietrich, I intuitively knew when I was doing too much, pushing too hard and neglecting my health. Yet I ignored many of these intuitive hints and allowed my subconscious to continue ruling most of my decisions. I know now that intuition is a feeling or knowing that I can trust. It is how our subconscious mind talks to our conscious mind, using gut feelings, strong urges, physical sensations, or dreams. My own intuitive messages usually warn me to do less and rest more. Whether I listen or not is up to my conscious mind and I then live with the consequences of my choices.

We can tell when our eight-year-old subconscious minds are in charge. You may notice an unnatural or seemingly *disproportionate* reaction to a person, place, or situation. For example, bursting into tears after casually bumping into a table may be an exaggerated subconscious response to feelings of clumsiness as a child, with the hurt and shame rushing back in an instant. In situations like this, compassion is the key. We all have wounds and fears from childhood. Healing the child inside each of us may require professional help.

Sometimes, our childhood wounds develop into stories we tell ourselves that lead to behaviors that are anything but self-caring. One New Year's Eve, I had plans to attend a game night at my sister's home. I love visiting family and playing board games, so I was really looking forward to the evening. Unfortunately, I was sick, yet my FOMO (Fear of Missing Out) was in high gear, compounded by concern over disappointing my sisters and being thought a flake. I almost drove my sick self to that party despite the obvious fact that I needed an evening of rest! Thankfully, my conscious mind took over and I put myself to bed instead of spreading my germs among those I love dearly.

Practice Acceptance

We're human. And humans are flawed, which is to say, we make mistakes. Acceptance of our humanness – and the humanness of others – is an integral part of self-care. It's also important for us to be aware of the outside forces that get in the way of accepting this simple, undeniable aspect of being human. Perhaps the strongest force comes through social media – the new "schoolyard" for bullying. From peer pressure to outright shaming, to public online attacks, I have long felt we all need to chill out when it comes to our online presence. If we wouldn't say something in a face-to-face conversation, then we shouldn't be saying it online. I believe we are all *perfectly imperfect.*

While we're talking about bullying, let's take a minute to dig into the mindset of bullies. Bullies – like, sexists, racists, and misogynists – tend to be insecure people who feel powerless. Bullies need to feel more powerful and secure, and putting others down gives them a (false) sense of power over others. As the victim of bullying in my younger years, it brings up not-so-fun memories. However, I can honestly look back on those painful years and say that the bullying happened *for* me, rather than *to* me. (And, no, I'm not endorsing bullying. Bullying and shaming in all forms are reprehensible behaviors.) In hindsight, I realized that my commitment to self-care came from a place of protecting myself now, when I didn't then. Unfortunately, before coming to this realization, I allowed the sense of victimization I felt as a bullied child leak into other areas of my life, creating a barrier to my own success and happiness. Working with a hypnotherapist, I was able to address and overcome my subconscious thoughts of victimhood, accept myself as I am, and take responsibility in all areas of my life. Acceptance of self is perhaps the greatest gift I received because of this experience.

There also exists a form of mild self-bullying that comes from our social media-obsessed culture. It's our tendency to *compare and despair.* It's important to remember that no one on social media is sharing the whole picture; most are creating an idealized version of themselves. Comparing our own imperfect lives to these idealized images often leads us to feel "less than" about our own lives. This is a form of self-abuse and should be nipped in the bud the minute you notice yourself playing the comparison game – a game in which there are never any winners. Shame, blame, criticism, and judgement of oneself deplete the soul. So, please stop that immediately! This is perhaps the most critical aspect of self-care – namely, the end of negative self-talk, replaced with genuine acceptance of who you are and what your life circumstances are in any given moment. It is only from this place of acceptance that we can begin to make positive changes to improve our lives. Start where you are. Do your best and forgive the rest. Our only competition is ourselves, no one else. We are meant to be who we are, not someone else, and not who advertisers tell us we ought to be. Accept where you are, who you are, right now, with gobs of self-compassion. Replace disappointment with acceptance, knowing that disappointment often stems from unrealistic expectations tied to perfectionism. Accept what is, as a starting point, and then map out a plan to change course as you desire. If we can master being our own best friends, then our other friendships and relationships will automatically improve.

If you do nothing else recommended in this book, please do this: *be gentle with yourself.* It's easy to fall victim to life's ups and downs, judging ourselves every step of the way. Being our own worst critic takes more effort than we think, which drains us. It also makes it difficult to hear genuinely helpful and constructive criticism from others or to accept others who have differing opinions and perspectives. Self-acceptance helps us to move forward, to be less defensive, and to take critical feedback in a positive manner. It allows us to accept another person's reality as legitimate, regardless of whether we agree with it. We can't give what we don't have, right? So, acceptance and compassion for others starts with acceptance and compassion for one's self.

Once we're able to accept our own lives as they are, it's time to move into accepting the greater world around us exactly as it is...and then working on contributing to its betterment. We may not be able to single-handedly change the way our government, or employer, or school system is run, but we can make some contribution to improving things. Even if the only thing in our power to change is our reaction to what is. Think about something right now that frustrates you and is also out of your control. What can you do to accept that current reality and to have more peace in your life? It is from this calm mindset that we can begin to see what positive changes we could contribute to the situation. After we accept what is, action is needed to make a change. Author of *25 Days to Living Your Happiness*, Dr. Zayd Abdul-Karim (Dr. Z) likes to say, "applied knowledge is power." I couldn't agree more. Simply learning about self-care doesn't make a difference...*applying* the knowledge by taking action does. Real power is in the *doing*.

Take Action

Actions speak louder than words. We must do something different to get different results. To start, let's work on being better today than we were yesterday. Take baby steps. The Power of 1% states that the big differentiators between great businesses and average ones is the commitment to keep evolving, to keep improving systems to make things 1% better, over, and over. The same applies to individuals. 1% improvement – that's all you need – over and over.

If we're dealing with major stress-inducing changes like loss or transition or even a series of unfortunate events, creating little healing rituals is one of the most powerful self-care actions we can take. Writing love letters to those we've lost, practicing meditation, expressing our gratitude out loud or in a journal, and using uplifting affirmations, are all examples of healing rituals that we can employ.

Affirmations are a popular healing ritual to make changes in our lives, even though they may not work for everyone. For some, they can put change in motion, jumpstart our confidence and potentially give us motivation to take action. To be most effective, customize affirmations to be specific to your needs and/or what you care about. They also need to be ones you can believe to be true. For example, if you are overwhelmed by the pressures at work, then you could attempt to change the spiral downward by stating an affirmation with conviction, *as if it is already true*. "I am calm and centered and my work flows smoothly" may work. Develop a consistent practice of saying them out loud, writing them down or reading them 2-3 times per day. How many times do you repeat the same one? As many times needed to feel better, or to jumpstart action. I've heard anywhere from 10 to 108 times is effective. People who repeat them 108 times use Mala beads to keep count. Otherwise, you focus on the counting and not the affirmation. Again, the power is in the action, the doing something different. Ideally, the words you use motivate you to do something calming to center yourself, like take a mental break to reduce the feeling of overwhelm.

Another powerful action step, that is also easy and free, is to consciously choose how we spend our energy and with whom. Some people in our lives are energy boosters; we feel energized and "boosted" in their presence. Great! Other people in our lives, however, are energy drainers, or vampires. A mere five minutes in their presence can make us feel depleted. (Keep in mind, this is a different form of depletion than, say, hanging with our 3-year-old – which can be physically draining, no doubt, but can also feed our souls like nothing else.) Being aware of these relationships and the energetic impact of them is key to self-care. Limiting time with drainers, while increasing time with boosters, is powerful. Similarly, the activities we participate in can be draining or boosting. One of the biggest draining activities ties back to the refusal to accept what is. Yes, that again! So draining! "Going with the flow" may sound a bit cliched, but it's cliched for a reason: it works! Plans changed at the last minute? What's more energizing – being bitter about the change – or being open to what might take place in lieu of those cancelled plans, such as a nice quiet evening with a good book? Or having a good laugh over yet another rerun of *Frasier*? Or taking a good long walk outside in nature? Or even sitting on that meditation pillow that's covered in dust from lack of use and going within to examine why we're so upset about the change in plans? Go with the flow, baby!

Remember that what we feel on the inside shows up on the outside, whether we want it to or not. Too often, what's on the inside is fear. Science tells us that the only two fears we come into life with are the fear of being dropped and the fear of loud noises. Yet somehow, we manage to develop so many additional fears. The good news is this: *Action cures fear.* Once we get moving, we often realize there was really nothing to be afraid of in the first place.

Small actions, consistently taken, can help us get where we want to go. These actions should be tied to our goals and values. Why? Because goals can shift yearly, weekly, even daily. The one constant is our values, which may evolve, but rarely change drastically overnight. And how do we know what our values are? Basically, they are the things we care deeply about and would go to great lengths to protect, such as family, love, fitness, financial security, and personal growth. (See also Core Values List in Appendix B) Thus, our values should be the inner guiding light for all our small actions, keeping integrity at the forefront every step of the way. Doing this will get us closer to the goal of better self-care.

We've all heard the saying that *life is about the journey, not the destination.* And we've all likely, at some point, rolled our eyes upon hearing this, especially if we weren't enjoying our journey very much. But here's the thing: ultimately, we all have the same destination – death. There's no escaping it. So why *not* enjoy the journey? Why not celebrate all the small successes along the way? Why not accept what we can't change and then dive into solutions for working around life's inevitable obstacles? LaTonia Taylor, author of *My Juicy Rebirth: A Journey to Healing the Feminine through Pleasure & Sacred Process,* says, "staying the course is not easy in a world where conformity is easy and non-conformity comes with fear." Stay the course. Being aware, accepting what is, and then taking action – not staying in worry mode – is the key. And the best news of all? Once you master this: *Oh, the places you'll go* and the peace you will feel!

Alicia, Revisited

Let's return to our example of Alicia. How happy and fulfilled do you suppose Alicia would be if she understood and embraced having a self-care habit of acting on awareness and acceptance (AAA)? Perhaps her situation would've played out more like this:

Alicia awakens with her usual sense of dread. She has that nagging feeling that she is in an unhealthy relationship and has committed herself to someone who doesn't respect or love her in a manner conducive to a long and lasting relationship. While reading over previous entries in her journal (which she keeps hidden in the spare bedroom closet, so her fiancé won't discover it and read it), she gains *awareness* of a pattern that makes her stomach lurch — namely, of abuses she witnessed in her parents' relationship for years before her father's premature death from cirrhosis. She *accepts* and realizes that she's been kidding herself for too long. She must choose between this unhealthy relationship or her own happiness, health, and peace. For too long she's denied the reality of her situation. Now, at long last, she can see it clearly for what it is: a relationship train wreck, one that will likely kill her spirit for good if she allows it. And for too long, she now realizes, she has allowed it.

Today is the day. She's already thought it through numerous times, but today feels different, as if the conviction within has come to a tipping point. She can not only see that this relationship is dangerously unhealthy, but she can finally *accept* that he will likely never change. Today is the day she will *act* and finally take her oldest friend up on her offer, made on numerous occasions, to move in with her. After her fiancé leaves for work, Alicia calls in sick to her employer, makes a call to her friend, and spends the day packing her most essential items. She feels nervous and rushed because she wants to be gone long before her fiancé's shift ends. It is time to act. It's time to value herself and her well-being much more than she was taught by her family's example. It is time to put her own needs and desires first. It is time to practice self-care to a degree she's never done it before. She's ready. She's moving on. Alicia hasn't felt this certain about a major decision in years. Her relief is palpable. And her new life has just begun.

Accept - then act. Whatever the present moment contains, accept it as if you had chosen it. Always work with it, not against it. Make it your friend and ally, not your enemy. This will miraculously transform your whole life.

— Eckhart Tolle

10

Intention:

I trust myself to take action after I know and accept what is.

Now, how about digging deeper? As a warm-up to this time for reflection, I suggest listening to "Scars to Your Beautiful" by Alessia Cara.

Invitation to Reflect:

What old habits and behaviors must you become aware of, and what will need to change so that you can get busy *really* living?

_____

_____

_____

_____

_____

_____

_____

_____

What do you need to accept in your life that will lead you to greater peace of mind?

_____

_____

_____

_____

_____

_____

_____

_____

_____

What will you do differently to achieve the material success and/or personal fulfillment you've always wanted?

_____

_____

_____

_____

_____

_____

_____

Here are some actions you can take now for your self-care:

○ Awareness: Record self-observations in a journal or as a Note in your phone labeled "ME."
○ Acceptance: Do a root cause analysis, as mentioned in this chapter, about what holds you back from acceptance. Based on what you learn, set up a Note in your phone or write in the *Other Thoughts and Reflections* section, at least one affirmation of acceptance like, "I love myself as I am." Or "I am who I am, and that's enough." Speak the affirmation with conviction, as if it is already true.

○ Action: Set an intention to create a goal for one or more chapters of the 26 self-care habits in this book. They do not all have to have the same deadline.

Commit to doing at least one thing differently based on what you learned in this chapter. Write out an actionable goal – with a specific deadline – to satisfy your commitment.

_____

_____

_____

_____

How will you celebrate or reward yourself if you reach the goal?

_____

_____

Other thoughts and reflections:

_____

_____

_____

_____

_____

_____

_____

For additional resources related to this topic, please check out my website: www.abcsofselfcare.com

Root Cause Analysis (5 Whys System) ① Worksheet

Use one worksheet for each challenge. In the spaces below, answer the question: *Why is this a challenge?* When you get that answer, ask *Why?* again and build on the last answer given. (See example in Letter A.) By asking the question *Why?* for each of the previous answers given, you drill down to the essence of a challenge. Keep asking *Why?* until you feel you have reached the root cause of each challenge. You may need to ask the question more than 5 times. Focus on <u>*you*</u> and your actions and feelings – not others and their actions) – during this exercise. Consider seeking assistance from a professional therapist or coach to facilitate the exercise for several challenges.

①Root cause analysis is often used in business to solve challenges at the root level as opposed to symptoms. It is an excellent way to reflect on challenges you face in developing a self-care mindset and lifestyle.

Challenge: _____

WHY?

WHY?

WHY?

WHY?

WHY?

Action I Will Take

B

BUILD BOUNDARIES

Your personal boundaries protect the inner core of your identity and your right to choices.

— Gerard Manley Hopkins

❧

When you think of the term "boundaries" as it relates to you and your life, do you conjure images of rigidity? Isolation? Fear? Standoffishness? If so, you, my dear, have been thinking of boundaries all wrong – and have likely been taken advantage of in the past by others who've exploited your lack of them.

Setting, and adhering to, personal boundaries is fundamental to a self-care mindset. Building boundaries is about establishing limits on the behaviors you are willing to accept from others as it relates to your life, your time, your energy. They help others understand how to treat you and, more importantly, how *not* to treat you. You may have subconsciously already set some boundaries without really thinking about it. But *consciously* setting boundaries is the key to consistently upholding them.

Bonnie and Building Boundaries

Let's consider Bonnie. She works long shifts as a nurse, hustling from patient to patient in the ER of her local hospital, caring for others and tending to their emergencies. Near the end of her workday, Bonnie gets a text from her brother asking her to babysit his kids that night so he can take his wife out to dinner on a whim. Bonnie already has plans to cook her favorite meal and enjoy it with a glass of wine and some Netflix viewing, maybe even soak her tired feet in a tub of Epsom salts at the same time. And then it's early to bed so she's rested and rejuvenated for work tomorrow. Bonnie adores her niece and nephew but was *really* looking forward to some peaceful alone time tonight. But how can she deny her brother the opportunity to take his wife out? How can she say no to family? So, she replies, *Sure*, as she lets out a sigh, and then she heads straight to his home from the hospital.

Instead of tortellini in Gorgonzola sauce with a glass of Chardonnay, she finds herself eating frozen chicken fingers and boxed mac-and-cheese, washed back with a juice box. Instead of another tearful-yet-enjoyable viewing of her favorite romantic comedy, Bonnie watches several episodes of *their* favorite show. Instead of tending to her feet, swollen, and aching from being on them for twelve straight hours, she practically twists her ankle stepping on loose Legos strewn across the floor of her brother's family room as she cleans up after putting the kids to bed. When Bonnie's brother and sister-in-law return well past midnight from their evening out, they apologize for being longer than originally planned and tell her they didn't think she'd mind since she "only has a cat" waiting for her back at home. Bonnie leaves her brother's home feeling depleted and angry, not to mention a bit gassy from the chicken fingers.

Did Bonnie demonstrate personal boundaries in this scenario? Absolutely not! And what's worse, now she gets to wake up in five hours for another 12-hour shift. How well do you suppose she will care for her patients tomorrow? And more importantly, how well do you suppose she will care for *herself?*

Bonnie's example clearly demonstrates why building boundaries – and adhering to them – is such an important element of self-care. Without boundaries, we *allow* ourselves to be taken advantage of. Sure, we care for our loved ones and want to support their needs. But we must be willing to support our own needs as well. We must be willing to say a loving "no" to others when our boundaries are being tested…and a very firm "NO!" when they're being flat-out disrespected.

Quick Check - Select all that apply:

- ☐ I'm a people pleaser (aka, the "disease to please"), sometimes to the extreme.
- ☐ I often have a hard time turning off my phone or ignoring calls and texts.
- ☐ I've set aside my own challenges that require extra attention (e.g., preparing for a move, working through grief, staying focused during a busy period at work) to help others with less pressing needs.

Healthy Boundaries Could Include:

- Reserving at least one night a week for pampering yourself at home.
- Limiting how much you're willing to baby/cat/dog-sit for someone, especially if they have the financial means to hire a baby/cat/dog-sitter.
- Asking others not to interrupt you for the next 3 hours while you focus on a project that's important to you.
- Setting your phone on Do Not Disturb mode whenever you choose not to be disturbed.

- Negotiating equal amounts of "me time" with your spouse on the weekends when the kids need supervision.
- Requesting that others not interrupt you while you speak.
- Politely declining an invitation that you genuinely do not want to accept, be it a dear friend who wants you to join them for lunch or a stranger in a nightclub who wants you to dance with them.

Healthy Boundary Statements

Initially, it can be uncomfortable enforcing the personal boundaries you've established. Practice saying the following statements until they roll off your tongue with ease:

- *I appreciate the invitation, but in the spirit of self-care, I'd better not. I hope you understand.*
- *I would sincerely appreciate you giving me a head's up when you're running late. Thanks.*
- *Normally, I'd love to help you out, but now is not a good time for me.*
- *I feel it would be more of a win-win to _____.*
  Or simply the age-old and direct:
- *No, thank you.*

Avoid Unhealthy Boundaries

When you have no boundaries – or unhealthy boundaries – they are often couched in the belief that you're "just being flexible." I suspect there are many reading this book whose kindness is being taken for granted to the extreme. If a friend is always willing to let you pick up the tab at a restaurant or constantly borrowing your car without refilling the gas tank or dropping in on you when you've explicitly told her you need to stay focused on completing an important project for work, guess what? That's not being flexible. That's being taken advantage of. Taken to the extreme, being taken advantage of is called abuse. And abuse is never okay.

Banish Boundary Predators

Think of the people in your life who seem to suck you dry of energy or resources. The coworker who wants to talk your ear off despite knowing full well that you're working under a deadline. The family member who asks for another loan, even though they recently returned from an expensive vacation. I'm not talking about people you choose to regularly help in a small way, such as the homeless man who sits outside your office building who could use a kind word or a cup of coffee. I'm talking about people who know you can't say no – *won't* say no – so they come at you constantly with requests. They prioritize their needs and wants over yours, even when it's inconvenient, taxing, or outright cruel to make such requests. I call these types of people Boundary Predators, and I advise you to steer clear of them – or, at minimum, set and uphold boundaries that are strong and clear enough to minimize their negative impact on your sense of well-being and balance. Boundary predators know you have a weakness for saying *yes* to others, for helping, for listening, for giving. They prey on *you* because they are looking for someone who will say yes to make *their* lives easier.

Trust me when I tell you that boundary predators are not going to like it when you begin to prioritize your self-care needs by setting boundaries. It will seem strange to them, and they may even respond a bit angrily at your initial attempts to keep your needs front and center in your life. If they're truly on your side, they'll eventually understand and respect your needs. And they'll learn, hopefully, to find other means of satisfying their own needs instead of asking you all the time. They'll respect your ability to say no graciously and kindly.

By learning to say no to others, you are also learning to say yes to yourself. Doesn't that sound nice? It is! And surprisingly, boundaries can often deepen a relationship because that relationship is now built on mutual respect, not on one-way giving to the point of depletion. Remarkably, when you show respect for your own time and energy, others will too. And if they don't, there may be no place in your life for them. They go on the "toxic person to be avoided list."

Adhere to Your Own Boundaries

But boundaries aren't just for other people. They're also for you. Sometimes (and I've been guilty of this myself), we mistreat ourselves in ways that we wouldn't tolerate from others, even if we're clear on what our personal boundaries are. A common example of not respecting one's own boundaries is not taking small refresher breaks throughout your day. I cringe whenever I hear a coaching client tell me that they are too busy to take breaks while working. Instead, they plow through the day like a tractor, ramming their way through fields of never-ending projects without a break, as if this somehow demonstrates a strong work ethic. Not true! The only thing it demonstrates is that you're not respecting yourself. You've not set boundaries or you're blatantly disregarding the ones you have set. You end the day feeling mentally and physically drained. This is not sustainable if you have committed to a life that prioritizes and consistently incorporates self-care. You might even surprise yourself at how much more productive you are.

Me? I'm a big believer in frequent breaks throughout my day. After completing a project, I take a brief break. After catching up on my email, I take another break. And so on. It can be something as simple as taking a lap around the office and/or doing a few deep breaths. It needn't be a two-hour bubble bath to rejuvenate. Anything simple and re-balancing will do. We think we're being more productive by powering through, yet our minds actually work better when refreshed.

Different Needs, Different Boundaries

When determining your own personal boundaries, it's important to be aware of any special needs you may have. For example, I am considered an HSP (Highly Sensitive Person). This is a genetic and sensory attribute. HSPs feel emotions – whether positive or negative – more deeply than non-HSPs. We are more likely to be intuitive and empathetic. We are sensitive to loud noises, our pain is magnified, and we get overwhelmed or overstimulated easily. Being aware of this hardwiring in myself allows me to be proactive about setting boundaries that will support my needs as an HSP. It's not unusual for me to politely ask a Lyft driver to turn the radio down; or to isolate myself occasionally when I'm in a hectic environment to recover my equilibrium; or to keep sunglasses handy to block the sun – all of which can overwhelm my senses. And horror movies? Don't even! I already know they are too much for my genetic predisposition, so I am very firm on that boundary. If you want to watch a movie with me, it is likely to be a fun action movie or a romantic comedy. There's no place in my psyche for Carrie or Chucky, let alone an exorcist, poltergeist, or zombie!

What predispositions do you have? They can be physical, mental, emotional, social, whatever. If you know yourself well and have a good understanding of your tolerance level (or lack thereof) for certain circumstances, you'll be in a better position to build boundaries. Plus, it is another opportunity to call on AAA – act on your awareness and acceptance. You have to know what you want and need to set a boundary to get it.

Bonnie, Revisited

Let's return to the example of Bonnie and see how she might handle her brother's request in a way that both acknowledges her love for him while also honoring her own needs. Her brother texts her with his last-minute babysitting request. Instead of immediately replying *Sure*, Bonnie takes a moment to close her eyes, take a few deep breaths, and check in with herself. *I planned this peaceful evening alone,* she tells herself. *It's been a long day and I've got another long day tomorrow. But after Thursday, I have three days off and I'd love to spend some time with my niece and nephew.* She opens her eyes and knows exactly what she will do. She texts her brother back: *Sorry, I have plans tonight. But I'd be happy to babysit for you on Saturday or Sunday if you'd like a Date Night. Just let me know. Xo.* And with that reply, Bonnie has shown support for both her brother *and* herself. Remember, in healthy relationships, everyone wins!

I am a master at setting boundaries that protect my time, energy, creativity, and emotional well-being.

— Cheryl Richardson

❧

Intention:

I have the strength to protect myself by building my boundary muscle.

Now, how about digging deeper? As a warm-up to this time for reflection, I suggest listening to "Me Time" by Heather Hedley.

Invitation to Reflect:

What would your life look like with better boundaries?

_____

_____

_____

_____

_____

_____

What boundaries could you set with the Boundary Predators you want to maintain a relationship with?

Person: Boundary to Set:

_____

_____

_____

_____

_____

What other boundaries do you want to set, in addition to those listed above?

_____

_____

_____

_____

_____

Here are some actions you could take now for your self-care:

○ Start to notice the feelings and physical symptoms you experience when you are not setting appropriate boundaries.

○ Set Do Not Disturb (DND) hours on your phone. Also use this feature when you need uninterrupted time. Most phones allow you to change the settings to accept calls from "favorites," or let anyone through who rings twice.

○ Choose one or two phrases to use as your go-to boundary setting responses.

Commit to doing at least one thing differently based on what you've learned in this chapter. Write out an actionable goal – with a specific deadline – to satisfy your commitment.

_____

_____

_____

_____

How will you celebrate or reward yourself if you reach the goal?

_____

_____

Other thoughts and reflections:

_____

_____

_____

_____

_____

_____

_____

_____

For additional resources related to this topic, please check out my website: www.abcsofselfcare.com

C

CHOOSE WISELY

We may have limited choices, but we can always choose. We can choose our thoughts, emotions, moods, our words, our actions.

— Stephen Covey

❦

The power of our choices as individuals cannot be overstated. Our choices define us, guide us, determine the direction our lives take – be it for the next five minutes or the next five years. Your choices, from the mundane to the magnificent, *matter*. Choices are at the root of our personal freedom. And choosing wisely means making the best choice in any given moment for yourself and for the world.

Response-Ability

I first became consciously aware of the power of our choices from existential psychotherapist, Dr. Lois Frankel, who promotes the perspective that all of life is about choice and taking responsibility for those choices. In other words, short of being the victim of a crime, accident, or illness, you create your life one choice at a time. By embracing this worldview, I've personally been able to own up to some of the bad choices I've made in my own life – uprooting myself and moving across the country five times being among them.

Sometimes, understanding whether a choice was right or wrong, helpful, or hurtful, happens in retrospect. Taking responsibility means accepting the consequences of those choices – the good, the bad, and the ugly. All of it. No exceptions. This is one of the true marks of a mature and evolved human.

Making wise choices requires a certain level of responsibility – aka "response-ability," the ability to respond. It is through owning and examining the outcome of past decisions that we can thoughtfully consider making different ones the next time around. In other words, it's about assessing past choices to make better, more informed choices in the future. Remember the adage: If you always do what you've always done, you will always get what you have always gotten. Basically, it is the tongue-in-cheek definition of insanity: doing the same thing over and over, each time expecting different results.

Carolyn and Choosing Wisely

Let's consider Carolyn. Carolyn grew up in a sports-oriented household and was used to getting lots of exercise, but her diet reflected her on-the-go lifestyle: heavy on processed foods, sugary "sports" drinks, and snacks. As an athlete, however, Carolyn didn't think twice about what she ate. After all, she'd run off all those (empty) calories at the next basketball game or track meet, right? After graduating college, Carolyn's level of physical activity decreased considerably as she moved into the business world with her first of many office jobs. Her diet remained much the same, as she was often under too many deadlines at work to break for lunch at a fresh salad bar nearby or to prepare her own food. Instead, Carolyn often opted for a frozen burrito from the break room vending machines, or worse yet, a couple bags of salty snacks washed back with a soda. In her early 30s, Carolyn noticed physical symptoms that were often painful and debilitating. Diagnosed with an autoimmune condition, Carolyn was advised to get regular movement and to cut the junk food from her diet, replacing it with healthful whole foods, and lots of fresh vegetables. And she did...for a few weeks. Until another big deadline at work caused her to skip lunch hours at the salad bar and working late each night meant her gym membership went unused. All too soon, Carolyn fell back into her old habits, relying on more and more ibuprofen to suppress her physical aches and pains.

Years later, Carolyn still begins each new year with a resolution to walk around her corporate office park each workday, and to improve her eating habits. *No more lunches of pretzels and soda at her desk! No more dinners of fast food in the car on her drive home. This is the year she'll change! This time she means it!*

And yet, by the end of every January, Carolyn is back to long hours in the office and "meals" that primarily come from vending machines. Instead of upholding her vow to take better care of herself, Carolyn slowly gets worse and worse, eventually relying on stronger prescription medications to numb the ever-increasing symptoms of her medical condition. In addition to feeling physically awful most of the time, Carolyn now feels emotionally awful as well, regularly chiding herself for being unhealthy and overweight, someone who deserves to feel as sick as she does. Any sense of self-worth she has comes from the accolades she receives at work, often celebrated by picking up her favorite fast food on the drive home. And so, the cycle continues year after year: broken resolutions, unhealthy food choices, little to no exercise, increased use of pain medication, and declining overall health.

Carolyn's example clearly fits into the definition of insanity – she makes the same choices over and over at each lunch break and at the end of each workday yet expects different results. Do you suppose the coming new year will result in Carolyn sticking to her resolutions? Heck no! Do you think Carolyn is on track to start making wise choices? Um, doubtful. There will always be one more vending machine burrito or one more drive-thru chicken sandwich standing between Carolyn and a wise choice. Unless she changes her pattern where making choices is concerned.

Quick Check - Select all that apply:

- ☐ I second guess my choices – especially if I don't like the way a situation turned out.
- ☐ I often make decisions coming from a place of fear.
- ☐ I often say I *should, ought to,* or *have to* do things in a certain way.

Different Emotion, Different Choice

Research shows that to change our choices, it helps to change the emotion tied to each one. And that's what allows us to make different and wiser ones. I'm not suggesting you ignore emotions, instead change your focus. Sometimes emotions are teaching us something about ourselves or a situation. However, if a negative emotion is not useful you can choose to let it go and focus elsewhere, perhaps on something more positive until the negative emotion subsides. For example, thinking of an upcoming vacation after a stressful period at work is much better than nervously focusing on an upcoming project. It takes practice and repetition to shift your attention. It also takes practice to not feel like a victim to your emotions. They are often sending us messages physically, for example through anxiety or a heaviness in our gut. Observe your emotions and do your best not to see them as being in charge. Take back control by experiencing them like an outside observer, determine the message your emotions are sending you, and then let them go as soon as possible. Getting distance from an emotion makes it easier to understand what it is telling us. Maybe the message is concern about an upcoming presentation, signaling a need to prepare more. If we can experience emotions and then let them let go, we are consciously making a wise choice to feel differently. It's up to you whether you want to continue to feel bad or move on. Either way you have the power to choose wisely.

One of the best emotional choices we can make is to choose love over fear. What does this look like? Check in with yourself at each choice point to determine if the choice you're leaning toward comes from an inner place of love rather than fear. Love-based choices come with feelings of abundance, self-love, love for others and love for life in general. Fear-based choices are often accompanied by feelings of scarcity, fear of the unknown or unfamiliar, fear of judgment, fear of others. If you really dig into the choices you've made in life, you will likely see that every significant one was made from a place of love or fear. Some examples:

- Staying with a love interest who disrespects you? Fear (that you'll never find someone better).
- Choosing to leave a disrespectful partner? Love (self-love, to be precise).
- Rejecting a fabulous job offer in a field you've always dreamed of working in because it would require relocation to a new city? Fear (of the unknown).
- Accepting the same job offer even if it means having to create a social life and network of friends in a city where you know no one? Love (of new adventures and possibilities).

It's helpful to remember that most of the things we fear typically don't come to pass. So why waste all that psychic energy being fearful? That which we fear only has the power we give it. We can choose to give it no power at all, thereby freeing us to make choices that come from love. Every event in life, every situation we find ourselves in, offers us the opportunity to choose love over fear. And by choosing *love* most of the time, we can make wiser choices overall.

Choose a Growth Mindset

If you really want to live your best life, I encourage you to develop a growth mindset. Those with a growth mindset believe that one's basic abilities can be developed through dedication and hard work; brains and talent are simply a starting point, not a guarantee. Developing a growth mindset also creates a love of learning that will keep you engaged in life and help you develop a level of resilience that allows you to bounce back from disappointments or challenges. By adopting a growth mindset, you will be open to learning new things and growing into a better version of yourself, day after day, year after year. Sounds good, right? I promise you – it is!

Being a better version of yourself means choosing *you* and therefore choosing healthy behaviors over unhealthy behaviors that work against you. Smoking, excessive drinking, abusing drugs, consistently eating a diet of unhealthy foods, burning the candle at both ends despite the obvious toll it's taking on your need for sleep and rejuvenation – these are all choices that will prevent you from growing into that better version of yourself, from *choosing you*. These choices work against your commitment to self-care. As you adopt the role of your own best friend, you may notice that you no longer want these unhealthy choices keeping you from a better, healthier life.

Choosing *you* is a supreme act of self-care, which is another demonstration of self-love. It involves checking in with yourself to determine what choices will make you happier, healthier, and more at peace. Not just "in the moment" choices (e.g., the temporary joy of that first bite of a Big Mac or first swig of a margarita), but also in longer term ones (e.g., how good it feels to be strong and healthy). It is a minute-by-minute, hour-by-hour, weekly, monthly, yearly practice of examining your choices and looking for signs that you might be tipping the scales against your own well-being. For example, if you've committed to giving 120% to a big project at work, you should avoid taking on any additional commitments that aren't critical. In this case, you should accept that this is a time to receive from others instead of giving to others. There'll be time for that when your big work project is complete.

Choose Self-Care

Whenever possible, I recommend you choose the self-care option over the non-self-care option. If the non-self-care option is important to you for other reasons, consider if it will add undue stress, inconvenience, or burden to your life. Catch yourself defaulting to your sense of obligation to others. Remember: you're obligated to yourself just as much, if not more. Sometimes, it's not necessarily an either/or choice, and finding a happy middle ground can be the healthiest path. An example of this from my own life involves the personal value I place on spending time with friends. I once received a call from a grad school buddy who was in town unexpectedly and invited me to meet him and another friend for dinner. Although I was tired and looking forward to a quiet night of self-care at home, I sought a creative alternative that worked for everyone: I invited the two of them to my home, where I could still be more relaxed and casual than getting gussied up for a restaurant. I then ordered a take-out meal to be delivered later before taking a brief and restorative nap. I also decided ahead of time when I would usher them to the door and stuck to it. We had a great time together and I didn't have to make an either/or choice. More like a win-win!

Keep in mind that throughout our lives, we are constantly making choices about what we need in any given moment: more activity or more recovery? Just as doing sit-ups once a month (activity) won't give you abs of steel, practicing self-care (recovery) infrequently won't give you the sense of peace and contentment in your life that you desire. Both require dedication. The trick with self-care is to keep your eyes open for any opportunity to practice it. A last-minute cancellation of a meeting or other event is a great opportunity to add more self-care to your day. Asking for help with your commitments and projects is another way to free up more self-care/recovery time. Instead of getting things done no matter the cost to yourself, seek to get things done in a way that is also healthy for you, e.g., building breaks or brief naps into your plan. Put yourself first more often. Avoid back-to-back meetings when you can or leave at least a 10-minute cushion in between. Add a self-care or pampering activity to your to-do list, knowing that its completion is as important as that report you need to finish for work.

Block out time on your calendar for self-care rather than leaving it vulnerable to others' gobbling up your "free" time by scheduling meetings on your behalf.

What any individual needs for good self-care really depends on them; there is no one-size-fits-all formula. One way I figure out if a self-care choice works for me is if I get the inner sense that sandbags have been lifted from my shoulders. For someone else it could be a deep, relaxing sigh that comes out naturally. For others, perhaps it's noticing that whatever they're doing has them smiling. Learn what your own cues are for knowing you're on the right track for making wise choices that support your self-care. Avoid measuring yourself against others' standards for self-care and create your own routine based on your unique goals and values. We're all different and that means we all come with different requirements.

Making choices is a constant in our lives. Some are big choices, like whether to start or end a relationship or find another job. There is no shame in asking for help with such complex matters. Cynthia James, Author and Christian Psychologist, encourages her "tribe" to ask a higher power when they don't feel like they can change a situation on their own. This is another way of asking for help. Either way, it is important to be aware of when a choice is in your best interest; in other words, when it supports your happiness, health and peace of mind.

Carolyn, Revisited

Let's revisit the example of Carolyn and the difficulty she has making daily choices that support her resolution to improve her health by eating better and exercising. First, let's jump into a typical workday, specifically at lunchtime, when she sees others leaving for lunch, but still hasn't completed an important project. Instead of dashing to the company break room to grab a soda and some distasteful vending machine "food," Carolyn closes her eyes to check in with herself. She imagines how good she will feel after eating a salad from that healthy restaurant six blocks from the office. She sits with this feeling, smiling at the thought of not feeling bloated or tired in the afternoon from indulging in junk food. She imagines how healthful food choices for lunch will negate the need for her afternoon coffee, and how that might help her get to sleep earlier that night. She considers that her supervisor may not be as impressed as he normally is if Carolyn takes time for a real lunch break, but then she reminds herself that she will be a better, more productive employee if she treats her body well. More importantly, however, is how she will be a better version of herself overall if she just chooses a healthy entrée over processed snacks.

While she's feeling good about how a healthy lunch will positively impact her, she pushes away from her desk and grabs her coat to leave before her negative habits have a chance to fight back. She walks to and from the restaurant and is pleasantly surprised at how much more quickly she completes her work after eating food that nourishes her. She also notices another benefit she hadn't anticipated – namely, that by giving her body the nutrients it needs, she no longer has a mid-afternoon candy craving and is able to work until quitting time without snacking. She has completed enough work to feel good about her day, so she leaves when others tend to leave, walking the quarter mile to the parking lot where she purposely parked in the morning, another trick to get more movement into her day. Feeling great by the time she reaches her car, Carolyn drives straight to her gym and pulls her gym bag from the trunk – another smart choice she made, to always keep gym clothes on hand. After working out, she grabs a smoothie from the gym's cafeteria and drives home, where she will sleep soundly through the night without pain, restlessness, or the need for pharmaceuticals. All because she made wise choices that day. Remember: over time, seemingly small or insignificant better choices add up to big positive outcomes.

We are not victims; we are "volunteers" to the choices we make.

— Pam MacGregor

❧

Intention:

I intentionally make wise choices that support my self-care goals.

Now, how about digging deeper? As a warm-up to this time for reflection, I suggest listening to "My Wish" by Rascal Flatts.

Invitation to Reflect:

What are some healthy choices you make that you'd like to continue making?

_____

_____

_____

_____

What are some unhealthy or unhelpful choices you often make that you'd like to change?

_____

_____

_____

_____

_____

What would your life look like with better self-care choices?

_____

_____

_____

_____

_____

Here are some actions you can take now for your self-care:

- ○ Today, make one choice based on *love* instead of *fear*.
- ○ Research the concept of Growth vs. Fixed Mindset by Carol Dweck.
- ○ Consciously choose the self-care option when faced with a dilemma.

Commit to doing at least one thing differently based on what you learned in this chapter. Write out an actionable goal – with a specific deadline – to satisfy this commitment.

_____

_____

_____

_____

How will you celebrate or reward yourself if you reach the goal?

_____

_____

Other thoughts and reflections:

_____

_____

_____

_____

_____

_____

_____

For additional resources related to this topic, please check out my website: www.abcsofselfcare.com

D

DISCIPLINE YOURSELF

For a man to conquer himself is the first and noblest of all victories.

— Plato

❦

Remember when you played your first sport as a kid and your coach started out by teaching the fundamentals? Every sport has them. As a child you were likely more interested in getting to the fun: scoring points! But your coach likely made you learn and practice the fundamentals of that sport before having you play the game. John Wooden, the famed UCLA basketball coach who won 10 NCAA national championships in less than 12 years, was notorious for demanding that his players always practice the fundamentals, right down to how to properly tie shoelaces. No kidding! Shoelaces! But hey, who's going to argue with his record of success? Not a soul!

And guess what? As your self-care coach, I'm going to encourage you to do the same: discipline yourself to do the fundamentals of self-care so you can win big in the game called Life.

Dennis and Discipline

Let's consider the case of Dennis. Dennis recently attended a workshop with his girlfriend Deborah on self-care and work/life balance and the important role it plays in living a fulfilling life. Although he went to support her, he left more committed to practicing self-care and re-creating his life with better balance. As the instructor recommended, he journaled, listing all the ways he could practice better self-care on a regular basis. As a writer, Dennis works from home, so incorporating his list of self-care actions into his daily routine shouldn't be too challenging, right? Wrong! With good intentions to start his morning with a brief meditation followed by a bit of exercise in his living room, Dennis awakens with a sense of dread about his current writing deadline. Still in his bathrobe, he quickly dashes to his home office and jumps on his laptop to double check the deadline his editor set for the latest chapter. While online, he checks his other emails, both personal and professional. One email includes a link to a *New York Times* article, and after reading that, he scrolls through the other headlines, captivated by all the important news of the world. Before he realizes it, hours have passed and he hasn't even showered, let alone done the morning routine he'd planned.

With his deadline just days away, he forgoes a lunch break and does a deep dive into his writing, stopping only to grab more coffee from the kitchen every hour or so. Before realizing it, it's 8 pm and Dennis hasn't eaten all day. But he's mid-paragraph and on a roll, so he dials the number for his favorite pizzeria, places a delivery order, and keeps jamming on his manuscript. Finally, on his way to the shower (at last!), the doorbell rings. Pizza delivery! Famished, and not a fan of lukewarm pizza, Dennis takes the entire pizza box to the living room, grabbing a bottle of cabernet and a wine glass from the kitchen as he goes. Plopping down on the couch, Dennis briefly feels remorse for another day gone by without meditation or exercising or even one breath of fresh air from outside. But that first cheesy bite combined with that first warming swig of the cabernet melts away that remorse, and Dennis settles in to watch his favorite superhero movie. He later falls into bed exhausted, vowing to start tomorrow the way he'd planned to start today.

How disciplined was Dennis about the way he both began and finished his day? If you said *not one bit*, you're absolutely correct! And how much self-care do you think Dennis will practice tomorrow? Again, *not one bit*. Not until he starts practicing better discipline, one of the fundamentals, will Dennis see the positive results of a commitment to self-care.

Quick Check - Select all that apply:

- ☐ I have difficulty sticking to intentions/goals/New Year's resolutions.
- ☐ My mornings often start rushed and chaotic.
- ☐ I am not sure what to do or where to start for better self-care.

The Fundamentals by Category

When it comes to self-care, there are plenty of important fundamentals, and they fall into six categories that you may have seen before in various self-improvement or self-awareness programs. Why do we see these categories so frequently? Because they are fairly standard in determining if you have a good balance in your life.

Below are the six categories along with some of the self-care fundamentals that fall under each:

Emotional

- Maintain a positive mental attitude.
- Manage change (When I'm going through a lot of unplanned changes, I minimize the changes I make – like I won't even choose a new moisturizer).
- Preserve mental health with the help of therapists and coaching professionals.

Practical

- Take sufficient time away from work (daily breaks, days off, vacations).
- Maintain household responsibilities (cleaning, decluttering, organizing).
- Stay current with financial responsibilities (bills, paperwork, etc.) and monitor your financial health (live below your means, spend less, and save more; save for retirement as if you will live to be 100 – with better self-care, it could happen).

Physical

- Eat healthier (more whole foods, less processed foods, controlled portion sizes) and drink more water (approximately ½ - 1 ounce of water a day for every pound of body weight).
- Stay active (regular movement or exercise, such as stretching or gardening or whatever feels good to your body).
- Sleep 7-9 hours per night and practice good sleep hygiene (powering down screens 1-3 hours before bed, avoiding stimulants after 4 p.m.).

Mental/Intellectual

- Set and achieve goals and work on your dreams.
- Read books (especially ones that improve career or personal knowledge).
- Adopt a Growth vs. Fixed Mindset.

Social

- Maintain healthy relationships, practice forgiveness and unconditional love.
- Balance social activities with rest.
- Set and maintain boundaries with everyone.

Spiritual

- Reflect upon and confirm or amend your spiritual beliefs.
- Do activities to support your spiritual beliefs.
- Develop a spiritual practice in line with your spiritual beliefs.

These fundamentals of a balanced life require discipline to consistently engage in them, as well as to adopt habits that may be new to you. Self-care is about more than the occasional spa appointment or nap. If you're new to these fundamentals, don't get overwhelmed by them. Start where you are, choose one thing from the list to focus on for the upcoming week or month. Once you feel you've incorporated that into your routine without thinking about it, pick another fundamental to practice, and so on. Avoid all self-judgment. Just do the work, at your own pace, and know that the more you practice the fundamentals, the more they'll become second nature to you. And remember to use the Three R's – Reminders, Rituals, and Repetition – to make self-care practices a part of your lifestyle.

Create a Morning Routine

Creating a powerful and supportive morning routine is one of the best ways to practice the fundamentals. My own morning routine includes ignoring email, text messages, and notifications from the apps on my phone until *after* I've had a cleansing drink of water and done my morning meditation. When I don't stick to this practice, I find that my mind focuses on whatever I just read rather than staying present and mindful during my meditation – which is the entire point of meditating! I hold off on any work communications until after I've had breakfast. Some mornings, I listen to motivational songs (I'm partial to Karen Drucker's music) while I stretch. The right music can be a meditation in motion. Notice I said "some" mornings. Why? Because I'm as human as the next person, and sometimes I'm seduced by an incoming text or email. Fortunately, I've been disciplining myself to do the fundamentals for so long now that I notice my misstep, accept it, and get back on track easily. You will be able to do the same soon enough. Do you have a morning routine? Does it support the fundamentals? Or is it a mad dash to your caffeine of choice followed by getting to work as quickly as possible? Is it time to review your morning routine and revamp it to be one that is more empowering and supportive of your commitment to self-care?

Create a Nighttime Routine

I find that my nighttime routine is more difficult to do consistently than my morning routine. Why? Because at the end of a day of go-go-go, it's often challenging to let go of all that energy and wind down. Our minds like to trick us into thinking that they can keep going till we drop. This is *not* a fundamental of self-care. Even if it feels like we're not ready to wind down for the evening, wind down we must! Trust me, you'll end up being even more productive during your days if you create and adhere to a healthy nighttime routine.

Having once been challenged by insomnia during a stressful period of my life, I am now conscious of the need to prepare for bed and practice healthy sleep hygiene. I avoid news, TV, Google, or other potentially negative information, in general. I also avoid sugar and caffeine after 4 p.m. I usually stop eating, drinking, and exercising three hours before bedtime. One hour before bedtime, I put my phone in Do Not Disturb mode to avoid getting into late night chats while I'm in wind-down mode. I usually turn off all the screens in my life: TV, phone, iPad, etc. Then I do less intense activities like tidying up, brushing my teeth, and reading. (I'm also careful about what I read because some material is too stimulating for me right before bed.) If I'm still wired, I'll take deep breaths or listen to soft music, or a calming meditation on Calm.com (I have a life-time membership). Ideally, I go to bed at the same time each night. And if all else fails, I'll take Melatonin or a sleep aid because I'm *committed* to getting my 7-9 hours of sleep.

Do the Fundamentals

Did you notice the fundamentals do *not* include scouring social media and the internet? How did we ever live without Google?! Like many of us, I am a frequent Googler. And I love apps! However, I've found myself lost in pages of social media and other websites, going down rabbit hole after rabbit hole while the minutes melt away. Sometimes, I don't notice how far gone I am until 45 minutes have passed. And trust me, I wasn't always looking at self-care related articles and posts. Social media has become an integral part of our lives and I'm not saying you should give it up. It's a great place to connect or catch up with your real friends. The internet is full of reliable and legitimate sources of information and data to help you make decisions about your health and well-being. Still, time spent online can rob you of hours better spent making real connections with people or attending to self-care. Discipline yourself to limit time spent on social media by setting a timer or an internal deadline for how long you'll spend online. Balance negative news with positive self-care or spiritual rituals to keep a positive mental attitude. Read positive messages and ideas to make social media and the internet work for, not against, your self-care lifestyle.

Disciplining yourself to do the fundamentals improves your quality of life. No doubt. That said, the fundamentals shouldn't preclude you from attending to your physical health as well. Have regular health exams and recommended tests based on your age or underlying conditions. I trust you will rise to the challenge – discipline yourself to create happiness, health, and peace of mind – one disciplined habit at a time!

Dennis, Revisited

Let's return to the story of Dennis and see how he might've practiced better discipline with the fundamentals of self-care. Dennis awakens, at peace and ready to launch his new morning self-care routine. Because he already wrote out his daily "to do" list the night before – which includes some for self-care – he knows what needs to get done today and at what time he'll handle each one. First on his list is meditation. Second, exercise. Third, shower. With a clear plan for taking care of himself before he takes care of "business" (in this case, his writing). Dennis can move through these supportive self-care plans without stressing about his impending deadline. At 10 a.m. he steps away from his writing mid-sentence and takes a brisk walk around the block. Why? Because it was listed on his daily to-do list with "10 a.m." written in the margin. He does the same again at 3 p.m. At 6 p.m. he shuts down his computer and writes out his plan for the next day, including small acts of self-care he intends to perform for himself. He marvels at how much further in his writing he got today, even though he stopped to take brief walks and eat a proper lunch in the kitchen. He then carries on with the rest of his daily plan, making a light dinner for himself before doing some pleasure reading. At 9 p.m., Dennis sits quietly for ten minutes before climbing into bed. He sleeps well and awakens the next morning, refreshed and ready to go.

We must all suffer one of two things: the pain of discipline or the pain of regret and disappointment.

— Jim Rohn

❧

Intention:

I have the discipline to commit to self-care fundamentals.

Now, how about digging deeper? As a warm-up to this time for reflection, I suggest listening to "Rise Up" by Andra Day.

Invitation to Reflect:

What are some of the ways you are already disciplined?

_____

_____

_____

What not-so-good habits keep you from being more disciplined?

_____

_____

_____

_____

Think of one area in your life where you'd like to be more disciplined. Describe the feeling and positive results of being more disciplined.

_____

_____

_____

_____

Here are some actions you could take now for your self-care:

○ Create and write down a *morning* routine you intend to follow, with time frames. It might include prayer, meditations, affirmations, journaling, reading, a drink of water, breakfast, hot beverage and/or exercise.
○ Create and write down a *nighttime* routine you intend to follow, with time frames. It might include setting an "in bed by" timeframe, prayer, meditation, affirmations, journaling, reading, turning off screens 1-3 hours from bedtime and/or stretching.
○ Schedule an appointment for at least one preventative maintenance activity: Schedule regular testing for your health (annual physical, mammogram, etc. and, depending on your philosophical views, typical vaccines: flu, shingles, and tetanus shots)

Commit to doing at least one thing differently based on what you learned in this chapter. Write out an actionable goal – with a specific deadline – to satisfy this commitment.

_____

_____

_____

_____

_____

How will you celebrate or reward yourself if you reach the goal?

_____

_____

Other thoughts and reflections:

_____

_____

_____

_____

_____

_____

_____

_____

For additional resources related to this topic, please check out my website: www.abcsofselfcare.com

$$\mathcal{E}$$

EMBRACE ENOUGH-NESS

I was told I wasn't good enough, but I just chose not to listen.

– Khalid

Did you know that you are worthy simply by virtue of being born? Scientists estimate the probability of being born is at least 1 in 400 trillion, if not 1 in 400 *quadrillion*! How miraculous is that! Despite these incredible odds of our existence, most of us have forgotten – or worse yet, never knew – this basic truism of our innate worthiness, of being enough. Somewhere along our journeys, we lost our sense of this, perhaps because someone or something in our childhood experiences made us feel as if we weren't enough. So, we grew up, consciously or subconsciously, believing this lie. It doesn't matter how you accepted this myth of unworthiness. What matters is changing this false belief.

Eva and Embracing Enough-ness

Let's consider Eve. After 24 years of marriage and caring for her triplet children as a full-time homemaker, like a bad cliché Eve's husband leaves her for a younger woman with whom he plans to start a new family. Eve is devastated. Sure, she and her husband had grown apart a bit as the demands of parenting and volunteering at the kids' schools. Add in his constant travel for work and, well, *life* got in the way. But divorce? Another woman? This was never a situation she thought she'd find herself in.

Eve had assumed that making it to the empty nest-stage of their marriage meant they could reconnect, spend more time together. Instead, Eve now spends her days feeling lost, alone, grief-stricken and like a loser. She chides herself for not having been aware that her marriage was falling apart. For not working harder to keep the excitement alive (while changing 3 sets of diapers, mind you). For not keeping as fit and toned as she was when she and her husband met at the company where he still works. For not trying harder to look her best. For not keeping her husband's interest. Eve can barely bring herself to get out of bed, let alone begin to reimagine a life without her ex-husband in it. Alone and devastated, Eve has spent the better part of the last 12 months barely leaving the house that was once filled with family activity and laughter. Most days are a mix of tears, chocolate, television, and lots of naps – sometimes not leaving the master bedroom at all. She sees no end to the emotional pain she feels, no possibility for happiness again. And it's all…her…fault. A self-destructive cycle has taken root: the more she condemns herself, the worse she feels. And the worse she feels, the more she condemns herself. More recently, Eve has fantasized about getting a diagnosis of terminal cancer. At least death would bring a welcome relief from the pain of living with herself, with all the mistakes she's made. And, she thinks, she would deserve it. How could she have messed everything up so monumentally?!

Clearly, Eve is still experiencing the grief that comes with loss, and her self-esteem is at an all-time low. By not recognizing that she is enough, regardless of her husband's decision to leave the marriage, Eve has trapped herself in a downward spiral of self-loathing and self-recrimination. In this mode, anyone would have a hard time believing that life could improve, that *this too shall pass*.

Quick Check - Select all that apply:

- ☐ I often compare myself to others then feel despair.
- ☐ I often feel like an imposter that doesn't deserve my success.
- ☐ I often feel inadequate as a spouse, parent, friend, sibling, coach, or leader.

Know the Importance of Being Enough

Why is the concept of being enough so important? Enough-ness is a necessary foundation for knowing – truly knowing with every ounce of your being – that you are deserving of self-love and love from others. Our enough-ness keeps us from "compare and despair" behavior, which is a form of self-sabotage. Embracing our enough-ness allows us to focus on our individual paths versus, say, trying to rival someone else's path or live up to another's expectations of us. We each have a unique destiny, our own individualized purpose. Embracing our enough-ness helps us realize that we deserve all the goodness life has to offer, including the experience of giving and receiving unconditional love.

And the beauty of enough-ness? It isn't something we have to earn. We're each born with it. We were born worthy. Yet as we allow the thoughtless comments or actions of others, or our own destructive self-talk, to chip away at our sense of innate worthiness, we develop a pattern of shame. And shame, as researcher Brené Brown, PhD, LMSW will tell you, can wreak havoc on the psyche. A steady diet of shame can cause us to believe we are worthless, damaged, and maybe even simply no good. If we feel shame on a regular basis, we begin to behave in ways that reinforce this shame, creating even more of it – and thus the cycle continues. To break this destructive pattern, I recommend repeating "I am good enough" or "I am enough" as often as you can. A friend of mine likes to write the initials "IAE" (I Am Enough) on her hand in the morning as a reminder that she is, indeed, enough.

Sometimes, the issue of not feeling like we're enough stems from over-identifying with external validation. Let's say you miss a goal or deadline, fail to get a promotion, believe you weigh too much, or feel you're not making enough money. Do any of these outcomes tend to make you feel that you're not good enough? For most of us, the answer is, sadly: yes. But what if you viewed things differently? What if a missed deadline actually saved you from making a big mistake by rushing to meet the deadline? What if a promotion you didn't get brought forth a different career opportunity that was even better suited to you than the promotion you coveted? The minute we over-identify with something we didn't achieve or receive, we subconsciously chip away at our sense of worthiness. Why not view the missteps and unachieved goals as just another "plot twist" in life rather than a reflection of our worthiness, or lack thereof? One result of this shift in perspective would be far greater levels of contentment and resiliency. And who couldn't benefit from more of these?

Eliminate the Imposter Syndrome

Imposter Syndrome, also known as Fraud Syndrome, is a psychological phenomenon in which we doubt our skills, talents or accomplishments and have a persistent fear of being exposed as a fraud. It manifests in feelings of not deserving all that we have achieved, often believing it was luck and that we're not as capable or intelligent as others believe we are.

I once attended a workshop conducted by The Bella Network, whose work supports female leaders and entrepreneurs. I was struck by how many successful women, with tons of accomplishments and accolades under their belts, felt they were not enough. Perhaps you know a few yourself, including one who can be found by looking in the mirror? When it comes to imposter syndrome, I can't help but recall messages I received in my younger years, such as *work twice as hard to be considered equal*. I also remember experiences of implicit bias when I did something that was viewed as odd by my white peers. I worked in toxic environments that reinforced my own feelings of being an imposter, as if someone was going to come find out that I really didn't belong in that leadership position or at that elite accounting firm. High achieving people, including Michelle Obama, have acknowledged their own experiences with imposter syndrome and feeling undeserving of the accolades bestowed upon them. Rather than being found out, those with imposter syndrome often work harder than most to convince themselves – and others – that they are deserving of their achievements. Yet if you looked at the accomplishments of those with imposter syndrome, you'd be blown away by their collective achievements.

So how do we rid ourselves of imposter syndrome? Realizing that we are worthy regardless of our accomplishments is a good place to start. Minimizing unrealistic or perfectionistic standards that perpetuate feelings of being a fraud helps as well. The inability to recognize our individual competence, combined with constant striving to prove oneself, robs us of feeling that we are enough as we are. Plus, let's face it – it's exhausting!

Own Your Unique Brilliance

You don't need to be Superwoman to prove what you already are: *enough*. You needn't try to become the next Mother Teresa to prove what you already are: *enough*. You are not loved for what you do or attempt to do. You are loved for simply being yourself. Living any other way drains us. So, take off the superhero cape, drop it to the ground, and never look back.

Here's an idea! What if you owned your own unique gifts and acted as if you had everything you need to showcase your unique brilliance? How do you know what these gifts are? By answering a few questions, such as:

- What makes me different?
- What stands out about me?
- What do I do differently than the masses?
- What gets me jazzed when I do it?
- What am I good at? (Notice I didn't say "great" or "expert" at)

Make time to learn the answers; they are likely clues to your unique gifts. Are you ready to own those gifts? Because until you truly own them, you can't share them with the world. So, own them...or not. The choice is yours.

And what happens if we own and develop our gifts to the point of gaining some notoriety? Well, typically this is when the haters show up – people who have their own issues like insecurity or maybe not embracing their enough-ness and so they feel the need to criticize others to feel better about themselves. Ignore them. You can't help them and they're not your problem. They're background noise, nothing more. The best way to protect yourself against the unwanted and unhealthy influence of haters is to strengthen your sense of enough-ness on a regular basis. When we see ourselves as good enough – no matter our results – we fortify ourselves against the inevitable judgment of the outside world.

Does embracing our enough-ness mean we can't strive to accomplish goals or be a bigger version of ourselves? Heck no! It simply means that you are worthy of love with or without that marathon finisher's medal, with or without that Ph.D., with or without that promotion or husband or ideal weight or whatever else you believe you need to achieve or obtain to be enough. Go for your goals... just don't tie your worthiness to their achievement. The two are not connected.

Eve, Revisited

Let's return to our example with Eve. Let's assume that Eve truly, in her bones, feels that she is, indeed, enough. Does her husband's announcement about leaving the marriage still devastate her? You bet! Why? Because divorce is devastating! However, with the sense of being enough, of truly claiming her enough-ness, Eve can feel her grief while simultaneously knowing that she will, eventually, move past this sense of utter devastation. She could gently review what may have caused her marriage to be vulnerable and to assess any behavior patterns she'd like to change in herself – not to "win" her ex back, but to fulfill her own needs and desires. With this sense of being enough, Eve allows a few close friends to take turns tending to her emotional needs, accepting the small comforts they provide, be it a homemade soup delivery or a shoulder to cry on. And one day, forever impacted but not broken, Eve realizes she is ready to engage in the world again, humbled yet stronger. Wiser. Content.

No one can make you feel inferior without your consent.

— Eleanor Roosevelt

❧

Intention:

I believe I am enough because I exist.

Now, how about digging deeper? As a warm-up to this time for reflection, I suggest listening to "You Say" by Lauren Daigle.

Invitation to Reflect:

When did you first feel unworthy?

_____

_____

_____

_____

_____

Name one situation where you felt that you were an imposter? How could you show up more empowered next time?

_____

_____

_____

_____

What people or situations trigger feelings of not enough-ness?

_____

_____

_____

_____

Here are some actions you could take now for your self-care:

- ○ Verify your answers to the reflection questions by doing a root cause analysis of your feelings of not being enough (See Letter A).
- ○ Create an affirmation (one you believe in, as if it is already true) about your enough-ness, it could be simply "I am enough." Keep saying it 10-108 times per day. Some other ideas are "I am capable of great accomplishments." "I am worthy of praise!" Speak it in your mind or out loud or write it down – consistently and with conviction.
- ○ Reflect and write about what makes you unique: talents, abilities, unique traits.

Commit to doing at least one thing differently based on what you learned in this chapter. Write out an actionable goal – with a specific deadline – to satisfy this commitment.

_____

_____

_____

_____

How will you celebrate or reward yourself if you reach the goal?

_____

_____

Other thoughts and reflections:

_____

_____

_____

_____

_____

_____

_____

For additional resources related to this topic, please check out my website: www.abcsofselfcare.com

$\mathcal{F}$

FORGIVE

The practice of forgiveness is our most important contribution to the healing of the world.

— Marianne Williamson

❦

The most common myth about forgiveness is that it condones bad, illegal, cruel, or unethical behavior of the perpetrator. Wrong! Even if forgiven, someone causing harm to another should still be held accountable. Accountability and forgiveness are not a package deal; one does not negate the other.

The second most common myth about forgiveness is that it serves the forgiven – the perpetrator of harmful behavior. Wrong again! The person who benefits most by forgiveness is the *forgiver*, not the forgiven. Sounds counter-intuitive, yes. But consider this: how much additional harm is being caused by all that anger being dragged around by the victim week after week, year after year? The answer? A lot. And given the now proven mind-body connection, it's highly likely that the stress of unresolved anger, over time, can lead to issues far beyond those created by the original misconduct. Forgiveness isn't about letting the culprit off the hook; it's about letting yourself off the hook, freeing yourself from the negative impact of all that anger, justified thought it may be. Let's see how unresolved anger and an inability to forgive can play out.

Fiona and Forgiveness

Let's look at Fiona's situation. Six years after "the accident" she still walks with a noticeable limp. During a long run in the countryside while training for her 10th marathon, Fiona was hit by a teenager who'd had his driver's license for less than two months. The driver had also been texting at the time. Fiona spent several weeks in the hospital before moving into a rehab facility for several more weeks, learning to walk again and, mostly, learning to deal with the new reality of her body. The accident had left her with no less than two dozen metal screws and rods in her right hip, femur, and knee. While at the rehab facility, the young driver came to visit, apologizing profusely, even crying about what he'd done. Fiona assumed that since his mother was with him, it was she who had made him come. Fiona lashed out at the young man, letting him know he had ruined not only her leg but her entire life. The meeting did not end well.

And now, years later, Fiona still can't shake her disgust with the young man. She secretly stalks him on social media, especially infuriated by any posts that involve physical activities – physical activities that she will never be able to do again. When he shares a photo of himself at the finish line of a 10K, Fiona comes unglued, hurling her phone across the room, shattering its screen on the far wall. She loathes this young man, now 23-years-old and seemingly doing well. She detests his apparent happiness, success, and *mobility*. A friend encourages Fiona to move beyond her anger and find a way to forgive him. Fiona abruptly ends the relationship, livid with her now former friend for "defending" the driver. Instead of the trauma of the accident dissipating over time, Fiona's inability to forgive has her trapped in a self-destructive loop, reliving the experience frequently and becoming more bitter month by month.

Fiona's example clearly demonstrates the wrong-headed perspective that many of us have around the subject of forgiveness. Namely, that withholding forgiveness is like drinking poison and waiting for the person who violated you to die. Insane, right? Well, that's figuratively what we each do when we refuse to forgive (notice I did not say *forget*) the person who caused us harm in life, be it a close friend, spouse, work colleague or complete stranger.

Quick Check - Select all that apply:

- ☐ I often hold grudges.
- ☐ I have lingering anger, bitterness, and/or resentment over past hurts.
- ☐ I suffer from mental turmoil due to unresolved trauma.

Overcome Negative Emotions...Before They Overcome You

One of the people who inspires me when it comes to the topic of forgiveness is Iyanla Vanzant. She has helped many people stuck in their anger and inability to forgive. She helps them discover the role they played in becoming victims to the bitterness and resentment they hold toward those who've harmed them in some way. So, let's just say Iyanla has an abundance of experience dealing with forgiveness. As she puts it, "only forgiveness can liberate minds and hearts once held captive by anger, bitterness, resentment, and fear." How right she is! And remember, forgiving someone doesn't condone or excuse what was done to you. Iyanla states it best when she defines forgiveness as "the intentional and voluntary process by which a victim undergoes a change in feelings and attitude regarding an offense and overcomes negative emotions such as resentment and vengeance."

I know, I know – easier said than done. You have every right to feel resentful and to desire revenge when someone does you wrong. But would this change what occurred with the original offense? No. Would it likely create even more problems in your life? Most likely. Is forgiveness a more powerful response to an offense? Absolutely! Over the years, my clients who have found a way to forgive those who've wronged them have also had to dig deep for levels of compassion they didn't realize they possessed, no matter how horrific their perpetrators' actions were. This may require the help of a therapist, spiritual counselor, or trusted friend. Whatever it takes, it will be worth it.

Be Neck-down Alive

If you avoid your uncomfortable feelings associated with a particular incident by staying in your head, it will be more difficult to forgive and move on. It's what Iyanla calls being in a state of "neck-down dead." Ignoring these uncomfortable feelings won't make them dissipate. In fact, quite the opposite is true – they'll likely fester and grow over time until they're shouting for attention to be resolved. So instead of being neck-down dead, aim instead for being neck-down *alive!* In other words, open your heart, allow yourself to feel the discomfort of something harmful that was done to you, feel the discomfort associated with the person who wronged you. Feel it...so you can release it.

Think of any resentments you harbor toward others, or even toward yourself, as being a large barrel of toxic gunk that you're carrying with you throughout every day. How much easier would your life be if you could tip that barrel over and pour all that gunk into the earth? Well, guess what? You can! Use this image when consciously practicing forgiveness and imagine yourself pouring all resentments you carry with you into the earth where they are absorbed. How much lighter do you feel now? This visualization can be used as often as needed until forgiveness has become second nature to you, until you realize you're no longer carrying that heavy weight. You'll be *happier* because you're no longer weighted down. You're *healthier* because you're no longer exposing yourself to toxic energy, which could lead to disease and illness. Letting go of that toxic gunk will absolutely contribute to the increased *peace* of mind you seek. Promise!

Practice, Practice, Practice

One of the best ways to develop the habit of forgiveness in your life is simple: practice, practice more, and then practice even more. Practice – whether in sports or penmanship or cooking or forgiveness – leads to mastery. Once you've practiced forgiveness to the point of mastery, it becomes as simple and natural as breathing. You won't even need to think about it; it'll occur as an instinctive response to any offense. Someone cuts you off on the highway? You'll be more inclined to have compassion for the rough day they must be having rather than flipping them the bird. Someone commits a more awful offense toward you? Perhaps it will take longer, but the path to forgiveness will begin much sooner if you have a strong forgiveness habit in place. Remember, the quicker you can move into a state of forgiveness, the quicker you can dissipate the ill effects of clinging to anger and resentment, and the less likely you are to get stuck in a vicious cycle of unhealthy and unproductive emotions.

So, how does one practice forgiveness? One of the simplest tools to cultivate the habit of forgiveness is to immediately (or as soon as you're willing and able) write down forgiveness statements after each offense, whether the object of your forgiveness is another person...or yourself. For example:

- I forgive myself for falling off my healthful eating plan last night.
- I forgive my coworker for slighting me in that meeting.
- I forgive the person who broke into my car and stole my valuables.
- I forgive my stepfather for the abuses he committed against me as a child. (Again: this does *not* in any way, shape or form mean you condone abusive behaviors; it means you're willing to let go of the hold these horrible formative experiences have had on your psyche for years.)

These statements, whether written down or spoken internally to yourself, are not meant to be shared with the person who mistreated you. They are intended for you, as a means of releasing the negativity associated with the mistreatment. They are for *your* benefit, not your perpetrator's. Should you choose to forgive your perpetrator in person or in writing, that's fine too. But it's not a requirement for forgiveness.

Practicing forgiveness in this one small way – i.e., writing or speaking forgiveness statements – will help you develop a lifelong habit of forgiveness. And that forgiveness is the key to consciously changing our thoughts and feelings about a person or situation to create greater levels of peace of mind. And who doesn't want that?

Fiona, Revisited

What if Fiona were able to forgive the young man who irrevocably changed her life by carelessly plowing into her during her training run? How would her outlook on life be different today if she were able to forgive and move on? Perhaps the outcome would look more like this: Fiona, in the rehab facility, listens to the young man during his visit with her. His tears and words seem genuine, and she can accept them. A year later, however, she still feels anger brewing deep within. *Why should I forgive that little jerk? He ruined my life!* Consumed with these post-traumatic emotions, Fiona realizes that she hates feeling this way. But how can she *not*? What he did was wrong! Instead of caving to her instinct toward hatred and anger, Fiona sets her first ever psychotherapy appointment. With the help of a trained professional, Fiona can see that to forgive someone is not to condone their actions. Nor does it require letting the person who hurt you know that you have forgiven them. Over regular therapy sessions, Fiona learns that all her anger will only hurt *herself* at this point. The young man responsible for permanently injuring her has served his jail time and his probation, and has, seemingly, moved on with his life. Fiona recognizes that she must move on with hers as well. And her refusal to forgive him – for *her* sake, not his – has been like a boat anchor she has dragged around far too long. In time, she is willing to let this anchor go, to forgive, though unlikely to forget, the young man's life-altering mistake. And when she finally does, she feels an immense and immediate relief. That relief allows her to stop focusing on what she can't do and more on what she still *can* do.

Forgive everyone of everything ASAP!

— Iyanla Vanzant

❀

Intention:

I am compassionate and forgive myself and others.

Now, how about digging deeper? As a warm-up to this time for reflection, I suggest listening to "Forgiveness" by Matthew West.

Invitation to Reflect:

Who have you already forgiven?

_____

_____

_____

_____

_____

Who else do you have to forgive for greater peace of mind?

_____

_____

_____

_____

_____

_____

What thoughts or stories are holding you back from letting go of anger, bitterness and/or resentment?

_____

_____

_____

_____

_____

_____

_____

Here are some actions you could take now for your self-care:

○ Add to your nighttime routine: Say to yourself every night before bedtime, "I forgive everyone for everything" or "I am a forgiving person."

○ Complete this sentences for at least one person:
I forgive _____ for _____

_____

_____

_____

○ Visualize right now a barrel full of hurts and disappointments. Now imagine dumping it into the earth. How does it feel now?

_____

_____

_____

Commit to doing at least one thing differently based on what you learned in this chapter. Write out an actionable goal – with a specific deadline – to satisfy this commitment.

_____

_____

_____

_____

How will you celebrate or reward yourself if you reach the goal?

_____

_____

Other thoughts and reflections:

_____

_____

_____

_____

_____

_____

_____

_____

For additional resources related to this topic, please check out my website: www.abcsofselfcare.com

G

GROW WITH GRATITUDE

Gratitude unlocks the fullness of life. It turns what we have into enough, and more. It turns denial into acceptance, chaos to order, confusion to clarity. It can turn a meal into a feast, a house into a home, a stranger into a friend.

— Melody Beattie

❧

Gratitude is one of the most powerful tools available to us all. And it's free! Do you make use of this tool on a daily, even hourly, basis? Have you already cultivated the habit of saying "thank you" to others, yourself, or whatever spiritual power you identify with? Do you regularly show appreciation for all that you're thankful for, including the little things like a short wait time when calling a customer service line or someone holding a door open for you in public? This sort of consistent mindset of gratitude is life changing. Just ask Oprah! Coming from humble beginnings, she credits her regular practice of gratitude – even when times were so tough that all she could find to be grateful for was the air she breathed – for her phenomenal success. And now she's one of the wealthiest women in the world. Okay, this isn't a promise that a few "thank yous" will instantly put your bank account on equal footing with Oprah's, but it is a promise that a consistent focus on gratitude will significantly improve your life.

Gayle and Growing with Gratitude

Gayle spent 12 years out of the workforce, caring for her children during their formative and less independent years. When the family finances get tight and she needs to return to work, a friend of a friend offers her a work-from-home business development job which requires lots of outbound phone calls. Gayle's thrill at receiving the position is quickly dampened when she realizes she'll be making about half of what she once made earlier in her career as a scientist. But she accepts the position, begrudgingly, solely for the paycheck. Now Gayle awakens each morning with a sense of dread about the day of phone work that stretches out before her. During the daily team meetings on Zoom to check in with everyone, she often complains about the factors blocking her from meeting her quota. She takes time during work hours to call her colleagues and fish for similar feelings of dissatisfaction. She understands that this job isn't the best fit for her education, experience, and personality…yet she sticks with it. Why? Because she deeply believes that no one else would hire her. *Why would they?* she asks herself. *Nothing good ever happens in my life.* Gayle continues to grind through each day, miserable and often crying during her lunch break, hating the work she does, but feeling dependent on the income she's receiving. Ultimately, Gayle's attitude – more than her low performance – gets her an HR warning. She brushes off the founder's offer to help her acquire more training that could increase her results. Gayle believes he only wants to get rid of her, that he doesn't respect Gayle's background. Several months pass with no change in Gayle's attitude or work results, and she is laid off. *See?* she tells herself. *Nothing good ever happens to me. Life is so unfair.* Gayle tries for months to find another job, and the pressure of needing to bring in more income becomes crushing. With each online application she pushes "submit" on, she reinforces this dangerous belief. *There's no way I'll get this job either. Nothing. Good. Ever. Happens.* True to her belief system, Gayle continues to suffer emotionally and struggle financially.

Quick Check - Select all that apply:

- ☐ I often feel as if nothing good happens to me.
- ☐ I often complain about what isn't going well.
- ☐ I often take things/people for granted.

Put Gratitude to Work

Gratitude works because it makes us feel good in so many ways. Gratitude sparks positive emotions. Positive emotions spark positive actions. Positive actions lead to positive outcomes. And gratitude for those positive outcomes starts the whole positive cycle over again! How cool is that?!

Many people struggle against a practice of gratitude because there are so many circumstances in their life they have judged to be negative that they never get around to finding and appreciating the positive. Yes, the climate crisis is devastating! Yes, there are evil people in the world doing evil things! Yes, we each have challenges in our lives that are genuine struggles. Gratitude isn't about sticking your head in the sand and pretending these tough situations don't exist. Rather, it's about intentionally focusing on things that you could be thankful for despite any undesirable aspects of life. It's not about denial, but focus. It's about putting energy toward that which is positive to expand the goodness in your life. Expand and increase enough goodness and guess what? The goodness will far outweigh the undesirable.

You can choose to look closely at situations that seem to hold no positive element. The singer, Jewel, claims that having profound amounts of gratitude helped her overcome her anxiety and panic attacks. She even wrote a song about it called "Grateful." Now *that's* putting gratitude to work!

In addition to overcoming anxiety or increasing one's prosperity, growing with gratitude can inspire us to:

- Be more generous.
- Do good for others.
- Be more optimistic.
- Feel more enthusiasm.
- Be more joyful in general.

And guess what? All these wonderful outcomes are contagious! The more gratitude you feel and express, the more gratitude those around you will likely feel and express. Have you noticed how much more enjoyable it is to be in the company of those who are upbeat and grateful vs. those who go through life with the pessimistic and gloomy attitude of Eeyore? Eeyores like to say they're being practical or realistic, when in fact, they're just being Eeyores. A good dose of conscious gratitude could help change that!

Even situations that are challenging in life can be viewed with gratitude if only for providing an example of what you choose not to have in your life or pointing out something that needs changing. Can you genuinely be grateful for family members who are primarily "takers" never returning a favor? Sure! They're great reminders of how you choose not to be. Can you feel sincere gratitude for a job that is soul-crushing? Absolutely! Be grateful for the motivation it provides you to seek a better work situation. Is it possible to appreciate the time you "wasted" in a dead-end relationship? You bet! Appreciate the contrast it offers to healthy relationships, knowing you'll never accept that sort of relationship in the future having experienced it.

A dear friend once told me how grateful she was for having insomnia during a particularly rough stretch of it. Her insomnia, she explained, was a gift that allowed her to be still and hear herself think. It gave her the opportunity to record her thoughts and empty her mind, something that didn't come naturally since she was someone who loves to stay busy. During these times of severe insomnia, she was able to receive powerful messages and insights about her life. And for that, she remains extremely grateful. There truly is no limit to the things you can feel grateful for. Try it!

Practice Gratitude

To grow with gratitude, we must practice! I know, I know – by now I sound like a broken record about the importance of practice, but I will continue to nudge you toward consistently practicing self-care habits until they become second nature to you. And growing with gratitude is likely the most important of all the self-care habits given its exponential impact on all areas of our lives, including all six of the self-care categories: emotional, practical, physical, mental, social, and spiritual.

Psychologist Rick Hansen teaches that our minds are like Velcro for negative information and Teflon for positive information. In other words, we tend to focus on that which we find undesirable, while underplaying the desirable and positive elements in life. Practicing gratitude can shift this default setting in our psyches. It can feel awkward initially, push through anyway. Practice expressing your gratitude for as many things as possible, as often as possible. Express this gratitude out loud or in your head or through written words in your journal or on loose bits of paper kept in a gratitude jar or box. A writer-friend of mine has a practice of ending all her general journal entries with a segment she calls "3 Things." It's just as it sounds – she must end each journaling session by listing three things for which she's grateful, from the simple (donuts) to the profound (another day of adventure on earth). The beauty of writing down all that you are grateful for is because when you're having a particularly rough day, you can reread all the things you've listed – a recipe for improving your mental state.

If writing things down feels too tedious, try staying in bed a few extra minutes each morning and run through as many things you can be grateful for in your head. Do the same at bedtime. It only takes a few minutes on each end of your day and the results will follow.

Remember that every single waking moment of your day offers the opportunity to be grateful. Try putting a "G" (for gratitude) on your hand as a reminder to think about something you can be grateful for every time you notice it. It takes less than 5 seconds! And that very small act every day can be a big step toward growing with gratitude.

Gayle, Revisited

What if Gayle had gone into this "workforce reentry" job with a greater sense of gratitude? How might that have impacted her results? Her options for advancement? What if Gayle had approached her need to increase the family income like this: Word gets out among her network that Gayle wants to go back to work. She is offered a role that doesn't look anything like her earlier career in astronomy, but she is genuinely grateful. She includes the offer in her Daily Gratitude Journal, writing *I am so grateful for this opportunity to return to work, and I know my income will continue to increase over time.* Then Gayle reiterates her gratitude for this opportunity each morning when she sits down at her desk in the guestroom-turned-home-office to repeat some affirmations about the day ahead. *I am so grateful for this job. I am so grateful for the potential clients I'm about to call today. I am so grateful for this amazing opportunity to update my business skills and grow.* And then Gayle begins her tasks with a positive attitude. Within weeks, Gayle has become one of the top performing business development consultants at the company. She receives her first commission check soon after, and again she expresses her gratitude for this additional income in her journal. Six months into the new job, the business takes a turn for the worse and the owner must lay off most of his staff, including Gayle. She thanks him for the opportunity he offered her, and her words are sincere. Gayle updates her LinkedIn profile and again takes to her journal to express gratitude for her next career move to unfold easily. She continues to express her gratitude as she applies for jobs online and reaches out to friends who might have a lead for her. She remains hopeful, open, and filled with appreciation for all she has, knowing that her next best career move will reveal itself in time.

When you are grateful - when you can see what you have - you unlock blessings to flow in your life.

— Suze Orman

❦

Intention:

I have an attitude of gratitude.

Now, how about digging deeper? As a warm-up to this time for reflection, I suggest listening to "Grateful: A Love Song to the World" by Nimo Patel featuring Daniel Nahmod.

Invitation to Reflect:

Who/What are you grateful for? _____ Why?

_____

_____

_____

_____

What thoughts do you have to let go of to have more gratitude?

_____

_____

_____

_____

_____

What is one thing that could be perceived as bad that you could be grateful for?

_____

_____

_____

_____

Here are some actions you could take now for your self-care:

○ Verbalize or write in a journal what you are grateful for during your morning routine and/ or your nighttime routine, ideally while you are drowsy and in a relaxed state when your mind is more receptive to suggestions.

○ Create a Gratitude affirmation you repeat over and over to hijack negative thinking, it could be as simple as "I am grateful" or "I have an attitude of gratitude." Speak the affirmation with conviction, as if it is already true.

○ Keep a gratitude jar (write what you are grateful for on a piece of paper and put them in a plain jar or container you dress up). Be creative. Or create/add to a gratitude journal. Update both, 1-7 days per week.

Commit to doing at least one thing differently based on what you learned in this chapter. Write out an actionable goal – with a specific deadline – to satisfy this commitment.

_____

_____

_____

_____

How will you celebrate or reward yourself if you reach the goal?

_____

_____

Other thoughts and reflections:

_____

_____

_____

_____

_____

_____

_____

For additional resources related to this topic, please check out my website: www.abcsofselfcare.com

H

HAVE HEALTHY SELF-ADVOCACY

Love yourself first and everything else falls into line. You really have to love yourself to get anything done in this world.

— Lucille Ball

❧

Self-advocacy is a term often used in relation to medical self-advocacy or advocating for oneself if you have a disability. I recommend that we talk about self-care in these terms too, because it is important to balance the wants and needs of others with our own wants and needs. It is a reminder to advocate for ourselves, have our best interests in mind when we make choices and decisions. It also applies if we are in a doctor's office or hospital and need to advocate for our care. An act of self-care would be to have a medical advocate in those situations, whether we are incapacitated or not. Someone who can be objective, ask good questions and quickly analyze the information being shared by medical professionals. Some medical professionals will not give you much time to process what they say. I'm the medical advocate for one of my sisters, and we believe the quality of her care has been improved by me sitting in on important appointments to listen for what is being said and not said.

Whether we have a medical advocate or not, one is more likely to practice self-care behaviors if they are self-aware, know what is important to them or what they need at any particular time. Awareness is of course the first step, then acceptance that you have this need, then being willing to act. Often that means expressing your thoughts and feelings to others. As we are making choices about how to spend our time, we can go within and have this somewhat difficult conversation with ourselves, then have the courage to ask for what we need. That is our natural born right. Sometimes that means asking for help when we would rather just do it ourselves. Getting past our need for independence could make the difference in the quality of our self-care and the quality of our lives.

In addition, healthy self-advocacy can also offer the following benefits:

- Resilience during times of difficulty and disappointment.
- Self-recognition of our talents and abilities as well as the talents and abilities of others (especially if you're not getting that recognition at work).
- The ability to be your own best friend.

Hanna and Healthy Self-Advocacy

Hanna's three children are at two different schools in town: elementary and middle. She has always prided herself on being involved in her children's schools, to help the greater community and to support those who support her kids. Whether it's a bake sale or an online auction or a cultural event, Hanna is always first to sign up as a helper. Lately, the number of parent volunteers seems to have shrunk, so Hanna picks up the slack, taking on even more tasks to support the two schools. Her best friend recently launched a nonprofit to help at-risk kids get the resources they need to engage in online education. A work colleague is chairing a gala to benefit cancer research. Both have asked Hanna for help, as her reputation for being a dependable volunteer is well known in the community. Unable to turn her back on a good cause, Hanna, of course, says yes to both efforts. She gives up her regular hikes to free up more time for volunteering. She forgoes her regular bubble baths with a good book.

Soon, her exhaustion shows and her temper flares – most often at her children and husband. With the gala completed and the project with her friend's nonprofit easing up a bit, another friend swoops in with a request for Hanna's help fostering rescue kittens. Hanna is a lifelong animal lover, so how can she say no? She is needed! This is important! Who else will help if not her? She says yes even though every bone in her body screams "No! No more!" She takes in three kittens, continues her regular volunteer efforts at the kids' schools, and becomes more bitter by the day. At the same time, she chides other parents – both behind their backs and to their faces – for not being more active volunteers. "A bunch of selfish folk unwilling to help others," she complains to her husband. Soon, the teachers and other parents at both schools start avoiding her and she feels like a pariah. A burned out, angry pariah. During the Sunday sermon, Hanna is told by her favorite minister that helping others is one of the best ways to serve God and self. "Bull," Hanna mutters under her breath.

Wow! Would you want to hang out with Hanna in this state? Would you aspire to be Hanna? I hope your answer was "not for all the kudos in the world!" Hanna clearly could benefit from a good dose of healthy self-advocacy.

Quick Check - Select all that apply:

- ☐ I am often willing to volunteer my time for a good cause, even if my life is already busy.
- ☐ I believe that once I became a parent, my life was not my own.
- ☐ I often do things for people who can do it themselves (personally and professionally) because it makes me feel good about myself; in fact, I depend on this feeling.

Avoid Extreme Selflessness

People who are selfless often have some very positive attributes. Some are even considered altruistic. George Clooney gave 14 of his good friends a million dollars each, even those who were already wealthy. That is truly a selfless act, even though George's bank account likely didn't suffer much. Being humble and respectful are also associated with selflessness. All good traits. The problem with selflessness, like many things, is when it is taken to an extreme. Said another way, a strength that is overused becomes a weakness.

Healthy self-advocacy is a self-care concept that is especially important to those of us (and I count myself in this category) who tend to take better care of others than we do ourselves. That is selflessness taken to a negative extreme. Why do we do this? It could stem from low self-esteem, or a sense of guilt instilled in us by others. Raise your hand if you've ever been rewarded for being "selfless." I can imagine there is no shortage of hands up. Being selfless is often an expectation for women in our society – at work, at home, and in our relationships. If we are truly committed to our own self-care then, honey, it's time to change those expectations! It's time to designate ourselves as being just as important as the other people in our lives, if not a tad more so.

Even if you are a caregiver you need to make your self-care imperative. Nadine Roberts Cornish, author of *Tears in my Gumbo: The Caregiver's Recipe for Resilience*, committed to advocating for herself because she didn't want to become a statistic or like her mom who died because she didn't make herself a priority. "When I realized self-care was a necessity, the guilt went away," she said. Some statistics reveal that 30% or more of caregivers die before the person they care for. Or they become ill or depressed. No doubt it can be challenging to shift your mindset, but it does get easier with – you know what's coming – practice!

Build Your Self-Esteem

We learn self-esteem from our parents/caregivers who are our first teachers. You tend to have high self-esteem if your parents showered you with love and attention, showed interest in what you cared about, and spent ample time with you. These highly engaged parents were probably parents with high self-esteem themselves. However sometimes life challenges or family history may get in the way of our parents being involved with us, despite their best intentions. Their low self-esteem or mental health may make it difficult to nurture our self-esteem because they are dealing with their own demons. Bless them for having done the best they could with the knowledge, energy, and experiences they brought to parenting. Forgive them. The good news is that the locus of control lies with you. You have within your power to take corrective measures to build your self-esteem. We all can make the choice to grow our self-esteem and thereby, our self-advocacy – for greater happiness, health, and peace of mind.

Research shows that self-esteem can indeed be built. Dr. Glenn Schiraldi, an expert on stress, trauma, and resilience, offers a sequence for building self-esteem over time in *The Self-Esteem Workbook*. Let's dive into each of the key steps in Schiraldi's approach:

(1) Unconditional Self-Worth. This is about accepting who we are, flaws and all. It involves knowing that we are worthy because we exist, not because some external entity or person says so. It's also about knowing – really believing in our gut – that we deserve all of life's goodness, regardless of whether we've "earned" it or not.

(2) Unconditional Love. This is about love without conditions, plain and simple. Experiencing unconditional love is the foundation of self-esteem. We know we're feeling unconditional love for another (or ourselves) when we want what is best for them without any strings attached. Unconditional love is both protective and compassionate. The most difficult, yet most important, time to practice unconditional love is when someone is being unlovable. Yes, you read that right. Like a muscle that continues to strengthen with training, offering unconditional love to ourselves and others is a great "workout" for building self-esteem.

(3) Growth Mindset. Growing in a positive direction, no matter how small each step is, helps build self-esteem. Having a growth mindset – i.e., being willing to learn and develop yourself on a regular basis – is what gets us there. We can learn and grow just as much from an unpleasant experience or so-called "failure" (which I prefer to view as a "growth opportunity") as we can from a positive experience. It's important to remember that our path to greater self-esteem will rarely be a straight line upward; it may zig and zag. The key is to *keep moving,* firm in the belief that we can and will develop aspects of ourselves depending on where we are on life's journey.

While degrees, trophies, awards, and other achievements are fine, we shouldn't depend upon this type of external validation for our self-esteem. We are worthy because we exist, remember? We don't want to be dependent on external validation that may or may not come. That said, our happiness tends to be greater when we're involved with people and situations that bring us joy and nurture our inner sense of self. By choosing more situations like this, we further develop the self-love and healthy esteem we have for ourselves, which leads to an increase in healthy self-advocacy.

Think Beyond Yourself

We all need a sense of purpose and meaning in our lives. Healthy self-advocacy involves giving back, not just feeling good about one's self. Thinking about the impact we're making in the world makes us more well-rounded. Giving our time and talent to a cause that resonates with us can be immensely satisfying. Offering compassion to those who are suffering is another great way to make an impact, while also creating connection within our communities. Volunteering has been one of the most fun and rewarding parts of my life. I felt needed, appreciated and like I was making a difference in the world. And I learned valuable project management, leadership, and presentation skills in the process, so it was win-win. It was only when I gave time to the causes in excess that it became "un-fun." That is when I could have used a dose of healthy self-advocacy or had healthier boundaries to prevent me from suffering through instead of calling it quits sooner.

Taking volunteering to an extreme can lead high achievers to put work and community service above all else. We take on extra projects without thinking about the implications to our current responsibilities. We work all hours of the day and night, committed to external forms of validation and seeking confirmation of our worth. For greater peace of mind, we need to shift our mindset from external validation to internal validation. We are born worthy of anything our heart desires. Worthiness is not bestowed. A healthy boundary for work and community service is to weigh the feel-good benefit vs. the cost to your self-care routine. Be selective about volunteering, and only choose organizations where you are passionate about the mission and future direction. Renegotiate deadlines and project timeframes when necessary. Balance out hard work with the fundamental self-care habits suggested for you in this guide.

Change Your Behaviors

Many of my clients over the years have complained that they don't have time to focus on self-care. They were already *over-giving* to others, often in ways that weren't healthy. For example, many parents equate love with removing all barriers from their children's lives, in essence becoming "snowplow parents." They remove every hardship, big and small, from their children's paths, which has the unintended consequence of impeding their ability to grow into self-reliant adults. Called "learned dependency," this is a classic example of over-giving. Having your children share in the family chores and learn to take care of themselves is actually more loving – and it frees up some of your time for self-care.

Years ago, when I worked at a Fortune 50 company, an internal study was conducted regarding the division of household chores among employees at the company's world headquarters, where 10 - 12-hour workdays were the norm. The results were stunning. In households where only the husband worked outside the home, the wives were, understandably, handling most of the household chores.

However, in households where both the husbands and wives worked outside the home, and even in households where *only* the wives worked outside the home, the women still handled most of the household chores. Is this the case in your household? Do you see where you might have, consciously or unconsciously, set up an imbalance of giving when it comes to the mundane tasks of home life? It might be time to reassess the division of labor in your household to ensure that every capable person living under your roof is contributing appropriately. You may have to set new boundaries to make this happen. Sometimes it helps to understand that some men and women were socialized to believe certain roles are expected based on our gender. It is healthier to think more broadly so the whole family benefits. Fathers can be more involved with their kids; moms will be less stressed out and in a better mood and kids will gain more confidence in themselves. And raising children to be confident, responsible, and independent adults will make the world a better place.

Another behavior to look out for is a knee-jerk response to compliments from others who are using them to manipulate you. How do you respond when you hear a colleague or family member say, "But you do it so much better than me!" If your inclination is to do the task this person could easily do for themselves, then it's time to change your own behavior. Learn to accept the compliment and not the task. Changing these ingrained behavior patterns won't be easy, but it will be worth it. It will result in a greater team effort at home and more balance in relationships overall.

Fall in Love with Yourself

Other than increasing your self-esteem and learning your self-care ABCs, falling in love with yourself is one of the greatest contributors to developing a happy, healthy, peaceful life. It involves loving yourself, warts, and all, whether you are crushing self-care or not. Since I love mnemonic devices to aid in memory, let me share one I created to help you F.A.L.L. in love with yourself:

F = *Filter what you say to yourself and what you hear from others.* How? By applying the TNK Technique (True. Necessary. Kind.), for both self-talk and for messages we're receiving from others. Ask yourself these three basic questions, in this order, of the messages you're giving yourself or hearing from another:

- Is it *true* (read: factual)? Or might it be an old story, not based in fact, that I've been telling myself year after year?
- Is it *necessary* (read: helping me/them grow or holding us back)?
- Is it *kind* (read: gentle and compassionate vs. critical and judgmental)?

If the answer to any of these questions is *no*, then I suggest having a go-to phrase or intention to pull yourself back to healthier self-talk. Mine is, "everything works out for my highest good."

Similarly, if we regularly receive messages from someone that are not true, necessary, or kind, we can ask that person to speak to us in a more respectful manner. This is a perfect situation for self-advocacy. There is no guarantee that they will, but ultimately, we are responsible for filtering out the messages we receive that don't pass the TNK test. We shouldn't allow others' insensitive remarks to steal our joy. We can prevent this by mentally putting up an imaginary shield to repel messages that don't serve our growth. Then forgive the offending person and move on. Remember that forgiveness is for you, the person harmed, not for the individual who did the harming. This is an important step because our spoken words are often formed from opinions, based on emotions, and justified with logic. Facts are where it's at.

A = *Accept what "is".* We often upset ourselves by wanting people and circumstances to be different than they are and then blaming ourselves (or someone else) for not making our situation match what's in our minds. We create these ideal scenarios in our heads and then allow them to crush our spirits when what we think should be happening doesn't. This is truly a recipe for misery. Wishing and wanting people and situations to be different is not going to change anything or anyone. Additionally, not accepting what "is" often results in our not being either protective or compassionate toward ourselves (or others). So, accept what "is". The peace it gives is well worth it.

L = *Live in the now.* Harping on our past mistakes often makes us anxious and less loving toward ourselves. Worrying about an uncertain future is just as destructive. The only thing we have is the precious present or *now*. Mindfulness, which is simply keeping our focus on what is happening now, in this moment, can help. Whether it's noticing the beautiful flowers on a walk or listening intently during a conversation, this moment and what's occurring *now* is the only thing we truly have control over. So how about we make good choices about how to spend this moment?

L = *Let it go!* Most of us hold onto soooo much baggage that doesn't serve us for waaaay too long. Sadly, we humans tend to hold on tight to things that are comfortable, whether they serve us or not. We replay old hurts to – weirdly – soothe ourselves in some dysfunctional way. Comfort becomes the subconscious goal instead of mental or physical health. But just because something we're holding onto puts us in our comfort zone doesn't mean it's good for us. We need to let that stuff go. And to do so, we may also need additional support – a good friend, therapist, professional coach, or support group – someone that helps us release old, harmful baggage. Letting go of old stories that don't pass the TNK test is a very loving act of self-care.

I strongly urge everyone to use the F.A.L.L. in love with yourself technique to practice healthy self-advocacy. Some days we'll get it right and others we won't. The key is to continue moving forward, take incremental steps. Be gentle with and have compassion for yourself along the way.

Hanna, Revisited.

In our earlier example, we met Hanna, who has a big heart, but lacks a true understanding of what it means to help others. What if instead of accusing others of being selfish for not helping as much as she does, Hanna was able to embrace and incorporate the concept of healthy self-advocacy? Perhaps Hanna's life would look more like this: Her oldest child begins his middle school years and at Parent Orientation several volunteer opportunities are offered. Hanna is particularly interested in helping with the theater program, so she signs up to chair one of its committees. She reviews her elementary school commitments from the previous year and informs the PTA president that she's going to take a break from volunteering with the elementary school for a year, focusing her efforts on her eldest child's new school. The PTA president says she'll miss her great work, but completely understands. When a friend enlists her help for a nonprofit she's launching, Hanna tells her friend that she's certain it will be a success, but she'll have to pass on helping for now due to her current commitments. Same goes for the gala her former colleague agreed to chair. Instead of signing up, Hanna limits her involvement to buying a few tickets and attending.

Hanna is loving her work with the middle school theater program and the results she's getting are fantastic. Because of her efforts, the school can increase their productions from once a year to once a semester. This makes Hanna feel amazing because she recalls what a positive impact her own middle school theater program had on her growing up. Because her enthusiasm for the theater kids is so apparent, more parents show up to help. And more kids than ever sign up to audition for parts in this year's Spring musical! Just as the musical wraps up, a friend asks Hanna for help fostering rescue kittens. While the little fur babies are adorable, Hanna recognizes that she needs a break from helping others – felines included – so she can restore herself. She puts out a call for fostering help on her favorite social media platform, and within hours she has two people willing to help her friend with the kittens. Hanna settles into her weekly "me time" bubble bath, content that she has done good work in the world. She relishes memories of the Spring musical, which wouldn't have happened had she not been involved. She gives herself a pat on the back for helping 80 young thespians develop their talent and confidence on stage. And now, she allows herself to close her eyes and enjoy a nice long soak in the tub. *Ahhh*, she thinks to herself. *Life is good*. And it is.

If you have found your purpose in life and experience a feeling of deep joy – doesn't have to be every minute of every day – you are following your bliss. Congratulations.

— Joseph Campbell

Intention:

I advocate for myself and contribute to the world.

Now, how about digging deeper? As a warm-up to this time for reflection, I suggest listening to "Man in the Mirror" by Michael Jackson.

Invitation to Reflect:

How often do you take better care of others than yourself? Give yourself a % and think about what percentage to strive for in the future.

_____

_____

_____

_____

_____

Rate yourself 1-3, with 1 being "not so good" and 3 being "I crush it" on each key step in Schiraldi's approach to self-esteem. What will you do differently because of what you learned?

_____

_____

_____

_____

_____

_____

What part(s) of the mnemonic F.A.L.L. in love with yourself do you need to work on most. Prioritize them by giving them a number.

_____

_____

_____

_____

Here are some actions you could take now for your self-care:

○ Think about one thing you had passion for when you were younger that you would currently like to make more time for in your life.

_____

○ Choose at least one commitment that you will give up within the next 1-7 days for healthier self-advocacy.

_____

○ Think about one task you don't enjoy and/or you aren't good at – delegate that task to someone else. I will delegate _____

to _____

Commit to doing at least one thing differently based on what you learned in this chapter. Write out an actionable goal – with a specific deadline – to satisfy this commitment.

_____

_____

_____

How will you celebrate or reward yourself if you reach the goal?

_____

_____

Other thoughts and reflections:

_____

_____

_____

_____

_____

_____

_____

_____

_____

For additional resources related to this topic, please check out my website: www.abcsofselfcare.com

I

INTERNALLY VALIDATE

When we learn to accept who we are right now and celebrate who we are becoming, we can kick the approval habit.

— Sue Patton Thoele

❀

Internal validation is the non-judgment, validation, or acceptance of our own feelings, attributes, actions, or accomplishments. In effect, it's a form of positive self-talk that prevents us from relying on the opinions and judgments (right or wrong) that others have of us. What we tell ourselves has the power to develop self-respect, self-confidence, and self-esteem — all great traits for happiness, health, and peace. Internal validation helps us get comfortable in our own skin. It allows us to be our own council. It relies on supporting oneself emotionally rather than relying on external validation (the opinions of others), which may or may not come.

Isabelle and Internal Validation

Isabelle works as an accountant, but on the weekends her true passion gets attention: painting. After working for weeks on a landscape oil painting, Isabelle posts it on Instagram, proud to share her creative efforts with her friends and followers. When the first comment comes in, she opens the app on her phone to see a supportive comment from a friend. Short and sweet, it reads: *Beautiful!* Isabelle smiles, inwardly releasing a sigh of relief. Like Sally Field's infamous "you like me" speech at the Oscars, Isabelle feels validated after years of classes and one-on-one lessons working in this medium. She hears the ping of her phone a few minutes later and reopens Instagram. Several hearts have been added to her post by followers. Isabelle is thrilled. She goes to bed, pleased that the world (ok, a few acquaintances, a few complete strangers, and an ex-boyfriend from back in high school) has acknowledged her talent. She's not just a bean counter; she's an artist!

The next day at work, Isabelle remembers her post and during her coffee break she decides to check her Instagram account. Over 100 hearts! And more comments! She eagerly scrolls through them: *Wow!* And *Nice!* And *I'm impressed!* And then she sees it, a comment from one of her former classmates from a painting class: *A good start, but a bit washed out.* Isabelle feels like she's been punched in the gut. She continues scrolling to read more one- or two-word compliments before coming upon another negative comment, this time from a complete stranger: *Looks like the cat ate a box of crayons and barfed on a canvas. LOL.* Ouch! Who would be so mean?! Isabelle returns to her current work project, the deadline looming, but can't shake the shame she feels from having read those negative comments.

By evening, her painting has received over 300 hearts! But one more nasty comment has been added, again from a stranger. Isabelle is incensed. And heartbroken. Despite the joy she herself felt while working on and then completing her latest painting, she can't shake her sense of being rejected by those few negative comments. *I guess I'm just a bean counter after all*, she thinks. Opening her Instagram account, she deletes the whole post and goes to bed feeling like a creative loser. She vows to never post her work again. Worse yet, it's months before she even enters her little in-home art studio. *What's the point?* she asks herself each time she passes the studio door.

Has Isabel's reliance on external validation negatively impacted her life? You bet it has! And I'll bet every person reading this right now can relate to Isabel to some degree. It's one thing to accept an accolade or compliment or validation of something about yourself from an outside source; it's quite another to depend upon it. The key is having a healthy appreciation of external validation vs. having an unhealthy reliance on it.

Quick Check - Select all that apply:

☐ I often have trouble making minor decisions without input from a trusted advisor.
☐ I often have trouble committing to decisions made.
☐ I often feel hurt by negative comments received on social media.

Seek External Feedback vs. External Validation

External feedback is not the same as external validation. With external *feedback*, we're seeking information or improvement – input that makes us (or our perspectives, beliefs, actions, or projects) better in some way. When you have a growth mindset, you will welcome feedback to continue growing. With external *validation*, we're seeking confirmation or approval – input that makes us feel okay about ourselves. See the subtle, but notable, difference? Feedback, when offered kindly from those whose perspective you value and who have the proper "expertise" in a relevant area, can be incredibly helpful. Even critical feedback is helpful – again, depending on how and by whom it is delivered. *Constructive* criticism is feedback that offers specific and actionable recommendations that can lead to positive improvements. Being open to, and graciously accepting, constructive criticism from friends, mentors, coaches, teachers, supervisors, and leaders is a valuable element of growth and development – especially for those who are younger in years and earlier in their careers. Seeking out constructive criticism can make a significant difference in the trajectory of our careers and lives in general. And if we've supported ourselves with internal validation and have consistently strived to grow both personally and professionally, it is unlikely someone else can destroy us with their criticism. Being able to discern between constructive criticism vs. criticism that is intended to dim your light (typically by someone who has low self-esteem), is a valuable tool. More on this later.

Know Your Worth

If you're like me, you've likely minimized your own gifts in the past based on the opinions of others – and, unfortunately, not the uplifting, supportive opinions. Often, I found myself "shrinking" to fit into others' perceptions of me, playing small so I could be more accepted and loved. Or so I thought. Trying to fit into someone else's smaller view of yourself results in neither acceptance nor love. So why do we do it then? Typically, it's because we don't have the confidence (at least in a particular area of our lives) to honor our own capabilities and individuality. We must learn to trust our intuition when it comes to our gifts and what we get to share with the world. The more we do, the more comfortable we'll be letting our lights shine in the world – even if others can't handle our brightness!

There will always be those who seek to be "right" in a way that makes you "wrong." Don't play that game. When you encounter people, whose self-esteem is so low that the only way they know how to pump it up is by deflating others, walk away. They are not worth your time or attention. You will soon learn how liberating it feels to bow out of a needless debate, not caring whether you win or lose. The key is refusing to even play the game.

The ability to detach from outcomes is also a good technique to use when you encounter people who wish to dim your light with their criticism or judgment. If you can learn to be okay with whatever happens, you're one step closer to mastering empowerment and resilience. The journey to empowerment will undoubtedly involve getting it right sometimes...and sometimes getting it, well, *not* so right. That's okay. That's life. If you've already learned to validate yourself from within, you'll have the resilience to roll with the inevitable missteps or "mistakes" (aka – opportunities to learn and grow) along the way. And the more you learn to trust your own inner wisdom, the more self-empowered you'll become. Internally validating will then become easy and a natural reaction.

Isabelle, Revisited

What if Isabelle were adept at cultivating internal validation versus external validation? How might the completion of an art project impact her? Let's see! Isabelle finishes her landscape painting after weeks of effort. After cleaning her brushes and palette and then showering the paint flecks off, Isabelle returns to her in-home studio with a glass of wine and sits before her painting. She smiles, full of pride and pleased with her efforts. She really likes this one! The next night, a close friend and fellow weekend artist comes for dinner, and they discuss their latest projects. When her friend asks to see her painting, Isabelle gladly walks her to the studio. Once inside, they both stand before the painting. Her friend admires it, pointing out specifically what she likes about it. Then her friend asks her if she'd like a little constructive feedback on the forest portion of the painting. Isabelle has a momentary pang of regret over inviting her friend in to see her work, but as an artist with far more experience, Isabelle knows her friend would offer accurate insights. She listens as her friend offers her perspective, much of which Isabelle realizes she agrees with. She makes a mental note to make a few changes to her piece, disregarding the suggestion she disagrees with. They return to the living room and enjoy the rest of their evening together. The idea of posting her painting on social media never crosses her mind. She's content to enjoy her artwork at home, thinking perhaps one day she'll launch a website to share and possibly sell some of her paintings. Until then, she is happy doing her art for the sake of art alone.

Once we give up searching for approval, we often find it easier to earn respect.

— Gloria Steinem

❁

Intention:

I rely on my own validation from within.

Now, how about digging deeper? As a warm-up to this time for reflection, I suggest listening to "This is Me" by Keala Settle.

Invitation to Reflect:

In what 2-3 situations could you improve confidence in your abilities?

_____

_____

_____

_____

_____

What will you do to become more confident in your abilities?

_____

_____

_____

_____

_____

In what situations could you validate yourself more instead of counting on external validation?

_____

_____

_____

_____

_____

_____

Here are some actions you could take now for your self-care:

○ Practice committing to small decisions without input from others.
○ Research more deeply one topic in any subject you care about.
○ Decide to ignore comments and "likes" to any social media for one day. Alternatively, ignore it for 1-8 hours. You can do it!!

Commit to doing at least one thing differently based on what you learned in this chapter. Write out an actionable goal – with a specific deadline – to satisfy this commitment.

_____

_____

_____

_____

_____

_____

How will you celebrate or reward yourself if you reach the goal?

_____

_____

_____

_____

Other thoughts and reflections:

_____

_____

_____

_____

_____

_____

_____

_____

For additional resources related to this topic, please check out my website: www.abcsofselfcare.com

J

JUST START

You can dance in the storm. Don't wait for the rain to be over before because it might take too long. You can do it now. Wherever you are, right now, you can start, right now; this very moment.

— Israelmore Ayivor

❧

As I write this chapter, I find myself procrastinating. Ironic, right? Why am I procrastinating writing about procrastination? I tell myself not to worry about getting the perfect words on paper; begin by getting *any* words on paper. In other words, *just start.* Truth be told, it wasn't just this chapter I had difficulty getting started with, it was the entire book. Why? Well, like many people, I had to deal with the fear of failure. Would my words be the right ones to motivate others to commit to a consistent self-care lifestyle? Sadly, this fear nagged at me for a long time before the actual work of writing began. And that fear didn't dissipate until I finally talked myself into putting a few words on paper...which led to me gaining some traction. At that point, the momentum kicked in and I was able to find my rhythm with the project. And therein lies the most useful tool to overcoming both the fear of failure and procrastination: *just start.*

I know, I know – sounds too simple, too pat. But it works. Starting doesn't mean whipping out an entire manuscript (or losing 20 pounds or going from entry-level worker to CEO) overnight. It means taking the first step toward a goal, doing that one small thing that will move you forward, no matter how insignificant. There is power – real power – in that first step. So, what are you waiting for? Isn't it time to just start that new habit you wanted to develop? The hobby you always dreamed of? That skill you wanted to master? Your commitment to self-care?

Just. Start.

Jada and Just Starting

Let's look at Jada's efforts on her own self-care program. Jada knows she's stressed out; knows she needs to take better care of herself. She's organized and keeps a running to-do list to stay on track with her jam-packed schedule as a literary agent. Over the years, she's become adept at juggling numerous writers, editors, and the scripts that arrive in her inbox daily. But somehow, despite Jada's best efforts to build some time for herself into each day, her self-care "to do's" are always the ones that never get crossed off her list. Her clients – both the writers and the publishers – love her because she is remarkably responsive. But that responsiveness comes with a price, and that price is always paid by Jada. Suddenly it's 10 p.m. and she is exhausted and ready to fall into bed, without having done that online yoga class or taken the five minutes she committed to sitting in silence away from her laptop and phone. Before turning out the lights, Jada makes her to-do list for tomorrow, again listing her self-care plans and even marking them with a specific time she'll perform them. Yet the next morning, Jada awakens to a new and busy day at work, and her self-care plans are once more superseded by the demands of her career. As an empath, Jada understands how nervous writers are about hearing back from her promptly and how much pressure editors feel to publish the next big bestseller. She cares deeply for her clients and publishing partners and wants to do her best for them. But what about what's best for her? Another day passes and Jada's self-care plans go undone. Again. Eventually, she stops writing them on her daily to-do list. *I'll rest when I'm dead*, she often jokes to herself. That may be sooner than she plans, given her inability to care for herself as much as she cares for others.

Quick Check: Check all that Apply:

- ☐ I often procrastinate about doing my self-care practices.
- ☐ I believe if I have a good enough excuse, I can justify my procrastination.
- ☐ I often avoid asking for help to handle my responsibilities.

Be Aware, Accept, Act

Some research points to the idea that procrastination is not about a lack of self-control or motivation. Instead, it's more about the negative thoughts we have about doing a specific thing, which leads us to do something else – even if that something else is nothing at all. Putting off the task that holds some sort of negative association for us provides a bit of relief, if only temporary. Thus, we are, in a sense, rewarding ourselves for our procrastination, which begins this self-perpetuating cycle.

Based on my years of coaching clients, I've discovered some common bad habits that need to be broken to free up more time for self-care. They include:

- Saying yes when you really want to say no (typically, this helps us feel busy and involved in life).
- Consistently putting others' needs ahead of your own to the detriment of your well-being.
- Allowing your independent streak to supersede your need for help from others (i.e., sharing the responsibilities for tasks that benefit all in your household, family, or work group).

Do any of these examples hit home with you? If so, can you honestly say you will have more happiness, health, peace of mind and energy by continuing on this same path? My guess? No, you won't. It may be a challenge to change our behaviors and assert our need for a greater commitment to self-care, but it will be worth it.

Ask for Help

If you find yourself procrastinating, especially where self-care is concerned, it is time to practice the self-care tenet *just start*. No matter how small that first step is. Digging into what is holding you back can be helpful, so long as it doesn't become another way to procrastinate. Answering a few simple questions may help you understand the source of your procrastination:

- Are you feeling anxious about a new habit or behavior you're trying to establish?
- Is there a difficult conversation you need to have with someone to move forward with the habit, behavior, project, or outlook you're trying to cultivate?
- Do you hold any religious, cultural, or family beliefs that may be impeding your ability to put attention toward the thing you've been procrastinating about?
- Is your schedule simply too full right now to incorporate something new? If so, is this a temporary situation or ongoing? If ongoing, what can you let go of to make room for the new focus you wish to incorporate?

Sometimes, identifying the root cause of our procrastination can help us move into just-start mode more easily. Too often, we beat ourselves up for procrastinating, calling ourselves lazy or stupid or unmotivated. Yet there may be an underlying issue that, once addressed, seems to magically dissipate any resistance we had to launching a new habit or project or self-care routine.

One of the most common roadblocks to getting started – with a self-care routine in particular – is the fear of asking for help. Perhaps we've lulled ourselves, and others, into believing that we have unlimited energy and the ability to do it all. And perhaps at one point in our younger years we did! I get it, I really do. I've been guilty of this myself...and suffered for it as a result. But this superhero approach to life is ultimately unsustainable and, over time, self-care becomes increasingly necessary. It isn't easy undoing our past patterns, but sometimes it's a must. Asking for help is the first step in making room for this new habit you would like to cultivate. Are there projects around your home, or even your office, that you could delegate or share responsibility for with others? You may find yourself getting resistance from others if you've suddenly decided that, no, you won't be the one who always unloads the dishwasher, cooks dinner, or tidies up the office at the end of the week. Is it time to ask for help? My guess is – yes! So, let's practice just starting by setting a date for when you have that first conversation with others who could share in daily responsibilities, thereby freeing up more of your time for self-care.

Time to call on AAA again. Once we become *aware* of these tendencies, we can see how we've used them as a form of procrastination. The next step is to *accept* that we derived some form of relief from that procrastination and forgive ourselves for that unhelpful behavior pattern. And then it's time to *act*. One small action: a conversation, a request for help, a chores schedule or an interview for paid help. One. Small. Step. Just start!

Jada, Revisited

Let's go back and see how Jada might have handled her self-care program launch more effectively, shall we? Fresh from reading an author's manuscript on self-care (you knew it was coming, right?), Jada commits to taking time for herself throughout her busy work week, which is currently Sunday through Saturday. She knows she has a bad habit of jumping on email first thing in the morning...as in, the minute she opens her eyes. So just to get started, she locks both her phone and laptop in a cupboard and gives the key to her partner. "Don't give me this key tomorrow morning until I've sat in stillness for at least ten minutes." Her partner laughs at her extreme tactic but agrees. The next morning, Jada awakens, remembering that today is when one of her editorial connections is supposed to have an answer for her about a client's manuscript. She wants to quickly check in to see if a decision came through in email overnight. Then she remembers that her partner hid the key to the cupboard and is still sleeping quite soundly. Jada sighs and wraps herself in her robe as she makes her way to the spare room, stopping by the kitchen for a drink of water while her stomach is empty to rehydrate, clear toxins, help with digestion and lubricate her joints. Look at her getting in another act of self-care. She starts to wake up.

Arriving in the spare room, she sits in the corner chair, the early morning sunrise streaming through the blinds. Closing her eyes, Jada takes four deep, slow breaths. Then...she sits. No email, no texts, no notification pings interrupting her. Her shoulders drop, her belly relaxes, her breath steadies into a quiet rhythm, and her thoughts...they begin to slow, releasing their grip on her psyche, letting go. Jada recognizes a feeling she hasn't felt in as long as she can remember: the peace of nothingness, that feeling on the fourth day of a vacation (not that she's had one in years, mind you) when your body and mind finally accept that this is a break, some time away from hectic living. Eventually, completely relaxed yet refreshed, Jada opens her eyes, thinking it's been close to ten minutes. The clock on the bed stand reveals that Jada has just sat quietly for forty minutes! She feels amazing!

Her partner meets her in the hallway, smiling, and drops Jada's key in her hand. Instead of charging to the cupboard to retrieve her devices, Jada heads to the shower. Because she started her day with quiet time alone, she feels more rested and recharged than she has in months. She then sets her phone alarm for 3 p.m., with a plan to go into a conference room at work, lock the door, and sit quietly for fifteen minutes. And she did it! That night she repeats the key trick with her partner and, again, has great results. Within two weeks, she's hooked and no longer needs to hide her devices to launch her day properly. She sticks to her afternoon self-care breaks and soon Jada has fully embedded a self-care routine into her busy life – without any loss of productivity. In fact, she's picked up two additional authors to represent and still finds time to "represent" *herself*. All because she made a healthy self-care decision to *Just Start!*

> *No matter how much time you've wasted in the past, you still have an entire tomorrow.*
>
> — Denis Waitley

❧

Intention:

I exercise self-control and commit to a self-care routine.

Now, how about digging deeper? As a warm-up to this time for reflection, I suggest listening "Never Give Up" by Sia.

Invitation to Reflect:

How will your life improve right away by adding more self-care habits?

_____

_____

_____

_____

_____

What is your biggest fear about enrolling your significant other or kids in you creating a self-care lifestyle?

_____

_____

_____

_____

What happens if your family is resistant to the idea of you making time for self-care? Hint: what can you control?

_____

_____

_____

_____

Here are some actions you could take now for your self-care:

- ○ Do a root cause analysis to discover why you procrastinate about self-care (See Letter A) and/or seek professional guidance to kick the procrastination habit.
- ○ Consider seeking professional guidance to address guilt in asking for help.
- ○ Set up a family meeting and create a family chores schedule that would allow you more free time for self-care.

Commit to doing at least one thing differently based on what you learned in this chapter. Write out an actionable goal – with a specific deadline – to satisfy this commitment.

_____

_____

_____

How will you celebrate or reward yourself if you reach the goal?

_____

_____

Other thoughts and reflections:

_____

_____

_____

_____

_____

_____

_____

For additional resources related to this topic, please check out my website: www.abcsofselfcare.com

K

KEEP YOUR POWER

There is no passion to be found playing small – in settling for a life that is less than the one you are capable of living.

— Nelson Mandela

Regardless of your goals in life, keeping your power will always lead to a more fulfilling life overall. It doesn't matter if you're a full-time homemaker or a CEO or a barista or a small business owner. Knowing your true power and cultivating it at every turn is a powerful tool for living the life you've dreamed of.

True power is not manipulative or controlling. It's not about how many people you oversee in your work or how much money you have or even how much you can bench press at the gym. The truest power is in acting as if you have power, finding your purpose, living a life that's consistent with that purpose, and then sharing the results with the world. This is exactly why I chose to write this book; it is absolutely in line with my life's purpose to help other people cultivate more self-care in their lives. Many of us chase degrees, jobs and even love to feel more powerful. True power comes from within, whether or not you have all the outward trappings of success.

Keisha and Keeping Her Power

Keisha is ten years into her career, having graduated at the top of her class from an Ivy League MBA program. She was proud to be a woman of color who beat the odds, educated herself out of poverty, and landed a job at one of the top financial institutions on Wall Street. She loves her work studying financial trends and monitoring the impact of world events on the markets. She loves working with data – numbers and graphs and the stories they tell excite her. (I know, right? Remember: to each their own.)

There are few people of color and not many in senior level positions at the firm. But she believes that if she keeps her head down and works extra hard, the rewards will follow. Given Keisha's strong results to date, she feels confident she'll make partner this year. She heads to her annual review appointment filled with anticipation. She already has a bottle of champagne in the fridge back at her apartment. One of the partners greets her warmly as she enters the room. They review her many achievements over the past year, congratulate her performance, and offer her a meager bump in base salary. The meeting is clearly over and Keisha thanks them, even apologizes for the meeting running a bit over the allotted fifteen minutes. She smiles warmly, though inside she's feeling anything but.

She recalls all the times she's been offered a patronizing smile from a senior male partner during an overly simplified explanation as to why a *minor* point of one of her reports was off, when she'd watched those same partners overlook even bigger issues with reports of her peers – to the point that even her peers pointed this out. Believing in API (Assuming Positive Intent), she had maintained a public display of brushing off their concerns on her behalf. She still believed that her hard work and undeniable results would eventually pay off. Clearly, they haven't. By working hard but not advocating for a promotion based on the value she's brought to the firm, Keisha allowed her power to be chipped away over the years. Here she is, after 10 years as one of the top performers, beating her quota year over year, being passed over for a promotion once again. Had she allowed herself to be too flexible? Too agreeable? Too...*powerless*? You bet! And now she's likely been pegged as a dependable "doer," lacking the ability to demonstrate leadership qualities – a must for partners within the firm.

Quick Check - Select all that apply:

- ☐ I am more concerned with being nice than with being assertive in my requests.
- ☐ I say "sorry" way too much – even if I haven't done anything wrong.
- ☐ It is more comfortable for me to avoid conflict rather than ask for what I want.

Act Powerfully

Often, instead of keeping our power, we subconsciously give it away. How? Here are a few common ways:

1. Considering ourselves the "victim" in too many situations.
2. Not sharing power or balancing power in relationships.
3. Prioritizing pleasing others to the detriment of our own well-being.
4. Choosing to ignore power dynamics.
5. Choosing relationships with others solely based on their perceived power.

6. Apologizing too much.
7. Speaking tentatively or in an unassertive manner.

How can we counteract these behaviors and beliefs to keep our power? I thought you'd never ask! Let's dive into some key areas:

1. **Eliminate the Victim Mindset.** Being a victim is the opposite of feeling powerful. And to be clear, there is a difference between being the victim of a serious crime and having an ongoing victim mindset. I'm speaking to the latter. Maintaining a victim mindset – assuming we're powerless in a given situation – can feel easier and more comfortable because it lets us off the hook for being our best, most empowered selves. Perhaps you've experienced sexism, racism, ableism, homophobia, or any other ism that assaults your self-esteem and self-confidence. Over time, enough of these small acts, called micro-aggressions, can take a toll, no doubt. However, by allowing ourselves to remain in a victim mindset due to the misdeeds of others, we give away our power. We can create a shield against these inevitable micro-aggressions by building our sense of empowerment on a regular basis – before we need it! Focusing on problem solving (at the root cause) and taking time to recognize our achievements and our positive attributes will help. Staying focused on your goals (instead of the misdeed) will help too, whether the goal is getting a promotion, making the sale, or gaining access. So, let's pump up the focus on affirmations and internal validation to be the victor vs. the victim!

2. **Sharing Power.** Sharing power is really about having a healthy balance of power in any relationship, be it a friendship, romance or business relationship. Not having this balance of power is a recipe for unhappiness despite the common desire to "go along, to get along." Keep in mind, there's a big difference between *submitting* to someone and *deferring* to them. Deferring is fine; it acknowledges what the other person brings to the table while maintaining your self-respect. In contrast, submission involves giving away our power, giving up something of ourselves. It's a win-lose situation, which is never healthy for either party. If there's an imbalance of power in a relationship dynamic, especially in romantic relationships, it's time to negotiate shared power.

3. **Take Responsibility.** Yes, we're returning to the concept of taking responsibility. Why? Because it impacts so many aspects of our lives and well-being. We cannot have power without choice, and taking responsibility for the choices we've made, especially the wrong-headed ones, is critical. For example, deciding to please others at our own expense is a choice we make. Also, instead of looking to place blame elsewhere when confronted with a tough situation in life, we would do better to look within. See how our own choices may have led to this moment, forgive ourselves and love ourselves unconditionally in the process.

4. **Understand Power Dynamics.** Like it or not, we all engage in systems that include power dynamics that impact our lives. Work, politics, and financial markets – all of these contain power structures that we can learn to work within to maximize our own personal power. Paying attention at work to who gets the visible projects, who gets promoted, are things to keep an eye on. Then decide if you want to do what is necessary to get them for yourself. How the influential people in the organization communicate with their bosses and subordinates can also help us better understand, and therefore navigate, the power dynamics in our organization. Engagement in world events can help us understand global and national political power dynamics that will, inevitably, impact us on a local level. A trusted financial advisor can help us better understand how to build financial security and wealth. We may not like dealing with the power dynamics of these larger groups; however, understanding them will serve us well.

5. **Develop Authentic Relationships**. There is great power in building relationships. However, care must be taken to ensure you're also building authentic ones. My philosophy is to build relationships with people I *like* and *connect* with, rather than targeting someone only because they might be able to help me achieve my goals. Despite some of the business advice books that were popular when I was entering the workforce, that has never felt aligned with my internal compass. This may have caused me to miss out on relationships with some who are considered power brokers. I'm ok with that because I believe I can and will meet anyone needed to achieve my goals, on my terms. By focusing on authentic relationships, we are less likely to feel that we've given our power to people who drain our energy and leave us feeling *less than*. Life is too short to spend time with people who don't contribute to our happiness, health and peace.

6. **Make Sincere Apologies Only.** Incessant apologizing is the most common form of depleting our sense of empowerment. Apologizing too much for things that have nothing to do with your choices and actions can inevitably lead to a loss of confidence and power. Some people have a knee-jerk reaction to apologize for anything someone else complains about. Why is that? Are we anxious about another's discomfort? Fearful of retaliation? Attempting to avoid a negative reaction? Whatever the reason, needlessly over-apologizing not only diminishes your power, but it also diminishes the power of your authentic apologies. Contrary to reactionary apologies, sincere apologies are effective at strengthening relationships. If you make a mistake, accept responsibility, and offer a sincere apology. There's no need to offer a bunch of long-winded stories and excuses. Most won't want to hear them anyway (or maybe it's just me). Just show your level of integrity by apologizing sincerely, and then move on.

7. **Use Decisive Language.** How often do we say "I believe" when, in fact, we know? Take an inventory of the common language you use in discussions and trade wishy-washy, self-deprecating phrases for ones that reflect your power. Replace *I believe* with *I know.*

Replace *I may* with *I will*. Adding, *based on my experience* or *research* makes a statement more powerful as well. Doing this avoids putting yourself on a lower level than others. Trust me, you don't belong there!

Find Your Purpose

Ok, figuring out your purpose could be an entire book. In my humble opinion, you find your purpose by reflecting on what is happening in your life or learning from past experiences. Look for signs that you are passionate about a cause or something that you would do for free if money were no object. Sometimes you have ideas for solutions to a problem that won't go out of your head. Consider if those signs and ideas fit with your purpose.

It doesn't have to be a contribution to the world, maybe just to your neighborhood, city, or state. Or maybe it is through your job. Some, like me, have already found their purpose. It took me a minute! It used to bother me, until I learned that many famous women and men found their purpose later in life. Vera Wang, Betty White, Julia Child, Maya Angelou, and Sam Walton are just a few who became more successful after age 40. Until you figure it out, it could simply be to give and receive unconditional love. Imagine a world where everyone had that as their purpose. Oh, what a joyful world that would be!

Use Your Power for Good

Once you are acting more powerfully, figuring out and living your life according to your purpose, I'd encourage you to use that power to help others. So many nonprofits need resources, be they time, money, or insights. They are always looking for volunteers who want to make a difference and live out their purpose. You've also likely met people who are "drunk with power" and seek more of it for their own benefit only. What a waste of personal power! It's much more rewarding to use your power in the service of others, in ways that help them gain their own power as well. Choose volunteer opportunities that give you a chance to satisfy a passion or develop new and valuable skills and it becomes a win-win. Keep your power and use it wisely – with heart.

Keisha, Revisited

Surely, Keisha did not take enough responsibility for her own career advancement. She also believes extreme flexibility is a virtue. How might Keisha have handled her career advancement differently, either from the start or when she noticed that her peers with less impressive results were getting ahead while her career remained stagnant? Let's see how this situation could play out differently if she were to keep her power. When Keisha first joins the firm, she believes she needs to keep her head down, not complain, and work hard to succeed. Keisha also decides to listen to and observe some of her peers for insights on succeeding at the firm, which primarily boils down to building relationships, doing excellent work, being a team player, and having a positive attitude. She is determined to maintain her authentic self in the process. Putting all of this into action, Keisha creates 360 relationships with her boss, senior leaders, peers, administrative support, and even the office cleaning crew (you never know when you may need them to keep you company when working late). She set up meetings and phone calls with key leaders instead of sending emails. She figured out authentic ways to communicate and showcase her talents. Rather than be a victim to those with negative implicit bias, she builds relationships (not to be confused with *friendships*) with people of *all* backgrounds. Her work is stellar, and she makes sure that anytime a minor issue is brought up concerning her work, she uses it as an opportunity to learn from the feedback and build another relationship.

Also, she still believed in API (Assuming Positive Intent), even when she is in one of the firm's all-team reviews and one of her reports is questioned. She calls on AAA and is *aware* this attitude is a choice, *accepts* the reality and *acts* with her best interest at heart. Listening to the partner's critique, she knows he's using old data to refute her report. She is certain his analysis is inaccurate but doesn't want to embarrass him in front of the group. Instead of her typical apology and backing off, she smiles and thanks him for the feedback, promising to follow up directly with him once she's had an opportunity to recheck her figures. She keeps her attitude positive and does not ponder what might account for their different assessments. She already knows. After the meeting concludes, Keisha pulls the necessary data and returns to the partner's office, walking him through her analysis. He clearly understands how wrong his critique had been. "How could I have overlooked this report?" he says good heartedly. She chuckles, glad he's more interested in being factual than being right. "Happens to the best of them," she says, acknowledging his error in a way that helps him save face without giving away her power. She's also just laid the foundation for building another valuable relationship.

A few months before her annual review, Keisha asks for an appointment with the partner whose error she corrected. Since the day she allowed him to save face in the meeting, she has sensed an ally in him, although they don't tend to work on many projects together. When she sits down with him one-on-one, she tells him she is interested in advancing within the firm and asks him what she could do to improve her upward mobility. He gives a brief informal review, complimenting her intellect, hard work and focus. She senses that he's holding back and gently pushes for any constructive feedback he can offer her. "Clearly, I'm not perfect, as I've not yet earned my way to being a partner." He smiles at her honesty. "Look, you're clearly one of the brightest associates at the firm. I believe you could improve your chances of making partner if you were more vocal about your results more often. Honestly, Keisha, I think you come across as a bit too modest, somewhat of a backup singer rather than the main act." Keisha is stunned and finds herself laughing despite herself. "Wow, I'm glad I asked." she says. "It's freeing to hear that I ought to be a bit more self-promoting." "To a point," the partner responds, and they both share a good laugh. "Show your competence and teamwork," he continues, "by highlighting not just your own accomplishments, but also the contributions of team members. That is the key to winning friends and influencing the partners, so to speak."

A few weeks later, when the opportunity comes up to lead a major project that offers visibility and the potential to increase the firm's ROI, Keisha volunteers. She then invites a diverse team of colleagues to join her project team, ensuring a diverse range of ideas, perspectives, and skills. She also asks an influential senior partner in the firm to offer advice along the way, to make sure the team progresses and achieves the goals of the project. This gives her an opportunity to build yet another relationship with the senior management team and to gain visibility with someone who could later influence her advancement within the firm.

As Keisha progresses in her career, she acts more powerfully by communicating and advocating for her career. For example, when her boss decides to talk to his boss about the progress of her project without including her in the meeting, she is hurt. After a cooling off period to let her disappointment subside and discussing it with a trusted friend, Keisha sits down with her boss one on one. She asks to be included in future discussions about the project so that, as the project lead, she can address any specific questions. Her boss wholeheartedly agrees. That visibility will serve her well later.

Keisha notices that the partner who had become an ally stops by her cubicle more often over the coming weeks to check on her and discuss her projects. When her annual review comes up, he is the most vocal supporter in the room. The other senior partner advising her on the project tells Keisha he's seen a noticeable shift in her confidence, which is impressive. "It's as if you've finally become the powerhouse we always knew you could be." A third partner signals his assistant and a cart with champagne glasses and an iced bottle of Dom Perignon is wheeled toward Keisha, as the firm's founder stands and clears his throat. "Keisha," he begins, "it would be our great honor if you'd accept a promotion to Partner today. We're all so very proud of you and your work." The champagne cork is popped and there are toasts all around.

In 20 years, Keisha will resign from that same firm. She had found her true purpose within her career, first by contributing to the firm's success and second, by increasing its diversity efforts. She will be recognized for increasing the firm's ROI tenfold and expanding its clientele to be more reflective of the diverse population they serve. Keisha's "pay it forward" approach to recruiting diverse employees and training them to mentor and recruit even more candidates of color has become a model for the entire industry. She speaks at business schools, making an extra effort to address students of color, whom she encourages to reach for the stars. She tells them about the importance of owning their power, seeking out allies, and then sharing power as it expands in their careers and in life. Keisha always receives a standing ovation at these events. No longer shrinking to fit, Keisha keeps her power and becomes a force for good.

Our deepest fear is not that we are inadequate. Our deepest fear is that we are powerful beyond measure. It is our light, not our darkness that most frightens us. We ask ourselves, 'Who am I to be brilliant, gorgeous, talented, fabulous?' Actually, who are you not to be? You are a child of God. Your playing small does not serve the world. There is nothing enlightened about shrinking so that other people won't feel insecure around you. We are all meant to shine, as children do. We were born to make manifest the glory of God that is within us. It's not just in some of us; it's in everyone. And as we let our own light shine, we unconsciously give other people permission to do the same. As we are liberated from our own fear, our presence automatically liberates others.

— Marianne Williamson

❀

Intention:

I choose to keep my power.

Now, how about digging deeper? As a warm-up to this time for reflection, I suggest listening to "No Playing Small" by Fearless Soul.

Invitation to Reflect:

What victim mindsets (if any) are you holding onto that keep you from showing up more powerfully?

_____

_____

_____

_____

_____

What is one way you could show up more powerfully at work or in your personal life?

_____

_____

_____

_____

In what ways could you add meaning and purpose to your life by using your power for good?

_____

_____

_____

_____

Here are some actions you could take now for your self-care:

○ Change at least one of your device passwords to "I am powerful" (no spaces) as a constant reminder. Add a number and/or character to make it stronger.

○ Keep track of when you put yourself down, in a journal or in your phone, to increase your awareness. Decide what positive thought or affirmation to say when this happens. Say it with conviction, as if it is already true.

○ Think of one project at work that could make a positive impact on your team or organization. Volunteer to lead it. Or seek out a sponsor at work that could advocate for your career advancement.

Commit to doing at least one thing differently based on what you learned in this chapter. Write out an actionable goal – with a specific deadline – to satisfy this commitment.

_____

_____

_____

_____

_____

How will you celebrate or reward yourself if you reach the goal?

_____

_____

Other thoughts and reflections:

_____

_____

_____

_____

_____

_____

_____

_____

For additional resources related to this topic, please check out my website: www.abcsofselfcare.com

LISTEN TO YOUR BODY

Listen with love to your body's messages. It is telling you all you need to know.

— Louise Hay

How often in your past have you heard the phrase *listen to your body*? Probably a lot. Now, how often did you actually listen? I'm guessing the answer is *not* a lot. There's always one last big push before the deadline, one more item on the to-do list, one more sit-up (not me!), one more show to watch to empty the DVR (now, *this* is me!), one more, one more, one more…

Add up enough of these moments of overriding your body's innate wisdom and you could end up with your body shouting at you – in the form of illness or an accident. Tuning into the small, still voice within is one of our greatest forms of guidance, but ignore these internal hints enough and your body will be forced to give you more physical hints: headaches, back pain, fatigue, insomnia, etc. Ignore enough of these physical hints from your body and you could be in for serious consequences. And where's the self-care in that?

Lori and Listening to Her Body

Lori is a classic Type A personality and proud of it! Growing up with four brothers in a highly competitive household, Lori subconsciously learned at an early age that to be a winner and achieve financial success, you have to push through challenges – no matter what. Her family had shelves filled with trophies and walls covered with various awards, symbols of the family's collective success. As an adult, Lori now has her own wall of achievements, reminders that she is a powerful and successful human being. She's a can-do woman who always does what she says she'll do. That is, until recently. Despite her lifelong determination, Lori has been feeling drained during her morning walks. She typically dictates memos to her staff or letters to prominent donors during that time.

Her work as the executive director of a charitable foundation, which used to energize her, now feels like an insurmountable burden with meetings being missed and major donors being disappointed. *If I can only push through this next month of fundraising events,* Lori thinks, *I'll be able to take a break afterward.* The month passes and Lori is now consumed with the next work crisis. She cares deeply about the foundation's mission and hates disappointing its various stakeholders, so she continues to drag herself through each day despite feeling physically off. *I'll rest when I die* has always been one of Lori's favorite lighthearted responses to those who encourage her to take a vacation, but recently she's been feeling so poorly, she occasionally wonders if that day won't come sooner than expected. Still, she continues to show up to work, staying long past the rest of her team. She ignores the tightness in her chest she's experienced lately, the insurmountable fatigue, the lightheadedness. "The Foundation needs me!" is her common excuse for not taking greater steps to support her well-being – or even to determine what's going on physically with her health.

During another late night at the office, alone, Lori feels a sudden tightness in her left arm. Strange indeed. Then she notices a feeling of indigestion, despite not having eaten since early that morning. The tightness in her chest, now a common occurrence that Lori assumes is just anxiety, increases. She makes her way to the office couch, where she flops down with her phone. Doubt consumes her. *What's happening? Why do I feel so awful?* she wonders. While Googling the symptoms she's experiencing, Lori drops her phone to the floor and hugs herself in agony. Her last thought before losing consciousness isn't about the upcoming board meeting or the need for more lead generation for her fundraising efforts. Her last thought is simply: *not yet!* In the morning, Lori's staff will find her body, the rigor mortis already having set in. Heart attack will be the official cause of death determined by the autopsy. And the foundation that Lori believed needed her specific involvement so badly will install a new executive director within the month.

Quick Check - Select all that apply:

☐ I usually don't pay much attention to minor health issues.
☐ I am tired most days, even if I get adequate sleep.
☐ I am often sick or already have a major illness.

Either take time for rest or you will take time for illness. Listening to your body can make all the difference in maintaining good health and a strong immune system. Not listening could lead you to illness or even a premature death. Many people feel that the ability to push through their bodies' signals is a show of strength. Quite the opposite is true. It takes true strength to listen to those little signals and address them before they develop into big issues. If you watch for the signals, you will notice them. Perhaps you're moving a bit more slowly and would rather take an elevator than walk up one flight of stairs – empty-handed. You find yourself reading the same paragraph of your book over and over and you just started reading five minutes ago. You awaken in the morning after eight or more hours of sleep and *still* feel tired. You've noticed a few ailments that have nagged at you for months. And let me guess – you didn't see your doctor because you don't think you have time. Or even worse, you don't always think it is important to check in on your physical health.

Medical research estimates that 90% of illnesses and diseases can be attributed to chronic stress. It can also increase the chances of you being obese, having heart disease, diabetes, high blood pressure, Alzheimer's, depression, and gastrointestinal issues. There are warning signs along the way, before the disease becomes chronic. Among the most common signals your body will give you is fatigue. Just ran a 10K? Sure, you're going to feel fatigue, but that fatigue should resolve with a hot bath and a good night's rest. Had a big presentation for work that just wrapped up? Again, fatigue would be normal, and again, a good night's rest should clear it up. As we age, we might need a few nights of rest to feel rested. The key is to look out for a growing and consistent sense of fatigue. That's a sure sign that you've not been listening to your body. Worse yet, perhaps you hear it...and tell it to shut up.

Experiment with a Different Approach

Let's face it, keeping busy can be seductive. It can make us feel more alive, even more successful. Many of us have been programmed to feel that being super busy makes us productive and that over-producing will make us feel better about ourselves and, therefore, happier. Wrong! Please don't fall prey to this false belief.

Try this. Imagine how you would feel if you were to do two different projects in a day rather than your typical goal of five. Can you feel your shoulders drop a bit into a more relaxed state? Do you breathe easier just thinking about doing less? Are you looking forward to that day rather than dreading it? Habitually evaluating the quantity of what you can realistically do in a day can help you create more healthy, balanced, and energetic days. And in the long run, you'll most likely end up accomplishing more by striving to over-achieve less. Sounds contradictory, right? Try it, you might like it.

Even participating in fun social activities can take a toll on your body, so pace yourself with them as well. Look ahead to the social activities you have planned and determine how you can build some down-time around those. When invited to participate in an additional social event, check in with yourself to determine how much energy it will require and what else you have planned on that day. Rather than offering a knee-jerk "yes!" to any social invitation, take a minute to determine if it's in your body's best interest to participate, given other time commitments you've already made. Some of my clients are hesitant to take a pause before committing to a social engagement because they worry about offending the person inviting them. Or some worry that saying 'no' will somehow keep them from living their best life. But taking time to consider invitations need not be stress-inducing or bring on the FOMO (Fear of Missing Out). A simple "That sounds fantastic; in the spirit of self-care, let me think about it and get back to you," will allow you to pause and determine if it's a good idea for you to accept an invitation. Pacing yourself and taking time for yourself between commitments is key. Already made the commitment and now your body is giving you clear signals that you've overcommitted? It's okay to reschedule with a sincere explanation, such as: "In the spirit of self-care, I need to reschedule our plans for a time when I'm less tired. Please forgive me for the last-minute cancellation. I promise to do a better job of not overcommitting myself next time." Then...keep your promise. This approach is ideally the exception, not the rule, lest you become the boy (or girl) who cried wolf. Done to excess, you may find yourself no longer receiving invitations from friends you've rescheduled too often.

Move Your Body

Sitting is the new smoking, and our society has become far too good at sitting. In the same way that smoking became a public health crisis several decades ago, the same can be said of too much sedentary time during our days. Also, like smoking, the damage evolves over time and gradually takes a toll. Staying active is a critical element of overall health and self-care. It's good to move our muscles and joints at least 30 minutes a day, and once every hour. Movement can be the elixir we need to get the most out of life. It's also a natural antidepressant (though I'm in *no way* suggesting you replace any prescribed medications you might be taking with exercise; that's a discussion for you and your healthcare provider). Have you ever tried dancing when you're feeling listless or in a foul mood? It does wonders for the soul! A friend of mine even dances preemptively each morning – no matter her mood – during what she calls her Daily Dance. She swears by it. A few minutes and one song is all it takes to launch each day with an upbeat state of mind.

Notice I haven't used the word "exercise" and this is on purpose. Some of us seem to have an allergic reaction to gyms. The thought of dealing with weight machines and cardio equipment alone is enough to keep postponing that first visit to the gym. But movement comes in many forms and not everyone's health is suitable to what we might call "traditional" forms of exercise. Just move! At work, walking over to someone instead of calling about a project can be just the break you need to recharge. At home, nature walks, dancing by yourself, even cleaning your home and doing laundry involve movement. Movement away from the computer or the couch is the goal. Adding variety to your daily movement is a great way to keep it interesting and engaging. Like all other aspects of establishing a self-care routine, take small steps to avoid overdoing it, burning out, or injury. When this happens, it's too easy to give up on making movement a part of every day. Listen to your body and you'll know when to ease up.

Lori, Revisited

What if Lori had listened to what her body was telling her? Could she have avoided the heart attack that had been brewing for months? That will never be known, but one thing is certain: she would've, at the very least, learned that she was at risk given her symptoms. Let's see how this might've played out differently. Lori notices odd physical sensations. Despite having a big fundraising event in the works, she asks her assistant to arrange a wellness appointment, which results in numerous tests being conducted. Her doctor tells her she's lucky she came in when she did, as her test results all point to evidence of heart disease. Lori recalls how her favorite uncle died suddenly of a heart attack, right at the height of his career as a lauded and well-liked doctor. She knows heart disease is exacerbated by stress, of which she has plenty! Lori puts together a proposal for the Board which involves cutting back her role to take more time for her personal well-being, while simultaneously promoting two of her most talented directors into higher levels of responsibility. The Board unanimously approves it. Instead of working 70 hours a week, Lori now works 40 – or less. She now takes a full lunch break away from the office, usually with a non-work-related friend, and has added a second walk at the end of her day, without her recording device. She schedules – and keeps – regular medical appointments and has added meditation to her morning routine, regularly checking in to see how her body, and mind, are feeling. Because Lori has always been driven, she expands her success mindset to include personal wellness. Soon, Lori realizes that both she *and* the Foundation she leads are doing better – by doing less and listening more. Having a less stressful, less hectic lifestyle leaves Lori with more time to manage her personal life. She sets up regular get-togethers with friends, spends more time alone in reflection, and most importantly, makes time for self-care. By listening to her body and her stress levels, Lori is committed to taking care of her whole life.

Symptoms are the body's communication system.

— Amy Scher

❀

Intention:

I stay present to and listen to my body.

Now, how about digging deeper? As a warm-up to this time for reflection, I suggest listening to "Move Your Body" by Beyoncé.

Invitation to Reflect:

What project will you give up or remove from your schedule tomorrow?

_____

_____

_____

_____

_____

How will you fit more movement into every day?

_____

_____

_____

_____

Imagine a life with more movement, flexibility and physical rigor. What activities would you be engaged in?

_____

_____

_____

_____

Here are some actions you can take now for your self-care:

○ Move more. Take a short walk – around the house or around the block – after completing this chapter.

○ Create a daily fitness regimen that includes movement and stretching (you'll thank me when you're older).

○ Google exercises you can do in your work area and try at least one.

Commit to doing at least one thing differently based on what you learned in this chapter. Write out an actionable goal – with a specific deadline – to satisfy this commitment.

_____

_____

_____

How will you celebrate or reward yourself if you reach the goal?

_____

_____

Other thoughts and reflections:

_____

_____

_____

_____

_____

_____

For additional resources related to this topic, please check out my website: www.abcsofselfcare.com

M

MAKE PEACE WITH YOUR PAST

We cannot choose to have a life free of hurt. But we can choose to be free, to escape the past, no matter what befalls us, and to embrace the possible.

– Edith Eger

❧

Whenever I discuss the topic of making peace with one's past, Idina Menzel's voice pops into my mind singing "Let It Go" from the movie *Frozen*. Those three simple words – *let it go* – are crucial to making peace with your past so you can put more energy toward the present and planning your future. Too much focus on the past can lead to depression. Too much focus on the future can lead to anxiety. Concentrating on what we have in front of us – the present – is best for peace of mind. However, when encouraging my coaching clients to let go of the past, the conversation often goes something like this:

Me: Isn't it time to let go of past disappointments, fears, and judgments so you can move forward?

Client:.   Easier said than done, Sheri

Me: Perhaps. But all we have is right now and what comes next, the future.

Client: But my past is my history! It defines me. It's part of who I am. It's impossible to just let it go!

Me: What would if mean for you to try harder? Please do. For your own sake.

Imagine if everything you've ever owned – clothing from childhood, textbooks and toys, trinkets that no longer interest you, that old pair of skates from your teen years and the skis you haven't used in 20 years, everything! – was bundled up in a giant sack and you were required to drag it with you everywhere you went, every day, every minute. Not much fun to haul around a bunch of stuff from your entire lifetime, huh? Not making peace with your past is similar. Only instead of material items, you're dragging around an imaginary sack full of negative emotions and bad memories, grudges, and judgments. Also, not much fun. In fact, even worse, it can inhibit you from moving toward the things you want to manifest in your life: joy, contentment, a new job, a healthy intimate relationship, improved health, or greater peace of mind.

Ming and Making Peace with Her Past

Ming is giddy when she receives a text from Michael, the cutie she met at her favorite coffee shop last week. Divorced and 36 years old, Ming hasn't flirted with anyone in a long, *long* time. It feels good to be noticed by a man she finds attractive, not just physically, but intellectually as well. She enjoyed a lot of fun banter via text before he popped the question: *Dinner this weekend? I'd love to get to know you better.* Ming has already done a thorough social media check on Michael, has even asked a mutual LinkedIn connection about him. It all checks out; apparently, he's as nice and decent as he seems. But somehow the invitation to dinner – an actual date – shuts down Ming's enthusiasm. Her best friend asks her why the sudden disinterest?

"You know why," Ming says.

"You can't be serious, Ming! Dustin? Does this have to do with Dustin?"

"Of course, it does!" Ming replies. "How can I ever trust men again after what Dustin did to me?"

"Girl, I get it. I really do. Being cheated on by your husband sucks. And he lost you as a result," her friend says. "But seriously, you can't hold Dustin's transgression against every man on the planet!"

"Oh yes I can," Ming declares. "Men can't be trusted – that much is clear. And I refuse to be hurt like that ever again."

"Ming, you know I love you dearly and I want you to be happy. But it's been over five years. Don't you think it's time to let go of that anger toward Dustin, so it doesn't destroy all your future relationships?"

"So, you're *defending* Dustin now?" Ming says, aghast.

"Not one bit! But Ming, you're already treating this Michael guy as if *he's* Dustin before you've even gone on one date!"

Ming is quiet for a few minutes. Then she simply says, "I'm done talking about this." Her friend drops it, weary of having the same argument with Ming every time her friend meets someone she's clearly interested in. Michael never gets a reply from Ming. After several days of one-sided texts and calls that go right to voicemail, he stops trying. Ming never hears from him again. *See?* She tells herself. *I was right. Men suck.*

Does it appear that Ming needs to let go of her past? Oh yes! What Dustin did was unconscionable. But it's done, they're divorced, and yet Ming can't seem to let go. She hasn't been on one date since her divorce, and while she misses male companionship and intimacy, she can't get past her past. She can't *let it go.*

Quick Check - Select all that apply:

- ☐ I often bring up the same stories over and over, both to myself and to others, with the same amount of feeling attached, as if it occurred yesterday.
- ☐ I feel like I'm stuck in a cycle of victimhood – to people, circumstances, and outcomes.
- ☐ I have a friend or friends I can regularly commiserate with about when I was a victim.

Deal with Unfinished Business

It is difficult to consistently create a happy, healthy, peaceful life if you're holding onto past hurts, mistakes, injustice, or pain. To be joyful and healthy in a holistic way means being physically, emotionally, and mentally healthy. This includes dealing with unfinished business, such as rage, hurt, unforgiveness or judgment against others...or yourself. To be clear, we can't change the past and may not be able to forget it either. But we can shift how we view it. The key to this shift is to examine the lessons, both painful and joyful, that we have gleaned from the variety of experiences we've encountered in life. We can decide that, in a sense, perhaps we needed to go through painful or disturbing experiences to grow. This in no way condones any wrongs that others have done to you or wrongs you yourself have perpetuated. We must all be held accountable for our actions. That said, there is a time to make peace with our past and move forward, to do better, and – again – to *let it go.*

Perhaps you'll need to undergo a catharsis prior to making peace with your past. If so, here's a simple process to do just that:

1. Identify the issue from your past that's holding you back.

2. Dig into the root of the issue: what brought it about, why did it occur, what role, if any, did you play in bringing it about? (Just to be clear, if you were the victim of a brutal crime, do not trick yourself into thinking you somehow deserved or caused your victimization based on things such as being in the wrong place at the wrong time, what you wore, what time of night it happened, etc.)

3. If you played a role in bringing about the past issue that still holds you back, determine how you can do better next time. Then vow to do just that.

4. If you did something "unforgivable" to another person, and thoughts of shame or guilt are holding you back, make amends. By gaining the forgiveness of those you hurt, you'll be in a better position to forgive yourself.

5. If someone did something "unforgivable" to you, write out your feelings about what occurred. Consider writing them a "Get to the Love Letter" using the form at the end of the chapter. Really dig in and feel every horrible thought or feeling you've had about it for this exercise. You need not track down the perpetrator, because this is about your internal mindset regarding the event. When you've written out an exhaustive detailing of it, and how it disempowers you even to this day, burn that piece of paper. As it burns, you may wish to tell yourself that you are burning away the binds that this element of your past has had over your life. It's truly freeing!

6. If an experience is holding you back, look at it from another angle and ask yourself what you learned from the experience. If we examine our lives closely enough and with sincerity, we often find that everything in our life offers us a gift, if only in the form of a lesson. And we keep getting the lesson until we learn it.

7. Finally, commit to moving on. Commit to never again allowing this experience from your past to have any power over you. You deserve more. You *are* more. We are each more than our pasts. This is how we evolve.

When dealing with unfinished business, I suggest you rip that Band-Aid off. Leap into the deep end. Just do it! There's no need to adopt incrementalism when it comes to making peace with your past. *Slow and steady* can end up being *long and drawn out.* Wouldn't you rather get it over with? Another dear friend shared an example of the benefits of this strategy by teaching me how cows and bison each respond to storms. Cows, apparently, run away from storms. And because they are slow, the storm always catches up to them, keeping them in misery for longer than necessary because they're moving in the same direction as the storm. Bison, on the other hand, react to oncoming storms by running directly at them, passing quickly through the inevitable difficulty. Like the cows, bison also experience the discomfort of the storm, although for a much shorter time. So, when it comes to dealing with unfinished business, embrace your inner bison! Face the storm head on and you'll make peace with your past much more quickly than all those silly cows.

Eliminate the Victim Virus

Over time, victimhood can be a seductive trap. It's a mindset that's also habit-forming, especially if you were indeed the victim of a traumatic experience, such as rape or a near-fatal accident or domestic abuse or war. Obviously, these experiences are far more traumatic than, say, dealing with an irritable coworker or not achieving a goal or deadline. As such, they may require deeper intervention than what I can offer you through this book. If this is the case, I highly recommend seeking out whatever form of therapeutic help resonates with you, be it psychotherapy, hypnotherapy, spiritual counseling, or any other means of holistic healing you feel drawn to, like EMDR, Eye movement desensitization and reprocessing or EFT/ "Tapping Technique." Yes, it will require a lot of emotional work to ensure that your past trauma doesn't end up defining you for the rest of your days. But it's worth it. And it's crucial if you wish to grow and make lasting peace with your past.

It's likely that many of us will be victimized at some point in our lives. The key is to not allow the victimization virus to take root. What do I mean by this? The victimization virus is a mindset, based in fear, that can be traced back to an original trauma. It's the false notion that if you ever find yourself in a similar situation, the same horrific outcome will occur. This false notion can be either conscious or subconscious. For example, a friend lost her father quite suddenly in a plane crash when she was six years old. In her 20s, she began to read about the abandonment issues that tend to go hand in hand with losing a parent at a young age. Susanne rejected this notion. She continued to have short-lived, ill-fated romantic relationships, which usually ended with their first disagreement. She was often the one to break things off. It wasn't until she was in her 30s that she began to examine this tendency to abandon intimate partners before they could abandon her. When she finally met the man she chose to marry at age 34, she had to work even harder to make peace with the death of her father so she could enter her marriage without dragging subconscious baggage with her. Recently, she told me that she still hears whispers of her childhood fears, especially when her husband is backpacking, out of cell-service range, and returns to civilization a few hours later than expected. She jokingly told me, "I've usually already planned his memorial service in my head because my 6-year-old self is certain he's dead." She and her husband have now been married over 20 years, which might not have been possible had she not broken out of the victimization virus where her most important relationships were concerned.

As my friend's example shows, the victimization virus can have small flare ups from time to time, no matter how much therapy or conscious letting go we've done. The memories are still in our psyches, and we never know what might cause them to resurface. When this happens, a helpful course of action is to refocus our attention on the present. Rather than reliving that awful past memory, we can choose to shift to something we have control over in the here and now, even if it's a simple reminder that the traumatic memory that came roaring back is from *before*...and things have changed. That was then, this is now. We can even thank our former selves for caring enough about us to bring up this concern, and we must also remind our former selves that things have changed, the danger is behind us, and – perhaps most importantly – we're *safe* in this moment.

By curing the victimization virus, we not only make life more pleasant for ourselves, but also for those closest to us. Your loved ones and confidants may not tell you they're tired of hearing the same old stories of past hurts...so I will. You're welcome.

Make Room for the Positives

We are all a combination of *all* our experiences, good and bad. By making peace with our past and ridding ourselves of old mental junk, we're actually making room for more positives to come into our lives – in every regard. In a sense, by committing to identify and make peace with our past negative experiences or traumas, we are, in effect, saying, "Moving on! Next!" This is like a spiritual invitation for more pleasant, happy, fulfilling, and joyful experiences to enter your life. But these new positives can't enter where there is no space. It'd be like trying to host a huge party in a tiny closet. No room, no party. So, clearing out the junk to make room for the new is critical. And just imagine how much fun it will be when these new positive experiences and attitudes start showing up in your life.

One important factor to consider is the people with whom you spend most of your time. If you have a history of victimization virus, then you've likely picked up some enabling friends who've also been infected with the virus. After all, misery loves company, right? You will need to dramatically alter, or possibly end, these relationships. It's worth giving those who have always supported your victim mindset a chance to no longer enable you – or themselves. An honest conversation about how you are choosing to make peace with your past is in order. You can even enlist their help in redirecting the conversation should you fall back into your old ways. Your example of conscious change may serve to help them break their own victim mindset. But that is a choice they must make for themselves. It's not up to you to tell your friends they need to change. Your responsibility is to clearly communicate your new approach and your boundaries where rehashing past hurts is concerned. A simple "I'm going to need us to talk about something positive now, Debbie Downer." (Okay, maybe don't throw in the "Debbie Downer" part.)

Model the behavior you would like others to use with you if you were to slip up and fall back into a victim mindset. Soon enough, I suspect you'll see healthy shifts in your former Misery Buddies' behavior. If not, you'll likely be seeing less of them as they seek out another like-minded, victim-mindset friend with whom they can relive their old grievances and traumas. And that's okay. Just because we've decided to cure our own victimization virus doesn't mean everyone is going to make the same choice. We each have our own path to walk and our own timing for personal evolution in life. They may not be able to stay on the journey with you. Put another way: you can lead a horse to water, but you can't make him make peace with his past. Something like that.

Ming, Revisited.

What if Ming had worked through the wounds left by her first marriage with a trained professional, who helped her move into future relationships without her emotional baggage? Her interactions with Michael may have gone something like this: Ming receives Michael's text invitation to dinner. Instead of suddenly becoming distrustful and fearful of him, she accepts his invitation. They have a lovely evening together, laughing and talking at the restaurant until closing time. During their third date, Ming opens up to Michael about her divorce and the fact that her husband had cheated on her, repeatedly. She tells Michael how hurt she was for so long after the relationship ended, and how she's had to do a lot of work on herself to be able to trust again. Michael lets her know that he's been in that position too and that he understands how painful it is. They both promise to be upfront and honest with one another, regardless of whether their relationship continues for a month...or a lifetime. By making peace with her past, Ming hasn't condoned her ex-husband's behavior. But she has made it easier for herself to enjoy future relationships with men, free of her past relationship wounds.

Time doesn't heal emotional pain, you need to learn how to let go.

— Roy T. Bennett

❀

Intention:

I choose to make peace with my past.

Now, how about digging deeper? As a warm-up to this time for reflection, I suggest listening to "Let It Go" by Idina Menzel.

Invitation to Reflect:

Think about one painful memory that has stuck with you for some time: How would you benefit from giving it up?

_____

_____

_____

_____

_____

_____

How might your current relationships improve if you let go of that painful memory?

_____

_____

_____

_____

What friend is enabling your victim mindset? What will you do about it?

_____

_____

_____

_____

Here are some actions you can take now for your self-care:

- ○ Write a "Get to the Love - Letter" to someone, living or deceased, who has hurt you in the past (see format at the end of the chapter).
- ○ If possible, make an appointment to read that letter to the person or file it away until you are comfortable sharing it with them.
- ○ Consider alternative therapies. Ted Moreno is a hypnotherapist I've personally worked with and his podcasts #165 and #180 give a great overview of hypnotherapy. You can find his podcasts online or on iTunes. Consider making an appointment for a free consultation with him or another hypnotherapist (Emma Dietrich) to work on subconscious beliefs about the past that could be negatively affecting your present circumstances.

Commit to doing at least one thing differently based on what you learned in this chapter. Write out an actionable goal – with a specific deadline – to satisfy this commitment.

_____

_____

_____

How will you celebrate or reward yourself if you reach the goal?

_____

_____

Other thoughts and reflections:

_____

_____

_____

_____

Get to the Love - Letter Format

Dear_____ (Add person's name, even if it is your own)

<u>Anger and Blame</u>

I hate it when

_____

I don't like it when

_____

You make me mad when

_____

I am fed up with

_____

<u>Hurt and Sadness</u>

I feel sad when

_____

I feel hurt when

_____

I feel awful when

_____

I feel disappointed because

_____

Fear

I'm afraid that

_____

I feel scared because

_____

I feel afraid because

_____

Guilt

I am guilty for

_____

I am sorry that

_____

Please forgive me for

_____

I didn't mean to

_____

Love, Gratitude, and Forgiveness

I love you because

_____

I love you when

_____

Thank you for

_____

I understand that

_____

I forgive you for

_____

I appreciate you when

_____

I want

_____

For additional resources related to this topic, please check out my website: www.abcsofselfcare.com

N

N-O IS YOUR NEW Y-E-S

No is a complete sentence.

— Anne Lamott

❦

When you say *no* to a request you can't or don't want to do, you're actually saying *yes* to yourself. Not only is this an act of self-care, but it is also setting a boundary for others. Typically, it is our innate desire to be accepted or loved by others that leads us to commit to doing things we'd rather not do. As a recovering (and no longer exhausted) people-pleaser, I am proud to say that I now choose myself most of the time. Notice I didn't say *all* the time. Sometimes, I will agree to do something I'd rather not do because the person making the request is in genuine need, I care deeply about them, and doing it will not harm me. For example, attending a friend's son's "graduation" from preschool with her because her ex-husband would also be attending; hmmm, a preschool graduation? Not exactly on my bucket list, nor does it sound appealing, but to support my friend? Sure.

It has been a long road for me to get this far in learning to say no, however. Perhaps being bullied as a child fed my need to please. Or perhaps it stemmed from living with parents who were so caught up in solving their own life problems that there was little energy left for them to reinforce my sense of worthiness. Or maybe being a black female in predominantly white undergraduate *and* graduate schools caused me to work too hard to be liked, accepted, and respected. No matter the root cause of my inability to say no, and no matter who may have negatively impacted my sense of self-worth in my younger years, it is my responsibility to create the life I want. It is my fault alone if I don't work to overcome those earlier influences and take steps to improve my situation moving forward. Learning to say no – gently and kindly – has been one of the most empowering self-care habits I've developed over the years.

Nuria and N-O

Nuria is thought of as the go-to girl in her friend group. All her friends know that Nuria is the most reliable person to call on when in need because she doesn't even have the word "no" in her vocabulary. And Nuria is proud of this fact. She tells herself that she loves saying yes to people, to adventures, to life! She often finds herself overbooked and exhausted because of her jam-packed schedule. People often comment on how busy Nuria is, which gives her a feeling of importance and acceptance. She attends more events in a month than most people attend in a year! She helps countless friends with their personal needs, from proofreading graduate school papers to babysitting young children to writing letters of recommendation. Nuria is moving to a new condo in town in a few weeks and is on a strict budget, so she's planning to invite friends and neighbors to help her with the move. Surely all the goodwill she's built up with others will pay off in the form of help moving.

She sends out an email with her request and almost immediately the excuses start pouring in: *Sorry, but work has been really hectic lately, so I need my weekends to rest...*or *I've got a date that night, so I don't want to tire myself out...*or *Lifting boxes isn't my thing.* Plenty of friends haven't responded, so Nuria assumes she'll still have plenty of help. Moving day arrives and Nuria finds herself hauling all her belongings solo, making 18 trips back and forth with her SUV. Ultimately, she must pay a few neighbors – the same ones whose pets Nuria took care of for free during their vacations – to move her large pieces of furniture. It's after midnight when Nuria finally finishes her move. She flops on the couch feeling abandoned by and angry at her so-called friends. Then she receives an email from a friend (one who never replied to her moving help request) asking if Nuria can help her plant her spring garden tomorrow. "No one knows gardening as well as you do," her friend writes. Nuria bursts into tears reading the email. Then she wipes her eyes and writes back, "Sure!" "Great," replies her friend. "Be here at 8. Can you swing by Starbucks on your way, too?" Nuria falls into bed angry and hurt, but unable to see a different approach. She's a good person. *To give is better than to receive,* she reminds herself. Why then does she feel so used, so depleted all the time?

Quick Check - Select all that apply:

- ☐ I like making others happy, even if, at times, it is inconvenient.
- ☐ I like to stay in motion and busy.
- ☐ I often say yes to something even if I'm exhausted.

Cure the Disease to Please

The "disease to please" takes root when we consistently find ourselves saying yes when our true desire is to say no. The most common driving force behind the disease to please is a need for approval.

What will others think of me if I don't agree to their requests? (The follow up question should be: Do I really care what others' think of me if I choose to do what's best for me? And the answer should usually be a firm *no*!) Other factors that lead to an unhealthy desire to please others are a tendency toward perfectionism and conflict avoidance. Perfectionists will often say yes because they, often subconsciously, believe that being perfect in the eyes of others will bring them happiness. Basically, the inability to let someone down. And those who avoid conflict like the plague are at risk. Because saying no to a request – even if it's an invitation for a fun event – may lead to a response they can't handle, such as anger or disappointment. These are the people who would rather be "nice" and please others to avoid having to deal with uncomfortable discussions or reactions from others. The quest to please others all the time is unrealistic and exhausting, so I urge you to put your *needs* above the *wants* of others. The disease to please is not an element of true self-care, so the sooner you cure it, the happier, healthier, and more peaceful you'll be. It takes practice and a firm commitment to your own well-being, and it's worth it.

In her groundbreaking book, *The Type E Woman*, Dr. Harriet Braiker asserts that women in particular all too often view down time and relaxation as a luxury, something to be earned once all of life's to-dos are completed. The Type E woman is, in Dr. Braiker's definition, a woman who is trying to excel in multiple roles and be everything to everybody – a surefire recipe for disaster. The Type E woman will attempt to "rise to each and every occasion, pushing herself beyond safe or reasonable limits, without adequate regeneration and rejuvenation of her resources until she is thoroughly depleted by her own good intentions." This is just the sort of anti-self-care behavior that can lead to unhealthy stress levels, chronic fatigue, illness and even a premature and avoidable early death. Sadly, I suspect Dr. Braiker learned these lessons the hard way; she passed away from pneumonia at 55-years-young. Her death haunted me for quite some time, as I could see my own approach to life reflected in her words. I vowed to do better, and I've made it my mission to help both myself and others to incorporate greater levels of self-care into their lives.

Live Fully, Not Busily

I used to fear that I would die before I did all that I came here to do. So, I turned myself into a real go-getter, committed to squeezing all the juice possible out of life. I thought the way to achieve this was to do everything! Surely my busy lifestyle was proof that I was getting the most out of life, right? *Wrong!*

When I read the marvelous works of Dr. Elisabeth Kubler-Ross, one of the world's renowned experts on death and dying, I gained an even greater perspective. Kubler-Ross claimed that the sign of a life fully lived is one in which you spent a lot of time doing the things you love. If you've done this, Kubler-Ross states, then "dying is nothing to fear. It can be the most wonderful experience of your life. It all depends on how you have lived." That statement alone gave me an incredible amount of peace. It gave me permission to stop being so busy. I learned to make the most of my life by being more discerning about how I chose to spend my time and talents. I listened to my heart's desire more and began shifting my work more directly into the areas I cared deeply about. I learned to say no more often. I replaced the constant activity in my life with living more fully and more deliberately. I had more fun. What a difference this all made to my health, happiness, and peace of mind. Brené Brown, PhD, LMSW has done extensive research on vulnerability. She has taken the notion of living fully one step further. Brown's research has shown that people who are – as she jokingly puts it – "crazy-busy" are often using this approach as a numbing strategy, like donning protective armor against their own vulnerability. "We are a culture of people who've bought into the idea that if we stay busy enough, the truth of our lives won't catch up with us." Yet it always does, doesn't it?

We can cure an addiction to being busy by scheduling more time to simply chill and by only accepting invitations that are meaningful to us. Saying no more often is a good starting point. Avoid activities that aren't in alignment with your goals, priorities, and values. Check in with yourself, your intuition, before saying yes to something. Bite your tongue, go within, even delay your response for a day or two to decide. These simple steps can mean the difference between doing something you'll regret or choosing the self-care option. And *how* you say no is what will allow you to preserve the relationships that are important to you.

Preserve Important Relationships

When it's time to say no to a friend's invitation or request, Dr. Lois Frankel suggests that you don't want to say the word no except in extreme situations. These extremes include issues of attempted sexual harassment or assault, impending danger, and anything that is flat-out harmful to your safety or well-being. In most cases, however, we're attempting to let down a friend or colleague gently, so as not to damage the relationship. Dr. Frankel suggests we practice using a variety of responses that allow us to decline a request graciously and kindly without using the word *no*. These include:

- As much as I'd love to attend, my calendar is already over-scheduled for that week.
- Thank you for thinking of me; unfortunately, I am not able to attend.
- If I could, I would. I really value our friendship and wish the situation were different.
- Although I've been able to help you out in the past, this time I just don't have the bandwidth.
- I'm just not able to be of help at this time.
- I'm flattered, yet I'm not able to accept your kind offer.
- I'm so sorry that this isn't going to work out. I hope it might in the future.

I suggest you practice using some of these responses in low-risk situations to get comfortable with incorporating this language into your repertoire of "saying no without saying no." You can even give your friends and family a heads up that you're going to be more selective in what you agree to do in the future, so they're not surprised when you begin using this language with them. You'll soon see how easy and comfortable it is to let someone down without deflating them or being unnecessarily blunt. Learning the art of subtly and kindly saying no will go a long way in taking care of you while also preserving the relationships that are important to you.

Now, let's be clear, learning to say no in the workplace is a different story. It's not always within your power to say no to a request by a senior colleague. It is within your power, however, to volunteer or to do special projects less often, especially if you know your plate is already full. Other ways to prevent over-committing at work include renegotiating deadlines or lobbying for another person to join a project team. The most important thing for you to recognize in the workplace is when you are reaching the point of *overwhelm*. When this occurs, step back and evaluate what you can do differently to ease the current demands on your time. Can you say, "time for a day off?"

Remember, your happiness, health and peace of mind are dependent upon your ability to kindly and diplomatically say "no" more often. You can do it!

Nuria, Revisited

Let's return to Nuria and see how she might have handled her situation in a way that was more supportive of her own self-care needs. After a full day of moving on her own, she receives a request for help from someone she considers a close friend. Instead of her typical knee-jerk response of "*Sure*," Nuria crafts an honest but kind response: *Sue - I am exhausted from my move today. I didn't get any help from the friends I asked...including you. I must tell you that it really hurt my feelings that you never responded to my request. I am going to take tomorrow to rest and begin unpacking. Good luck with your garden. Nuria.* Before pushing send, Nuria reads and rereads her response, knowing that her friend will likely be shocked by the pushback Nuria is giving her. Strong in her sense that it's time to learn to say no more often, Nuria pushes send. The next day, she will review her calendar and cancel any future commitments she made looking for acceptance and approval. She will keep only those activities that she genuinely has an interest in doing. *No* has just become Nuria's new *yes* – to herself!

I've learned that there is nothing more consistent with unhappiness than spending your time in a way that doesn't serve who you are.

– Scott Dinsmore

❀

Intention:

With kindness, I say no to others so that I can say yes to myself.

Now, how about digging deeper? As a warm-up to this time for reflection, I suggest listening to "N-O Is my New Yes!" Written by Karen Drucker, music by Karen Drucker & John Hoy.

Invitation to Reflect:

What good self-care choices are you currently making that provide you comfort, are nurturing and fulfilling?

_____

_____

_____

_____

What projects or tasks could you let go of to free up more time for your self-care?

_____

_____

_____

Is it possible that you are staying busy to avoid vulnerability and/or difficult emotions? If yes, how could you be more vulnerable and/or address the difficult emotions?

_____

_____

_____

Here are some actions you could take now for your self-care:

- ○ Practice saying no in low-risk situations.
- ○ Adopt a rule that you will wait five minutes, up to five days before saying yes to a new request.
- ○ Journal about commitments you need to scale back on or bow out of gracefully. Strategize on an approach.

Commit to doing at least one thing differently based on what you learned in this chapter. Write out an actionable goal – with a specific deadline – to satisfy this commitment.

_____

_____

_____

_____

How will you celebrate or reward yourself if you reach the goal?

_____

_____

Other thoughts and reflections:

_____

_____

_____

_____

For additional resources related to this topic, please check out my website: www.abcsofselfcare.com

$\mathscr{O}$

OBSERVE RELATIONSHIPS

One of the most crippling things we can do to ourselves is expect someone else to make us happy.

— Sue Patton Thoele

❧

It should come as no surprise to us that research shows the #1 predictor of happiness and health comes down to social support. In other words: our relationships. Our peace of mind is directly proportional to the degree to which our relationships are healthy. I'm talking about real, in-person relationships – not those virtual "friendships" we develop online through the "happy" narratives we put forth to the public in our social media accounts or in a chat app. (Because, really, not everyone feels like posting about their lives when they're not so good, amirite?) Relationships create an opportunity for each of us to learn about and practice true intimacy – and I'm not talking about sex here. Let's be honest though: sex can be a great aspect of a relationship as well. I'm talking about the type of intimacy that involves sharing personal thoughts and feelings, which leads to forming a genuine closeness or bond – sex, or no sex. True intimate relationships are supportive, loving, and authentic. They generate the type of happiness most of us are looking for, regardless of whether those relationships are platonic or romantic. It is only through stepping back and observing our various relationships, and then honestly assessing them, that we can determine if they are worth keeping and nurturing...or letting go.

Olabisi and Observing Relationships

Olabisi loves her boyfriend, Omar, with whom she recently relocated to Tucson – him to complete his undergraduate degree, her for graduate school. They set up a nice little apartment near campus and settled in to begin their classes. And that's when Olabisi began to observe signs that troubled her. While hanging out at the Student Union one day, Olabisi saw a notice in the school newspaper about auditions to be the new campus mascot, Wilbur T. Wildcat. Olabisi was ecstatic! She'd been her school mascot for three years in high school and had a blast making people laugh and cheer. She immediately signed up for an audition and brought the application home to complete. When she excitedly told Omar about her plans, he looked forlorn and said, "What about us going to the football games together? If you get this, I won't have anyone to sit with in the stands." Olabisi was disappointed, although he had a point. Afterall, they knew no one in town, having moved from New York.

She was a no-show for her audition the next day. Then Olabisi made some new friends in her classes, some of whom were male, and Omar flipped out. "I don't want other guys thinking they can get their hands on my girl, Olabisi," he said to her, before going onto their patio and pouting. She hated seeing him this way, so she reassured him that she wouldn't see any of her new male friends outside of the classroom. When her mother, with whom she was very close, asked how the whole "living together thing" was working out, Olabisi fudged the truth a bit and told her everything was great. But *was it?* she wondered.

As the holidays approached, Olabisi was excited to fly to Texas to visit with her family, who had relocated there from New York a year earlier. Omar was incensed. "I thought we were spending the holidays together! In New York! Where all your old friends still are!" Did he really think she wouldn't want to see her own family over Christmas? Apparently so! Ultimately, Olabisi acquiesced and changed her flight to New York, flying into Texas only for a few days before New Year's Eve. Olabisi is upset that Omar always seems to be pushing her to do things she doesn't want to do, but she knows he loves her... and she believes he will change when he feels more secure about her feelings for him. She just needs to show him more love.

Does Olabisi's relationship seem like a healthy one to you? Do you suppose she and Omar are long termers? And if so, how do you suppose the power dynamics will be in 5 years? 10 years? 20 years? The answers? Bad, worse, and unbearable. In other words, this relationship is doomed, and the real question should be: does Olabisi have the emotional maturity to see it and, if so, to act on it?

Quick Check - Select all that apply:

- ☐ I have difficulty maintaining healthy friendships and/or romantic relationships.
- ☐ I am estranged from one or more family members.
- ☐ I am unhappy in many of my relationships.

Classify as Healthy or Unhealthy

Relationships can make or break us. Taking a closer look at each of our core relationships (beyond mere acquaintances) to determine which to keep and which to bow out of is a great way to make sure our relationships don't break us. It's likely that we instinctively know the difference between a healthy and unhealthy relationship, even if an unhealthy relationship feels "normal" to us at the time we're in it. Sometimes, it is only through hindsight that we see all the glaring signs of an unhealthy relationship that were there all along. Unhealthy relationships are those with a noticeable imbalance of power. They lack a sense of mutual support. If allowed to exist for any significant length of time, an unhealthy relationship can break us – our spirit, our aspirations, even our sense of self. An unhealthy relationship can hold us back by invalidating who we are and who we choose to become. They can minimize our potential and discourage us from living our best lives. They leave us feeling more alone than ever, even when we're with that other person. Often, when we come from a place of self-criticism, not enough-ism, insecurity, or hopelessness, we set ourselves up for attracting unhealthy relationships into our lives. Been there, done that! And guess what? Never again!

In a healthy relationship, on the other hand, our needs and wants matter. We feel supported. We feel our self-esteem and self-confidence being bolstered, not torn down. We sense that we have a true "partner" – be it a romantic relationship or dear friend. Healthy relationships make us better people and increase our happiness. They allow for both parties to grow in the relationship, at their own pace. In healthy relationships, both parties are actively demonstrating love for the other person. Things like spending quality time (i.e., phone-free), showing affection, listening attentively, expressing appreciation, and giving thoughtful gifts. Whether romantic or platonic, the unhealthy relationships feel different, as if we're in jail, not free to be our most authentic selves. Perhaps we have one or two of those relationships in our lives currently. We'll know by more closely observing each one.

Wait for True Love

Too often, people feel that being in a committed partnership or marriage reflects their worth. I assure you; it does not. Nor is it a badge of "enough-ness" or external validation. No relationship can make us enough because we already *are* enough. We were born enough, right? No marriage license or tenure in a relationship can "endorse" us either. Yet many people, especially women, feel they are less than because they aren't "chosen" by a spouse. Perhaps it wasn't your destiny or perhaps, you aren't ready yet for true love. Can you honestly say you've made the effort to find it?

And divorce? I can tell you from firsthand experience that it can be an incredibly soul crushing experience. Better to go through life single and surrounded by a strong, authentic friend group than to jump into an unhealthy marriage. Yet if we do find ourselves in an unhealthy long-term relationship, we should never assume there's nothing to be done about it, that we must stick it out for the sake of (fill in the blank: our children, our professional reputations, our religion's expectations, the mortgage, "couples friend group," etc.) Instead, we can reframe the dismantling of a significant relationship as "our – spiritual and/or emotional – work together is complete." Isn't that a much healthier and self-supporting way of viewing a breakup than to call it a "failed marriage" or "a waste of XX years"? Of course, it is. And it also happens to be the truth. We come together in a relationship to grow, be it for a lifetime, a decade, a year, or five minutes. Okay, I'm being slightly tongue-in-cheek about the five-minute relationship, but hopefully you get my point.

Never be ashamed to step away from a long-term relationship that is clearly unhealthy. I'm not talking about a couple bad days or even a longer stretch of feeling disconnected from one another due to work stress, a major life challenge, or a hurtful misunderstanding. I'm talking about genuinely ongoing *unhealthy* relationships. Remember, those of us who have experienced divorce took the risk to be vulnerable in the name of love. Okay, so it didn't work out as planned. We get points for trying, and even more points for recognizing when it wasn't working and moving on. No one can determine for you if your significant relationship is healthy enough to survive a current tremendous challenge or unhealthy to the degree that it's best to part ways. We're each on our own unique journeys, after all. We must each determine what is right for us based on our own needs, resilience levels, desires, and goals.

One thing I've observed over the years is that those who set an intention to be in, and stay in, a lifelong relationship will do all the things it takes to honor that intention. That's a great place to start. For me, personally, I've vowed to only move forward with a romantic relationship with someone I am already good (and healthy!) friends with, someone I like, care for, and can share difficult feelings with. I also observe whether this special someone is the sort of person who has worked through life's plethora of lemons to make lemonade. Because once we go deeper into an intimate relationship, there are bound to be more lemons. Personally, I want a good partner with whom to share my life/lemonade and I've learned that nothing less is acceptable. To me, that is true love and I'm willing to wait for it. Better to be alone and not lonely than to be in partnership with someone yet feeling very alone. Can I get an *amen*?

F.L.Y.

Okay, now that we've reviewed the warning labels that come with a committed, romantic, and intimate relationship, let's dive into the most powerful starting point for having one: FLYing! What the…?! Yep, you read that right. For us to be ready for a lifelong commitment to another, we must F.L.Y. – First. Love. Yourself. Why? Because, truly, the most important relationship in our lives is always the one we have with ourselves. Like the famed Queen of all Drag Queens, RuPaul, is always telling her audiences, "If you can't love yourself, how in the hell are you going to love somebody else?" Amen! Such a simple, yet powerful, observation. And how do we first nurture the relationship we have with ourselves? Master the three S's: Self-Acceptance, Self-Love, and Self-Care. This book, as you've figured out by now, aims to help you with all of these. In other words, it helps you become your own BFF. This is the foundation for all other relationships, be they platonic or romantic. Being your own best friend means you must love yourself enough to *not* need external validation or a relationship to achieve happiness. It means you love yourself enough to clearly, yet kindly, teach others how you wish to be treated. And yes, the "golden rule" about treating others as you wish to be treated absolutely applies here. As well as practicing the "platinum rule,"– treat others like *they want* to be treated.

Once we've shored up our relationship with ourselves, we can feel confident in our ability to observe and assess our romantic relationships for clues as to whether this one may "go the distance." As relationship expert, Barbara DeAngelis, so eloquently puts it, "The more connections you and your lover make, not just between your bodies, but between your minds, your hearts, and your souls, the more you will strengthen the fabric of your relationship, and the more real moments you will experience together." For a more in-depth look into recognizing and building long-term, intimate life partnerships, I highly recommend checking out her books or many available online talks. I heard someone else say to make sure you let the relationship progress naturally from Acquaintance, to Friend, to Intimate Partner (or AFI). Most importantly, always remember to FLY – First Love Yourself.

Determine Needs and Wants

Conflict can arise in romantic relationships when we don't get our needs, or even our wants, met. Perhaps we don't feel worthy enough to expect our needs to be met. Or maybe we're confused about whether something is a *need*...or just a less important *want*. Needs are those things that are extremely important to us; wants are more along the lines of preferences. If we find ourselves discounting our needs to avoid conflict, this may be a sign that the relationship is unhealthy.

Research has shown that conflict in relationships can come from the subconscious baggage we each carry into them from our past traumas, including all the way back to childhood. A good relationship goal, according to Imago relationship experts, Drs. Helen LaKelly Hunt and Harville Hendrix, is to avoid shame, blame and criticism. Unfortunately, our past traumas sometimes propel us into those exact behaviors in romantic relationships. Their decades of fascinating research demonstrates that we tend to be attracted to people who have similar negative traits to one or both of our parents. We bring to our relationships the expectation that we'll get what we need in a relationship from our partners, or we may recreate painful patterns we experienced in childhood. Our partners – assuming they are up for the challenge – can help us heal our earlier wounds by having the tough conversations that arise when we recognize this subtle reflection of our parents in our partners. Dealing with conflict, communicating, and working through challenges brought on by these old wounds, is a great way to build and nurture a healthy lifelong partnership.

Assess Your Friendships

Whether or not we find ourselves in a partnership, friendships are a key ingredient in a life well lived. When we hit a bump in the road and need some perspective, who do we call? We need close friendships to give us perspective, speak truth to us, hold us accountable, and encourage us to be our best. And yes, good friends are also terrific companions to hang out with. Bonus!

Just as with our romantic relationships, it's important to observe and assess our friendships. Are the people you spend time with simply "good time" friends? Or are they also friends you can share your difficult feelings with, such as shame or doubt or guilt? Are they friends who will jump in and help in a time of need? Or are they more of the "fair weather" variety? If you're like me, you have both biological sisters and sisters from other misters. Both are incredibly good for the soul. The key is that these relationships have unconditional love as their foundation, regardless of any blood relation. It's okay if not all your friendships are lifelong. Remember, some people come into our lives for a reason, some for a season and some for a lifetime. All are valid, but, man, what a blessing it is when we find ourselves with a lifelong friend!

Lifelong healthy friendships don't necessarily come without any conflict whatsoever. Ironically, some of the closest friendships in my life currently are people I've had major beefs with in the past. I even tried to "divorce" one of them! Yet today, she and I laugh ourselves silly about those hard conversations we had back when things were anything but smooth sailing. Friendships that have weathered the inevitable storms are often the ones that turn into lifelong relationships. Others – regardless of any storms or conflict, may not be fulfilling enough for us to keep investing our time and energy into. That's okay! Remember – reason, season, or lifetime. Our intuition often tells us when this is a one-season friendship. Which, again, is valid and ok.

Once we've become our own BFFs, our friendships become more like beautiful accessories. They enhance our lives, but don't define them. This perspective makes it easier for us to make self-care choices around the time we wish to invest in them. And of course, if we recognize that we're in an unhealthy friendship, as with an unhealthy romantic relationship, don't be afraid to kindly back out.

Friendships are an important aspect of work-life too. The key is to seek empowered ones. Some colleagues may become treasured friends outside of work as well. Others are friendly work relationships that are mutually beneficial. If we find ourselves in a work friendship that feels dysfunctional, we shouldn't hesitate to back off.

Regardless of whether a relationship is with a family member, lover, friend, or work colleague, if we want to keep them healthy and long-lasting, we must nurture them. This means making time for them, making them a priority. It could also mean being more generous during conversations with them by asking more questions instead of giving information or telling stories. Observe if you are often having a dialogue or a monologue when communicating with someone important to you. Be curious about what they are thinking and feeling, which demonstrates interest in them. This "intentional generosity" in conversations builds a foundation for better, more meaningful relationships that are, ideally, also mutually beneficial. What this looks like is up to the people in the relationship, yet it should be empowering, nurturing, and loving. Does it look like a periodic FaceTime or Zoom call? A shared vacation? An occasional lunch date? Including them in your prayers or meditations? Setting aside a work project to take a call from them? The ways in which we can nurture our important and healthy relationships are endless. It's remembering to do so that is key. The bottom line is that if you carefully observe your relationships, you will be better equipped to nurture the ones that contribute to your happiness, health, and peace of mind.

Olabisi, Revisited.

Olabisi, Olabisi, Olabisi. Of course, her closest girlfriends could tell that her relationship with Omar was unhealthy. But now that she's moved across the country with him, as well as backed away from nurturing her friendships to avoid conflict with him, she's also having doubts. What can she do differently going forward? Over the new year holiday, Olabisi spends a lot of time helping her mother with a project. While simply in one another's company, Olabisi realizes how much more relaxed she is being with her family vs. the time she spends with Omar, mostly trying not to upset him. Time away from Omar – even just a few days – has increased Olabisi's doubts about the relationship. In addition, she's come to the realization that the relationship she has with Omar doesn't square up with the lifelong relationship she imagined for herself.

Soon after, she blurts out, "I think I'm going to break up with Omar." There. She said it! She acknowledged it to her most trusted advisor. Her mother doesn't cheer (though later she will admit that she was happy with Olabisi's decision). Olabisi spends a great deal of time journaling through her feelings during her family visit. By the time she reunites with Omar in Tucson, she is clear about what needs to happen. Sadly, with many tears shed, she tells him she wants them to part ways. She loves him yet doesn't see a healthy long-term relationship with him. He is devastated. They talk for hours, Omar emphasizing how much he loves her. She loves him too, she tells him, but this is not a relationship she wants. She shares with him the many ways she has observed that they are unhealthy together, despite having plenty of talks about both their needs and wants. Both Olabisi and Omar are exhausted from the sheer sadness of breaking up. When he is at the door, luggage in hand and ready to leave he asks her, "Are you sure?" She hesitates, takes a minute to go within, and feels in her heart that this is the right move. They gave it their best, but their best wasn't at all what she wanted. "Yes," she says. Olabisi then spends the entire next day crying, alternating between feeling empowered and feeling lonely.

But as each new day unfolds, she starts to reclaim her former sense of self, her confidence blooms. She feels no need to rush into dating again, instead opting for time spent alone or with Ruth, the one new friend she'd made in Tucson during the entire semester. They become roommates and forge an even stronger bond. She has one solid friendship in her new hometown. And for now, that's plenty for Olabisi. In 14 years, she will meet the man she'll create a healthy, lifelong partnership with. After more than 20 years of marriage – not without its challenges, but stronger for having undergone them together – Olabisi will look back and chuckle at what she was once willing to put up with. *That* Olabisi is long gone...and in her place is an Olabisi who has developed a strong relationship with herself, her mate, and her important friendships. This is the version of Olabisi she was meant to be.

The depth of our love can be measured by our efforts. We demonstrate our love when we take that extra step.

— Harville Hendrix

❧

Intention:

I observe my relationships and choose to keep fulfilling ones.

Now, how about digging deeper? As a warm-up to this time for reflection, I suggest listening to "Roar" by Katy Perry.

Invitation to Reflect:

Which of your current relationships are fulfilling and nurturing (either friendly or romantic)?

_____

_____

_____

_____

_____

In which relationships do you feel you are not treated as you need or want (friendships or romantic ones)?

_____

_____

_____

What are you tolerating in your relationships that needs to change (friendships or romantic)?

_____

_____

_____

Here are some actions you could take now for your self-care:

- ○ Consider an important friend or romantic relationship. Set an intention for that relationship by stating how you want that person to see you.
- ○ Ask a romantic partner the questions from the *New York Times* article entitled "The 36 Questions That Lead to Love."
- ○ Have a conversation with a friend or romantic partner about how the relationship can be enhanced.

Commit to doing at least one thing differently based on what you learned in this chapter. Write out an actionable goal – with a specific deadline – to satisfy this commitment.

_____

_____

_____

_____

How will you celebrate or reward yourself if you reach the goal?

_____

_____

Other thoughts and reflections:

_____

_____

_____

_____

_____

_____

For additional resources related to this topic, please check out my website: www.abcsofselfcare.com

P

PREVENT PERFECTIONISM

Understanding the difference between healthy striving and perfectionism is critical to laying down the shield and picking up your life. Research shows that perfectionism hampers success. In fact, it's often the path to depression, anxiety, addiction, and life paralysis.

— Brené Brown

❀

In a nutshell, perfectionism is the refusal to accept any standard short of perfection. And we all know that "perfect" doesn't exist, right? So, perfectionism is a no-win way to go through life. Harboring perfectionist tendencies and standards negatively impacts everyone in your orbit: your kids, family, friends, colleagues, and yes, even yourself. Although many well-intentioned people say they are a perfectionist with pride, it can lead to controlling and judgmental behaviors. After all, who can live up to that standard? Those behaviors could lead to strained relationships...not to mention others avoiding you when they've had enough of not being able to achieve your unrealistic standards. Perfectionism is also the root cause of much of the procrastination we each experience in our lives. After all, the subconscious mind of the perfectionist tells us: *if it's not perfect, why bother?*

A whole host of emotional factors can feed perfectionism – shame, anxiety, lack of confidence, low self-esteem, and unrealistic expectations, just to name a few. Clearly, perfectionism isn't so perfect after all, is it? Rather than striving to be "perfect" – which is unattainable anyway – perhaps the healthier and more productive goal would be striving for excellence, becoming wiser and more confident in the process. You should never allow "perfect" to be what keeps you from "good enough."

Padma and Preventing Perfectionism

Padma was over the moon when she landed the role as the annual gala chair for a cause near and dear to her heart. She'd been volunteering with this nonprofit for years and had been named Volunteer of the Year *twice*. She regularly promoted the organization's efforts on social media. Now she had responsibility for the biggest fundraising event they host, which brings in several hundred thousand dollars each year. Padma was determined to make this the biggest, most successful gala in the charity's history! Everything would be absolutely perfect. She didn't want to just increase the monies raised last year; she wanted to triple them, breaking a million dollars in proceeds. And why not? Hadn't her mother always told her to reach for the stars? Aim higher? And her mother should know – she'd been a successful corporate CEO...before succumbing to cancer at the age of 47, when Padma was just 16 years old.

Now at age 33, Padma wanted to pull off an event worthy of making her mother proud, even if she could only be there in spirit. The board asked for a report from Padma concerning her plans for the gala, including assignments for the various board members, administrative personnel, and volunteers. Padma promised she'd have it soon and told herself that this week would be the week she'd finally dig into planning. Weeks passed and still no report, no updates, no delegated assignments. The charity's Executive Director asked Padma if she'd like help tackling the initial planning, but Padma declined. She knew no one would share her commitment to executing the best gala yet, so she wanted to manage the entire process herself. After all, as her mother used to say, "If you want something done right, you have to do it yourself." More weeks passed and still no gala plan. Padma continued imagining how amazing, impressive, and successful the gala would be, but never seemed to find the time to outline her plans on paper. The board chair sent emails requesting updates and a written plan. Padma ignored them, concerned that the board might want to use the same old approach with the gala. No way! This event was going to be perfect...even if it meant that Padma would have to oversee each committee herself.

Two more weeks passed, and no venue had been secured, no plan outlined, no committee assignments made. At this point, Padma felt the pressure of being behind on her commitment, so it was too late to ask for help. The board thought she was close to finishing the plan. Little did they know that nothing had been outlined yet. Not one detail. Padma began to skip her volunteer hours at the facility to avoid running into any of the leadership team. She knew they'd only bug her about the event. Padma still believed she could pull off the best one ever, but she felt exhausted every time she carved out time to work on the details. She began feeling awful about the months that had lapsed with no plan in place. Her mother would've never allowed this to happen!

How did Padma manage to screw up the biggest honor she'd been given? She started to worry in earnest that she couldn't do what she'd promised to do, which made her feel awful. She hated the idea of letting everyone down, so she'd just have to work extra hard once she finally got started. But Padma never did get started because a week later the Executive Director called her to let her know that the board had voted to replace her as gala chair. Padma wasn't even invited to head up a committee. She was so angry – and, though she wouldn't admit it, ashamed of herself – she didn't even attend when it took place four months later. In fact, Padma never returned to the charity's facility, not even to take her belongings out of her volunteer locker. She continued to stew over being fired from a volunteer position, often grumbling to herself *It would've been perfect if they'd just let me handle it.* Padma orchestrated her own downfall due to her perfectionism.

Quick Check - Select all that apply:

- ☐ I often feel bad for a while when I make a mistake.
- ☐ I review my work over and over to make sure everything is of the highest quality.
- ☐ I am often stuck and do nothing toward achieving my dreams, fearing imperfect results.

Confront Your Shame

There is nothing inherently wrong in striving for the best possible outcome. Healthy striving has to do with judging our performance against realistic standards. Unhealthy striving involves overthinking things based on the opinions and anticipated judgments of others. According to researcher Brené Brown, PhD, LMSW, currently the foremost authority on the subject of shame, perfectionism is a "self-destructive and addictive belief system that fuels this primary thought: *If I look perfect, live perfectly, and do everything perfectly, I can avoid or minimize the painful feelings of shame, judgment, and blame.*" Sounds crazy, right? Well, I invite you to think back on a time in your life when your own perfectionist tendencies were strong and then dig beneath the surface. What made you behave this way? Why did you feel it was so important to be perfect?

Dr. Brown asserts that we may all have a bit of perfectionism within our personality make-up. Learning to notice when we lean toward perfectionism, and then gently, nonjudgmentally nipping it in the bud, is the key to preventing its ongoing presence in our lives. To do this, we're likely going to have to confront some deep-seated emotions, such as shame. Perhaps there was a formative moment or time when we were shamed or criticized for not being good enough, smart enough, athletic enough. Perhaps we were held to unattainable high standards as a child, or unfairly compared with a sibling, thereby always falling short and feeling like a failure. Stack up enough of these emotionally traumatic experiences and we're bound to suffer from a certain degree of shame, no matter how long ago our wounds occurred. Experiences can also include the absence of any feedback or acknowledgment whatsoever – leaving us feeling lacking in some way. Recognizing this underlying shame allows us to explore it...and then release it. Releasing the shame will make it that much easier to also release any patterns of perfectionism. It will require work though.

Sometimes, we continually push ourselves to do something perfectly, regardless of the task's relative importance or urgency. Why? Because we may not have enough self-esteem to realize that we can let go, chill out a bit, accept "good enough" rather than kill ourselves chasing after the ever-elusive "perfect." We've all likely witnessed this sort of behavior, either in ourselves or others. It's that person who goes the extra 10 miles in every situation, even if it's not warranted. To curb my own tendencies toward perfectionism, I finally had to make and hang a sign that read: *Done is better than perfect*! This urged me to not ruminate *ad nauseum* over a simple email or a small project; it helped me put my work out there without overthinking every little detail. And if I made a mistake, confirming my humanness, so be it. I forgave myself right away. Most importantly, it reminded me that a successful life is not about perfection.

Increase Confidence

Understanding the distinction between competence and confidence can positively impact our ability to overcome innate perfectionistic tendencies. Sometimes we women strive extra hard for perfection because we want our competence to be recognized – especially in male-dominated work situations. In a nutshell, competence is the ability to do something successfully or efficiently. Confidence, as it pertains to our performance, is the *feeling of* or *belief in* our ability to do something successfully or efficiently. See the subtle difference? One is built on proven evidence, the other on personal belief. Renowned organizational psychologist, Dr. Tomas Chamorro-Premuzic, says that our self-esteem is strongly influenced by our level of confidence (or lack thereof). Additionally, his research shows that our confidence is rarely a sign of actual competence, as we tend to overrate our skills and talents. Regardless of how confident we are internally, if we come across as confident to others, they will assume we are competent...until proven otherwise. The good news? If you're in a situation in which you need to be seen as competent, you can *fake it till you make it*. Obviously, "fake it till you make it" isn't a sustainable long-term strategy, but if needed in a pinch, then do it!

So how do we increase our confidence levels for real? Here are some tips to increase your confidence over time:

- **Get things done**. Even little goals accomplished will feed your sense of confidence.
- **Monitor progress toward goals**. The more you can break a large goal into smaller steppingstones, and then monitor your progress with each step, the greater the likelihood that you'll accomplish the overall goal, thus increasing your confidence.

- **Live by your values**. If you know what you care about or value and you're always striving to be the best version of yourself, you'll likely be prouder of who you are, which is a surefire confidence booster.
- **Care less what others' think of you**. Haters gonna hate, and there will always be haters (who are typically reflecting their own lack of self-esteem by harshly judging others). The more you can release your dependence on the opinions of others, the more your confidence will soar.
- **Follow through**. Even on those commitments you don't feel like doing, either something for yourself or for another person. Following through reinforces your ability to take action, thereby building confidence. By the way, no matter how good your excuse, people may not remember it, but they will remember that you didn't follow-through.
- **Act fearlessly**...even if you have fears. Fear of failing can take a real toll on our confidence level. Yet it isn't failing itself that's the issue; it's the *fear* of failing. Accept that we're all going to fail now and then, so take action anyway. Confidence comes from taking fearless action. And consistently taking action builds courage. Imagine what you could accomplish by living a more courageous life!

It's important to remember that few people feel confident every minute of every day. So don't panic if you're just not "feeling it" all the time. Take these moments of self-doubt as a sign that it may be time to journal a bit about your strengths and achievements. Tell yourself, "*I know how to host a good dinner party! I've made it to director-level at work! I'm fun to be around! I still have friends from childhood, so I'm capable of maintaining relationships over decades!* Remember, this is a conversation with yourself, so don't worry about how awkward it may feel to pat yourself on the back. This is how you strengthen your self-confidence. I keep an "atta girl" file with cards and accolades that remind me of what I've done well. This is a great way to rebuild confidence when it wanes.

Adjust Expectations

I'm not asking you to lower your expectations – well, perhaps just a little. It depends on how unrealistic and perfectionistic your current standards are. Are you holding yourself and others to unrealistically high standards? Are you able to shift expectations so that you (and others) can *meet standards* without *expecting perfection*? Remember, perfectionistic expectations are not only unrealistic, but they are also unattainable. They lead to burnout, anger, and lost relationships with others, be they family, friends, or colleagues. Obsessing about making things perfect robs us of time we could be spending on more important things, including self-care. Very often, good enough is enough. By not demanding perfection, we regain valuable time that could be spent having more fun and focusing on the things that bring us greater happiness, health, and peace of mind.

Work with Affirmations

If you could use some help reigning in perfectionist tendencies, try working with some of the affirmations below. Said aloud, with conviction and consistency, they may help alleviate any shame, anxiety, lack of self-esteem or other unhelpful emotions that are keeping you stuck in the unsustainable cycle of perfectionism. The power is in the belief that it is already true – you are speaking it into existence. Replace unhealthy thoughts with these – right away. Our brains can only hold one thought at a time, retrain the brain by feeding it positive thoughts often. Then take appropriate action to curb perfectionistic habits. Consider the ones at the end of this chapter.

- I love and approve of myself.
- Mistakes are a part of being human.
- I have many successes to be proud of.
- I give myself credit for my efforts and results.
- I am reasonable and realistic with my expectations.
- I am gentle with myself and others.
- I am enough.
- I can live with disappointing others.
- I save my time and energy for the most important things.
- I forgive myself.
- I appreciate feedback that helps me learn and grow.
- I love myself unconditionally.
- I know when to say, "done is better than perfect."

One other tip to prevent perfectionism is to remind yourself that you don't have to apologize for being human. That has helped me cope better when I feel I am less than perfect.

Padma, Revisited

Let's return to Padma's situation to see how she might've better dealt with her perfectionist tendencies. She's been granted the honor and huge task of chairing the upcoming annual gala. She wants it to be the best ever and spends weeks fantasizing about how perfect it *needs* to be. Deep down inside, however, Padma is beginning to have doubts. *What if she can't pull it off? What if donations don't beat last year's proceeds? What if it's not perfect?!* When the Executive Director meets with Padma for an update on the initial planning, Padma admits that she hasn't pulled together a planning document yet, nor has she made any committee assignments. In fact, she admits, she's feeling a bit overwhelmed because she appreciates the trust they've put in her.

The Director tells Padma that these feelings are normal and that every gala chair before her has felt them. "In fact," she says, "I still have to fight off those feelings each year when the gala comes around. You know why? Because, like you, my mom was a huge success in her field. And I'm guessing that, like me, you want to do your mother's legacy proud. Am I close?" A figurative lightbulb goes off over Padma's head and she begins to feel her confidence returning. She continues, "The trick is overcoming those fears and accepting that you and the team you assemble will all do your best...and the outcome is up to fate. Regardless, everything will be just fine."

Feeling better after this talk, Padma reaches out to various people at the charity to see who's willing to head up the various planning committees. She drafts a timeline for executing the gala, breaking the planning into smaller goals with deadlines and assignments for those responsible for each element. Just doing this makes her shoulders drop a bit with relief, while simultaneously increasing her confidence that she – and the entire planning team – can, in fact, pull this off. While the gala doesn't end up breaking a million dollars in proceeds, it does show a respectable increase over the prior year. More importantly, those in attendance enjoyed it immensely while supporting a good cause.

There's no space for peace when perfectionism is a priority.

— Christian Bosse

❀

Intention:

I do my best and accept that "done" is better than "perfect."

Now, how about digging deeper? As a warm-up to this time for reflection, I suggest listening to "Imperfect Is the New Perfect" by Caitlin Crosby.

Invitation to Reflect:

What situations bring out the perfectionist in you the most?

_____

_____

_____

_____

What situation in your life right now requires more courage? What will you now do differently?

_____

_____

_____

_____

_____

In what areas would you like to be more competent? What will you do about it?

_____

_____

_____

_____

_____

Here are some actions you could take now for your self-care:

- Write "Done is better than perfect" on sticky notes and post them in strategic places to remind yourself to stop "perfecting" something sooner than later.
- Practice changing your thoughts immediately to positive self-talk and self-compassion when you notice perfectionism rearing its head. Pick 1-3 affirmations to replace the thoughts. Review them daily 10-108 times, until they are 2nd nature, then pick more. Speak the affirmation consistently with conviction, as if it is already true.
- Decide to change your mindset to strive for excellence instead of perfection.

Commit to doing at least one thing differently based on what you learned in this chapter. Write out an actionable goal – with a specific deadline – to satisfy this commitment.

_____

_____

_____

_____

How will you celebrate or reward yourself if you reach the goal?

_____

_____

Other thoughts and reflections:

_____

_____

_____

_____

_____

For additional resources related to this topic, please check out my website: www.abcsofselfcare.com

$\mathcal{Q}$

QUESTION YOUR TIME MANAGEMENT

It's not enough to be busy, so are the ants. The question is, what are we busy about?

— Henry David Thoreau

❧

Many clients tell me – initially, anyway – that they don't have time for self-care. It certainly is hard if you are not prioritizing the right things, or if you feel the need to do everything for everybody. Or you're driven to do everything perfectly. Of course, self-care won't fit into your schedule if you go through life this way. You're too busy fighting fires (usually someone else's) like a boss! You thrive on the reputation of being a superhero, the feeling of having been productive at the end of each overscheduled day! And yet – you're also depleted by then, no time or energy remaining to take care of your own needs. This is where questioning your time management approach can help. But first, let's peek into the life of Quinn to see how she spends her days.

Quinn and Questioning Time Management

Quinn prides herself on being a list maker. She's always has her to-do list handy, which she updates daily. When she rewrites her list each morning, there are a number of items she ends up transferring from the day before. Her lists tend to be long because, too often, Quinn's friends or coworkers request her help. Why? Because they know how driven she is, how willing she is to help others. They know they can count on her to get sh*t done! So, Quinn has earned the nickname "Go-To Girl" at work, a moniker that secretly gives her great satisfaction. Unfortunately, Quinn's willingness to help anyone who asks means that she often must work over the weekends. That's when the office is quiet and no one else is there to ask for her assistance. On Mondays, when her coworkers are refreshed and ready for the week, Quinn is often exhausted. With a lot of coffee and a shift in attitude, she powers through, refusing to let her guard down or admit that she needs a break. Quinn loves the sense of accomplishment she feels by being an overachiever at work – and in life!

Quinn's 40th birthday is coming up on Saturday and she realizes she has no special plans. She also has no special someone with whom to spend the day. In fact, Quinn realizes she's been out of touch with most of her non-work friends over the past six months. Birthdays aren't a big deal at the office, so she's not even sure any of her work pals know that her birthday is coming up. No one has mentioned anything about getting together to celebrate with her over the weekend. Midday on Friday, another coworker comes by Quinn's office to bemoan a Monday deadline he has. Would Quinn mind helping him out with part of his project over the weekend? Of course she wouldn't mind. After all, she has no plans, and this colleague's deadline is urgent. He needs her help. Instead of taking Saturday to celebrate herself – her *birthday*, for crying out loud! – Quinn finds herself exchanging emails with her colleague, who texted at the last minute to say he'd be working on the project from home. Quinn spends her entire birthday alone at the office, and when she finally leaves for home, she's too exhausted to even think about cooking dinner or even buying herself a birthday cupcake at the corner bakery. Instead, she pulls into Taco Bell and orders a Meal Deal at the drive-thru. Alone in her car, Quinn holds a taco up in a mock toast. "Happy freaking birthday to me," she says aloud, totally deflated. "The big 4-0. Whoop dee doo."

Quick Check - Select all that apply:

- ☐ I often say I don't have time for self-care.
- ☐ My life feels like it is fully scheduled all the time.
- ☐ I feel like I am constantly fighting fires.

Make Time for Important Things

I'm guessing you're wondering why I'm talking about questioning your time management. *So basic! I know how to do time management.* So let me explain. Over the years, I've studied the concepts of human potential, time management, self-care, and many other "self-help" areas that impact both our performance and our happiness. One of the most influential thought leaders in my life was Dr. Stephen Covey, author of the internationally best-selling book *The 7 Habits of Highly Effective People*. If you haven't read this classic yet, I urge you to do yourself a favor and pick up a copy of it. When Covey passed away in 2012, I felt I'd lost a family member, as his books and teachings had guided me as a parent would.

The cornerstone of Covey's teachings revolves around living your life based on principles and purpose, not on getting more done. It's about focusing on Quad II, the important, but non-urgent, things in your life, to create more peace and happiness. Covey asserts that all activities or "to-do's" fall under one of four quadrants (or "quads"), which are as follows:

	URGENT	NOT-URGENT
IMPORTANT	**Quad I Activities** • Emergencies • Deadline driven projects and assignments • Last minute prep • Problems needing immediate attention • Medical crises	**Quad II Activities** • Proactively preparing for projects and assignments • Prevent burnout with self-care • Clarify values and what you care about (like volunteering) • Plan more • Relationship-building • Be empowered • Have fun!
NOT IMPORTANT	**Quad III Activities** • People-pleasing activities • Some emails & calls • Frequent interruptions • Other people's "emergencies"	**Quad IV Activities** • Too much TV • Too much social media • Too much gaming • Procrastinating activities • Reading junk mail • Some "quick" conversations

Adapted from Stephen Covey's: "First Things First" Covey Leadership, Inc. ©2007

So, questioning your time management is all about reflecting on how you're choosing to spend your time. Ideally, make time for the activities you would list in Quadrant II above, namely those that are important but not urgent. Self-care falls squarely in this quadrant. You have 26 habits in this book to practice self-care. Plus, taking a walk or doing affirmations or giving yourself a day of pampering is important, but not necessarily urgent. Guess which tasks tend to fall by the wayside during a busy week? That's right – those in Quad II. Too often, we are motivated to perform tasks based on their urgency rather than their importance. We may fall prey to things important to other people by agreeing to do too many Quad III tasks, putting other people's priorities above our own. Worse yet, we may waste hours upon hours doing Quad IV tasks – those that are neither important nor urgent – such as scrolling through social media to read posts from people we're not even close with anymore. Do we really need to know what our ex-boyfriend from high school's politics are? Or what college an acquaintance's kid got into? Um, no!

Quad I activities – those that are both important *and* urgent – are, well, important. And urgent. It is a seductive way to live because you feel productive. But there's more to a well-rounded life than Quad I alone. Enter: Quad II. The key to creating a more meaningful and fulfilling life is to put more energy and attention toward those things in our lives that fall into Quad II, such as tending to our important relationships, participating in fun activities, and yes, self-care. It may be tempting to put all your energy into Quad I activities, but too much emphasis on Quad I, to the neglect of Quad II, may get you the promotion at work...but it could also lead to burnout, unhappiness, or poor health. The key is to stop looking at the clock and instead look at the compass – your own internal compass, that which tells you what your values and priorities in life are. If you use your compass as your guide, you'll find a way to fit more Quad II activities into your life. As the old saying goes: *Busy people make time for the things that are important to them.*

Plan Recovery Periods

Perhaps you need more self-compassion to allow yourself to *not* get things done. Recovery periods are critical for long-term success and happiness. As Covey puts it, "you can't cut down trees with a dull saw!" Rejuvenation is what sharpens that saw. Additionally, you can't give what you don't have – like energy. Making time to refill your energy fuel tank on a consistent basis is key. Limiting Quad I activities, and saying no to Quad III and Quad IV activities, will free up more time for Quad II activities – namely, *self-care!* And guess what? There's a nice bonus to taking more time for yourself and your self-care routine. It will actually result in greater productivity when it's time to focus on a Quad I activity. What?! That's right - you can accomplish more by attempting to accomplish less.

Let's say you're in a job that demands heavy travel. One way to counteract the ill-effects of being a road warrior is to schedule aggressive self-care upon returning from each work trip. Another friend, while on a full-time speaking tour for 6 years, always scheduled a professional massage the day after each trip. She would do this prior to even writing follow up emails from the trip she just completed. Self-care first, follow up second. Even if you're returning from pleasure travel, your body still needs time to recover upon your return. Different climates, time zones, and altitudes all require adjustments for the body when you return home. Respect that by helping your body with some good physical pampering – a spa day, extra sleep, a gentle walk in nature, binge watching tv, breakfast in bed with a good novel, whatever floats your boat. Or sharpens your saw.

Prioritize Self-Care

It's probably pretty obvious where I'm heading with all of this. I want you to prioritize self-care, a Quad II activity – to prevent burnout. But more than that I want you to prioritize it not just to survive, but to *thrive*! Question the Quad you are operating in I, II, III or IV, and refocus on Quad II so you can thrive.

In surveying my clients, as well as family and friends, most claimed that self-care was a necessity. Yet the majority of those same people who told me they don't have time for it, also did not prioritize it enough to *make* time for self-care. My guess? These folks are likely looking more at their clocks and calendars than their compasses. Prioritizing our actions based on what matters the most to us as individuals is considered "Quad II living." Focusing on the six areas of self-care – emotional, practical, physical, mental, social, and spiritual – is Quad II living. Self-care will coax the calmer, healthier being within you (who also has more energy and clearer thinking) to come out. Set them free! I promise you will feel less depleted and more fulfilled. That is what Quad II living has to offer. Below is an example of how to apply Quad II living to your desire to create a self-care lifestyle:

- **Preparation**. Prepare for chores, assignments, or projects by asking for help ahead of time, making it a joint effort.
- **Prevention**. Anticipate what will be stress-inducing and be proactive in managing your mindset.
- **Values Clarification**. Assess how much self-care fits into your values for physical, mental, and emotional health.
- **Planning**. Schedule self-care "Me Time" into each day by putting it on your calendar.
- **Relationship Building**. Plan activities/quality time to connect and bond with family, friends and colleagues.
- **Empowerment**. Focus on solutions, not barriers, and the things you can control.
- **Fun.** Decide that fun is a priority for self-care and schedule it in to keep your saw sharpened.

Self-care is not something you *have* time for, it is something you *make* time for. Question how you spend time now to make room for more health, happiness, and peace in your life.

Quinn Revisited

Let's return to Quinn's situation. How might she handle her upcoming birthday differently? Her "big 4-0" is upon her. She has no significant other or local family. She's ignored her non-work friends for so long due to the demands at work, she knows they're not planning anything. Her coworker appears in her office the day before her birthday asking for help. Instead of agreeing because, after all, she *is* the Go-To Girl, Quinn thinks for a moment, checking in with herself internally. She wonders how it would feel to put herself first for once, to actually turn down a coworker's request for her time. She realizes that for too long she's enabled her coworkers by rescuing them in the final hours before a deadline. She's enjoyed a certain level of esteem from being the superhero at work, but she's now realizing just how fleeting that feeling is. Is this really what life is about? Work and everyone else's work on top of that? Quinn decides to do something she's been wanting to do for a long time, but never had the courage to. Until now. She's facing a milestone birthday with no one special to share it with. "I understand you're up against a tight deadline, Bill," Quinn says, "but tomorrow is my birthday and I plan to spend all day – actually all weekend – celebrating. I know you'll find a way to get it done." Bill, staring at her in disbelief, doesn't even bother to say "Happy Birthday" as he turns and leaves her office.

Quinn then picks up her phone and texts an old friend. *I've been a bit of a terrible friend, haven't I, Amy? I allowed work to take over my life and ignored the people who were most important to me, people like you. I'm sorry. I miss you. And I'm turning 40 tomorrow. Any chance you'd be willing to celebrate with me?* Quinn pushes send and then hopes her friend will forgive her for having been incommunicado for so long. Minutes later her phone pings. The text reply reads: *I miss you too, Quinny! And I would LOVE to spend your birthday with you. What would you like to do? Let's go paint the town red, my long-lost friend! Xoxo Amy.* Quinn is thrilled. She feels a bit like George Bailey getting a second chance. Amy is still her friend! It's not too late to reprioritize her life and how she spends her time and energy. No more office weekends! No more falling prey to others' self-inflicted work emergencies. She's done with being the Go-To Girl. And she feels lighter already.

During Quinn's birthday celebration the next day, Amy gives her a book. Can you guess which one it was? Ironically, Stephen Covey's *The 7 Habits of Highly Effective People*, of course! From now on, Quinn will commit to Quad II living.

If you want something bad enough, you find a way.

— Ruth Bader Ginsburg

❀

Intention:

I consciously decide how I spend my time.

Now, how about digging deeper? As a warm-up to this time for reflection, I suggest listening to "Eye of The Tiger" by Survivor.

Invitation to Reflect:

What Quad IV activities could you avoid doing regularly, or eliminate completely?

_____

_____

_____

What Quad III activities could you avoid doing more often?

_____

_____

_____

_____

_____

_____

What Quad II activities could you add to make a difference in the quality of your life?

_____

_____

_____

_____

_____

_____

Here are some actions you could take now for your self-care:

○ Manage your calendar. Schedule only 1-3 big To-Do's per day. Include preparation time slots on your calendar so you can see how new projects fit into your day, realistically, based on what is already there.

○ Schedule one 15-minute self-care or pampering activity per day, at least 3-7 days a week.

○ Adjust at least one routine at home to allow more time for self-care (e.g., a child's bed-time routine or study time).

Commit to doing at least one thing differently based on what you learned in this chapter. Write out an actionable goal – with a specific deadline – to satisfy this commitment.

_____

_____

_____

_____

How will you celebrate or reward yourself if you reach the goal?

_____

_____

Other thoughts and reflections:

_____

_____

_____

_____

_____

_____

For additional resources related to this topic, please check out my website: www.abcsofselfcare.com

REDUCE STRESS

There is no glory in a grind that literally grinds you down to dust.

— Elaine Welteroth

Stress, stress, stress! How often have you heard warnings about stress and its impact on our lives? Quite a bit, I'd bet. But what exactly *is* stress? Stress (as we're referring to it here) is a state of mental or emotional strain or tension resulting from adverse or very demanding circumstances. A certain amount of stress is not only to be expected in life, but it can also propel you forward toward achieving your goals. So, all stress is not bad. However, too much stress can actually prevent you from reaching your goals, not to mention the grave toll it can take on your mental and physical well-being.

Stress is the underlying cause of upwards of 90% of disease, according to Bruce Lipton's *The Biology of Belief.* How is this possible? Because so many illnesses are the result of compromised immune function, and nothing compromises immune function quite like a mega dose of stress. One stressful day isn't going to send you to the oncologist, but string too many of these stressful days together, to the point where "stressed" becomes a chronic state of existence, and guess what? You could find yourself dealing with the stress of a life-threatening disease as well. Small, manageable levels of stress are a part of life. There's no avoiding that, nor should you try. It's stress as a *way of life* that leads to problems. Chronic stress increases our chances of developing bad habits, the kind that can increase the chance of developing cancer or some other debilitating health issue.

Stress also shuts down the part of the brain responsible for reasoning and problem-solving, so excessive levels of stress can be like trying to complete a complicated project while drunk or on mind-altering drugs. The outcome would not be pretty. The mind and body communicate constantly, so one informs the other and vice versa. What our minds think, perceive, and experience directly affects how our bodies perform. In other words, healthy mind – healthy body. Consequently, an unhealthy, stressed mind can lead to an unhealthy, stressed body.

Ryan and Reducing Stress

Ryan has been on a very tight budget since his divorce and, unfortunately, he was laid off several months ago by his employer of 22 years, a tourist-driven hotel chain where he worked as a concierge. An ongoing economic downturn has taken a toll on the travel industry, and Ryan was one of thousands who were let go as part of a workforce reduction. These stress inducing situations created even more stress – one of the worse kinds – financial stress. He has been dipping into his savings to cover monthly expenses, including the mortgage on his condo. Soon, though, his savings dwindle to nothing, and his job prospects remain grim. Most of the other hotel chains have also gone through layoffs and none seem to be hiring. With each passing week, Ryan's stress level increases.

With so much of his career invested in the hotel industry, Ryan feels he has limited job opportunities. After all, who in their right mind would hire him into a different industry at this point in his career? He *needs* the economy and the hotel industry to make a recovery, and fast! His brother offers to let his move in with him. He can have the entire walk-out level of his home to himself if he'd like. He can sell his condo, he argues, and use the proceeds for living expenses while also returning to school to make a career pivot. But Ryan doesn't see that as an option. First, he loves his independence. Second, at 44-years-old, he feels as if his career is set in stone. *A career change at my age? Not possible!* he tells himself. He digs his heels in, rejecting his brother's offer and advice. Instead, he spends each day scanning the online job boards for openings in his field that don't exist. His stress level is through the roof, yet he continues to only recognize one path forward: the hotel business *must* rebound, or else. Five months after his layoff, Ryan is broke...and broken. A recent medical workup shows that Ryan has developed pre-diabetes, likely the result of all the junk food and sweets he's been stress-eating to combat the anxiety of being unemployed and short on cash. He can barely pull himself out of bed these days. And when the first foreclosure notice comes in the mail, Ryan loses it. On days like this, he wishes he'd simply have a heart attack and "get it over with." Stress has clearly impacted Ryan's life to the point that he now sees no way out. At all.

Quick Check - Select all that apply:

- ☐ I have regular tension or stress related headaches.
- ☐ I'm often rushing to and from places.
- ☐ I often react badly if things don't go as planned.

Reduce Stress with Options

Having multiple options is a fantastic way to combat the negative impact of stress. Having only a "Plan A" is a surefire way to exacerbate it. According to Dr. William Parham, psychologist for the NBA, *options reduce stress*. For example, if you applied for a job you really wanted and didn't get it, take a little time to nurse your wounds. But then move on to Plan B...and then Plan C, and D, if necessary. Don't limit your opportunities by not considering other options. Are there similar companies you could apply to? Is there additional training in the form of a certification or an advanced degree that you could get to broaden our career opportunities? Have you considered launching your own business? Do you see how many more options are available to us if we look for them? How you *respond* to the inevitable challenges and disappointments in life will determine whether you keep your stress level manageable or whether stress will wreak havoc in your life.

Having multiple options gives us more freedom. A double major in college means you've doubled your career options upon graduation. Having two or three close friends you feel comfortable calling during a crisis is less stressful than having only one. Creating more than one source of income reduces stress of being dependent on only one income stream. Do you see how options can reduce stress while increasing freedom? The key here, of course, is choosing healthy options. Some people choose to smoke as a means of stress reduction, yet this isn't a healthy choice. Choosing to meditate or workout as a means of stress reduction is a much healthier option. Choose wisely!

Get to Know Your Stressors

Knowing our personality type can sometimes aid in stress relief. For example, Type A's – those who are more intense, impatient, competitive, and used to keeping tight schedules – may not enjoy passive activities like meditation. What might be more relaxing is listening to music, exercising, or journaling. Type B's, on the other hand, tend to be less intense, more patient, less competitive and not as time conscious. The biggest difference between the two types is how success is defined. Type A's competitive nature may require a higher standard to feel successful than Type B's. That extra pressure on Type A's may cause greater internal chatter that, in turn, causes more stress.

Understanding Introversion and Extroversion can also help us determine the best stress relieving plan. Although many think the difference between the two personality types is gregariousness or social skills, the real difference between the two is where you get your energy. Introverts recharge their energy by taking time alone, while extroverts are rejuvenated by being around people. I've met some talkative introverts who enjoy being around people unless they are tired and stressed out. It's good to understand your preferences to know the best way to relieve stress. Like many personality traits, where you are on the spectrum will help you determine what stress relieving methods are best for you.

Both personality types can use the same methods, of course. For example, journaling is good for both types. Meditation may be better for introverts and going to a gym may be better for extroverts. Research shows that introverts may have to work harder at mood control, positive thinking, and optimism. Therefore, intentionally focusing on being better in these areas could help relieve stress. Expressing gratitude is a multiplier for enhancing mood and thoughts for either personality type. Having a peaceful, organized retreat space may be more important for introverts, although we can all benefit by having that. The most important part of stress relief is being conscious of when you are drained and knowing your limitations when considering certain activities.

Finally, if you're an HSP (Highly Sensitive Person), you should also be especially attentive to your stress levels. HSPs tend to feel things far more deeply than others, and therefore have stronger reactions to physical, mental, and emotional stressors: pain, emotions, noises, etc. As an HSP myself, is it any wonder I'm so passionate about self-care?

Manage Your Energy Instead of Your Time

We must remember that life is a marathon, not a sprint. To maintain high performance, we must balance the stress we put on our bodies with sufficient recovery time. Jim Loehr and Tony Schwartz, authors of *The Power of Full Engagement,* call this oscillation. Too much expended energy without recovery time is a bad idea. Similarly, too much recovery without enough expended energy is also a bad idea. The key lies in the balance of expending energy (a form of stress) with recovery (stress reduction). As such, Loehr and Schwartz believe that full engagement and high performance in life are about monitoring our *energy*, not our time.

Our recovery periods will be enhanced if we participate in activities that we enjoy. Based on research conducted by the Mayo Clinic, only 20% of our activities need to be "red threads" to reduce the chance of stress-induced burnout. What are red threads? They are activities that we absolutely love, that uplift us, that we look forward to doing with great anticipation. Red threads are those activities that we "get lost in" while engaged in them, perhaps an exciting project at work or a hike in the mountains or meeting good friends at a favorite restaurant. Only 20% of your daily activities have to offer this level of joy for you to protect yourself against the pitfalls of stress.

So how do you discover what your red threads are? Observe how you feel throughout a week of activities. Keep a running list of each activity under one of two headings: *Brought Me Joy* and *Drained Me.* Ok, those headings might be a bit exaggerated, but you get my drift, right? The *Drained Me* column would include any activities you found yourself procrastinating about or not enjoying one bit or feeling stressed while engaged in it. The *Brought Me Joy* column would include any activities you lost track of time doing or actively enjoyed or felt content while performing.

Soon those red threads will make themselves apparent. They needn't be earth-shattering activities to be a red thread. One of my dear friends claims that doing laundry is one of her red threads. Why? Because it's simple, easy to accomplish, useful, and she feels a sense of order folding all those clean clothes and putting them neatly back in her closet. Weird? Perhaps. But who are we to judge another's red threads? To each their own! (Psst. I'm with you, though. Enjoying laundry does seem strange.)

Another way you can manage your energy is to use a methodology created by Dr. Zayd Abdul-Karim (Dr. Z) in his book *25 Days to Living Your Happiness.* Dr. Z concludes that our various energies are points of attraction; thus, whatever we focus our energy on we attract. Given this, we want to put our attention on those things that will create more happiness for us. For example, let's say you are encountering bad customer service at a health spa. I'm sure you would agree that spa employees should have phenomenal customer service skills. Perhaps the front desk person got up on the wrong side of the bed and is being rude and unpleasant. Instead of being frustrated, you could choose to be patient, which is the contrasting energy to frustration. Choosing patience is considered a Spirit Energy (per Dr. Z), which is motivating, vs. an Ego Energy, which is draining. See the difference? This simple tool of constantly assessing and changing our energy will create greater happiness and less stress in our lives.

Recognize Good Stress

Another important aspect of understanding stress in our lives is accepting that not all stress is bad. We need a certain amount of stress to motivate us to do better, to be better. Think of a deadline. Stress! Yet without that deadline, we might never launch that project that's important to us. Or go on that first date. Or finish that manuscript that the publisher is expecting from us. (Who, me?) Good forms of stress can be viewed as the motivational fire beneath our butts. Good stress encourages us to make more effort while also helping us develop our mental and physical muscles. Let's consider Dwayne Johnson, aka The Rock. Got a mental image of him in your head? Are you admiring those massive biceps? That carved form? The Rock achieved his stellar physical shape by "stressing" his muscles with each workout. Stress...recover. Stress...recover. Works like a charm.

Like our physical state, our mental state improves with stress and recovery as well, leading to more mental strength. The most essential form of mental strength is resiliency, which is the ability to bounce back from setbacks and to respond with emotional intelligence when under stress. Resiliency allows us to focus on what we can control and influence. It allows us to let go of trying to control that which is beyond our control. Think of someone you know who melts down at life's little inconveniences: a long line at the grocery store, a minor injury that interrupts their workout routine for a couple of days, slower service at a restaurant that's unusually busy. This person suffers from a lack of resiliency. Now think of another person you may know, someone who seems to have a strong sense of being okay despite major challenges – perhaps living life in a wheelchair or experiencing prolonged unemployment or surviving a horrific attack. This person has obviously developed resiliency. Resiliency allows us to focus on what we can control and influence rather than complain about what is out of our control. Letting go of what we have no control over, as well as letting go of past mistakes, heartaches, or other unpleasant experiences, is not only a sign of resiliency, but also a path to building even greater resiliency. We may not have control over everything in our lives, but we do have control over how we *react* to everything in our lives. Once we recognize and claim this power, we let go of a victimization mindset, undue stress, and feelings of powerlessness. Who doesn't want that?

Obviously, different stressors come with varying degrees of stress. The *Holmes-Rahe Stress Inventory* lists death, divorce, illness, and job loss among the most stress-inducing events we humans will encounter. Our *reactions* to these life events can impact the degree to which we are "stressed out." Even experiences that tend to cause massive amounts of stress can sometimes be reframed to reduce the level of stress we're feeling. A lost job could be a push into a new position that's more in line with our goals. A hurtful divorce could lead to a healthier relationship with someone new. And yes, even a near-fatal illness that creates lifelong physical challenges can be viewed as a blessing in disguise. Another friend experienced a near-fatal disease that landed her in the ICU for several months, with multiple organ failure, surgeries, and she fell into a coma. She never fully recovered and still deals with ongoing medical issues related to that experience. However, she used that experience to reevaluate every aspect of her life: her work, her commitments, even where she lived. While she's admitted that she never wants to experience that level of pain and suffering again, she also claims that she wouldn't trade it for the world. It gave her an expanded perspective on her life, not to mention a new career that is much more rewarding! Reframing negative or stressful situations as "growth opportunities" will take us far in reducing our stress levels. Depending on the degree of trauma involved, it may require the help of a trained professional. It's all about taking responsibility to change the one thing we each have complete control over – our *reactions* to every circumstance: the good, the bad, and the oh-my-God-over-the-top-stressful!

Anticipate and Manage Stressful Situations

To manage our reactions to stress, it's also important to anticipate stress-inducing situations. If certain circumstances tend to add undue stress to our lives, we can look for opportunities to do things differently. Perhaps do them less "perfectly," or find other ways to minimize our stress. I'm speaking to those of you who think you can do more than humanly possible in little or no time. You know who you are. Some examples of the most common self-inflicted, stress-increasing habits are below, along with suggestions for adjusting those habits to decrease unnecessary stress.

1. Multitasking to feel more productive, which is a myth. It actually makes us less productive because our brain is designed to focus on only one task at a time. Stress is the result because it takes more time to do the task in a quality way.
   Alternative habits:
   1. Focus on one task at a time.
   2. Be present in meetings or avoid ones that you don't need to attend.
   3. Schedule *working* meetings where the objective of the meeting is to get tasks done.

2. Responding to a text while driving or in a meeting because it's a text, so it must be urgent.
   Alternative habits:
   1. Setting up auto-reply to manage incoming texts while behind the wheel or in a meeting.
   2. Turning off your phone before driving or going into a meeting.
   3. Staying present while driving or in a meeting.

3. Knowingly overcommitting to unrealistic deadlines because you feel pressured to do so.
   Alternative habits:
   1. Pausing before agreeing to a deadline; checking your calendar, and only agreeing if it's realistically doable.
   2. Blocking out chunks of time on your online calendar (that others have access to) so they can't schedule meetings on your behalf; there's no need to explain what those blocked out times are for.

4. Consistently arriving late to appointments to get the most out of your time.
   Alternative habits:
   1. Listing appointments in your calendar 15 minutes ahead of their start-time so you arrive early.
   2. Going to your appointment early and bringing a small task with you to do while you wait (answer emails on your iPad, read a book, return a call).

5. Reaching for food, alcohol, cigarettes, or drugs at the first sign of stress.
   Alternative habits:
   1. Taking a walk outside, breathing deeply, and focusing on things you are grateful for.
   2. Calling a trusted friend to vent and keeping healthy snacks on hand in case they are busy: apples, bananas, nuts, or carrots.
   3. Sitting quietly in a vacant room to allow your thoughts and emotions to calm down.

6. Going to your gym at the same time you know your ex will be there even though seeing them creates stress and heartache.
    Alternative habits:
    1. Picking a new workout time.
    2. Picking a new gym.
    3. Accepting that it's over and that casually running into them isn't going to bring you true joy.

7. Getting upset at people who are driving too fast/slow/erratically on the highway.
    Alternative habits:
    1. Keeping your road rage in check by Assuming Positive Intent (API) and moving away from their car (without flipping them the bird; I know some of you were thinking that weren't you?).
    2. Giving them the benefit of the doubt that they're having a bad day and it's impacting their driving.
    3. Remember that you sometimes unknowingly make mistakes while driving too.

Self-awareness about the things *we do to ourselves* that increase our stress is the first step in replacing those bad habits with healthier reactions. Then consider what you do to others in that state of mind. If you are stressed out, it can impact how stressed out those around you are, especially children. To raise more peaceful kids, you may have to avoid mental stress that impacts them. One way we can do this is to notice our mental mind chatter – or "monkey brain" as some like to call it – which creates stress in our bodies. Resentment, self-criticism, and guilt are some of the most damaging mental patterns we can develop, according to Louise Hay, author of *You Can Heal Your Life*. These mindsets, often running on repeat through our brains, can settle into our bodies in the form of discomfort or disease. This is not to say that anyone with disease or discomfort has created it themselves by their thought patterns. Sometimes disease just happens. That said, you can influence the health of your body through the health of your mind. Avoiding mental stress is one such tactic to improve the health of your mind, and therefore your body.

Over the years, some of my clients have told me that they feel stressed about the mere concept of launching a self-care routine and better self-care habits. They already have too much on their plates. They tell me that just *thinking about* changing their behavior to include self-care is too stressful. I always call their bluff. Then I begin to point out the many ways they can get through their self-inflicted obstacles to self-care. Why am I so adamant? Because our lives and our well-being depend on it. Stress, if taken to extremes, can make us ill...or worse. Keeping our stress levels within a reasonable range through self-care habits can do just the opposite: make us happier, healthier, and more peaceful.

Ryan, Revisited

What could Ryan have done to prevent the unhealthy stress in his life? Well, he couldn't control the economy and its devastating impact on the industry in which he worked. He had no control over getting laid off either; workforce reduction was inevitable with the drastic changes happening in travel. But let's return to that moment and see how he might've responded differently to being laid off and worrying about his career and finances. Ryan meets with a few friends from work who were also caught up in the sweeping layoffs. Over dinner, they shed a few tears together, talk about the good times they had, and express their concerns about unemployment. After a bit of cathartic discussion, one of Ryan's former co-workers suggests they each list some of the options they're going to explore, and even suggests they imagine how their firing could end up being a blessing in disguise.

Ryan is taken aback because he loved his job, and he has a mortgage and other bills to pay. He needs an income because his savings aren't as hefty as he'd like it to be. But he decides to play along, pulling out a piece of paper and jotting down some ideas: *apply to jobs related to the hotel industry, finish coursework for real estate license I began last year, apply for unemployment as a short-term safety net; rent out condo and ask my brother if I can stay with him (we always said we'd love to be roommates again one day); rent out condo and take up BFF on offer to come stay with him in Spain for a couple months*! Then Ryan thinks of his worst-case scenario: *Sell condo (it's more than doubled in value since I bought it).*

Looking over his list, Ryan lets out an audible sigh as he realizes he has more options than he thought! In fact, perhaps this layoff was Life's way of telling him he was in a rut. A comfortable rut, but still a rut, nonetheless. Who stays in the same job with the same company for 22 years anymore?! He begins to imagine owning his own real estate agency, or perhaps teaming up with a friend who's been trying to hire Ryan into his agency for years. He realizes how his experience as a concierge – namely, his ability to help others, as well as the vast network of business contacts he's built up, would be super helpful in the real estate world. And he *loves* working with a variety of people; that's why he was drawn to being a concierge in the first place. A career pivot into real estate could be just what he needs! And if it takes a couple of years to build up his clientele and sales results, then perhaps renting out his condo to save money while living with his brother would be ideal, not to mention fun! Wow, he thinks, this unexpected "plot twist" in my life might turn out to be a great thing in the long run. Excited about the possibilities, Ryan eagerly shares his list with his pals, who all cheer his ideas and his optimistic perspective. Clearly, pre-diabetes and foreclosure notices will *not* be a part of Ryan's future. Because Ryan has good options and a great attitude.

Forces beyond your control can take away everything you possess except one thing, your freedom to choose how you will respond to the situation.

– Viktor Frankl

✿

Intention:

I manage my reactions to stress with optimism.

Now, how about digging deeper? As a warm-up to this time for reflection, I suggest listening to "Conga" by Gloria Estefan and Miami Sound Machine.

Invitation to Reflect:

What options can you create for yourself that would make your life easier or less stressful?

_____

_____

_____

_____

_____

How can you tell when something brings you joy? What physical and mental changes do you notice?

_____

_____

_____

_____

_____

How can you tell when something is draining you? What physical and mental changes do you notice?

_____

_____

_____

_____

Here are some actions you could take now for your self-care:

○ Just breathe. Take four deep breaths in increments – breathe in for 3 counts – hold for 3 counts – exhale for 6 counts. Make sure you can feel your belly expanding as you breathe.

○ For every two hours of work, take a 10-15-minute break (or listen to your body and determine the right combination). When you feel stressed, consider dancing or exercising for at least 10 minutes, or long enough to increase your serotonin levels. Play a song or two or three from the playlist in Appendix C.

○ Go on a "news diet" for 1-7 days.

Commit to doing at least one thing differently based on what you learned in this chapter. Write out an actionable goal – with a specific deadline – to satisfy this commitment.

_____

_____

_____

_____

How will you celebrate or reward yourself if you reach the goal?

_____

_____

Other thoughts and reflections:

_____

_____

_____

_____

_____

For additional resources related to this topic, please check out my website: www.abcsofselfcare.com

$\mathcal{S}$

SURRENDER TO SPIRITUAL PRACTICES

Religion, science, and spirituality help us make sense of the world. Life without at least one of them is a lonely and confusing place.

— Naval Ravikant

❧

Some people are resistant to the term "surrender" because they associate it with weakness. However, in its truest sense, surrender simply means to *cease resistance to.* As it pertains to spiritual practices, it means simply to *let go of any resistance* we may have to the notion of engaging in spiritual practices. I'm not talking about religious practices – that's an entirely different topic and one I'm not including in this book because I feel it is a personal decision to be (or not to be) affiliated with a particular religion. For the purposes of this element of self-care, "spiritual" is defined as *relating to or affecting the human spirit or soul as opposed to material or physical things.* So, we're talking about embracing the idea of engaging in spiritual practices, little ceremonial habits that support you in non-physical ways. Spiritual practices focus on ways of *being* vs. acts of *doing*.

If it helps, think of spirituality as that which operates at the energy level, no "gods" necessary. You can be an atheist and engage in spiritual practices. A friend of mine describes her husband as a "secular Buddhist" due to his deep connection to meditation, his leaning toward atheism, and his deep interest in stoic and existential literature (don't even ask!). But I digress. My point is, you can engage in spiritual practices as a part of your self-care routine *regardless* of your religious affiliation...or lack thereof. Another friend describes the *opposite* of surrendering to spiritual practices as *leading with the ego and believing you can and will make everything happen in your life.* This implies that we are on this remarkable life journey alone, with no higher wisdom or guidance to help along the path. No matter which one you choose, spiritual practices that nurture

163

our mind, body and spirit will significantly improve your ability to cope when life's inevitable challenges arise. This, in turn, builds overall resilience and fortitude for the next challenge. And who couldn't use more of that?

Suri and Surrendering to Spiritual Practices

Suri has had a rough go of it lately. She lost her job just before receiving a diagnosis of breast cancer. As if that didn't challenge her enough, one month into her chemotherapy treatment, her fiancé was killed during what appeared to be a random robbery. This last challenge has broken her, and she finds it difficult to even get out of bed in the mornings, let alone go back for her next round of chemo. *What's the point?* she yells in frustration, as tears stream down her face. Friends have attempted to offer comfort, but the constant *he's in a better place* and *this was God's will* do nothing to ease her deep emotional pain. In fact, it makes her angry to the point of rejecting her religious upbringing. What sort of God would allow something so horrible to happen to someone who had a heart of gold? *Screw God!* she thinks each night as she cries herself to sleep.

Suri's parents have tried to coax her into visiting their priest, but she has refused. Her best friend has given her the name of a reputable psychotherapist who specializes in grief, even offering to cover the cost of as many visits as she needs. But Suri has rejected this as well. Each day is the same: no shower, no real meals, no face-to-face interaction. Just tears, anger, and hopelessness – alone in her small apartment. When Suri's mother finally demands that she take a bath while she tidies up and makes her a grilled cheese sandwich, she gives in. Once in the tub, she notices her fiancé's razor; it's the removable blade kind. She thinks of how she used to tease him about his "old-timey razor" even though she loved watching him shave in the shower, using a horsehair shaving brush and a wall-mounted mirror. That simple memory brings on the tears again, the stark reality of never seeing him shave again. A thought comes to her, a way to end the relentless pain that has haunted her for two months since his death. Suri picks up his razor and removes the blade. She turns it over and over in her fingers, asking herself *Do I really have the guts to do this?* After all, she thinks, she'll never get over his death so what's the point in carrying on? I'm just making everyone I love miserable, so why not end the pain for *all* of us?

Quick Check - Select all that apply:

- ☐ I often feel like I'm in this world alone without support.
- ☐ I believe religion is the same as spirituality.
- ☐ I feel like I need to make things happen in my life.

Distinguish Religion from Spirituality

I used to think of religion and spirituality as interchangeable terms, basically the same thing. I've come close to being agnostic at one point in my life and devoutly religious at another. Over the years I've learned to distinguish between the two and have concluded that religion falls under the greater umbrella of spirituality. So, it's absolutely possible to be spiritual without being religious, but if you're religious then I'd put you in the category of spiritual as well. Religion is the manmade construct that allows people to identify more clearly with others who share their specific spiritual beliefs. Or as *Psychology Today* puts it, "The purpose of religion, in general, is to unite a group of people under the same values and principles and to facilitate their collective and individual communication with a Higher Power and/or philosophy. In other words, religion was meant to enhance spirituality." Make sense? So spiritual practices *and* religion can both enhance your overall self-care efforts. The choice is always yours.

I like to use the metaphor of driving a car when I think of spirituality. Imagine you are in a car on a road with plenty of twists and turns, rocks and gravel – all of which need to be navigated to continue your journey. The views are terrific along the way, but at times you need to focus on overcoming various hazards. Gravel could be the small things in life, such as meeting a tight deadline or having to juggle competing demands on your time. Rocks could include dealing with a failed test or discussing the fact that it's time to move a parent into an assisted living facility. Boulders are the big, hairy obstacles, the ones that can stop us in our tracks, both figuratively and literally: the death of a loved one or a life-threatening illness. Spiritual practices are those behaviors, beliefs, and activities that help us get past the obstacles on life's highway, allowing us to move forward.

Shift from EGO to a Purpose Led life

Having a strong sense of purpose is one way to navigate the twists and turns of life. I was deeply moved by watching a movie that included an interview with Dr. Wayne Dyer, *The Shift*. He defines the EGO as Edging God Out. He believes we are living from our ego when we live our life trying to control what happens instead of listening for our calling and living a life guided by meaning and purpose. He calls *the shift* (from ambition to meaning) as something that happens after we experience a *quantum moment*, an epiphany that makes us stop seeing who we are as what we do, have, or achieve or what others think of us. If those things go away, we can feel lost. On the other hand, a more spiritually balanced life occurs if we believe our worth is a given, because of who we were born to be, this unique human being, living out our calling or purpose. He urges us not to ignore that calling. Once we are living with purpose, winning, and competing with others goes out the window. You are doing what you were meant to do – what is yours alone to accomplish.

Non-ego living means you live as if you are connected to everyone and anything you want, by figuring out how to align yourself with it. You then don't have to make things happen. Instead, you will be guided towards what is meant for you to do. You'll know it when you feel good and happy about your life's direction.

Expect Synchronicity

Throughout my life, I have witnessed special moments that led me to believe in a higher power. There were also times I could see things work out with such synchronicity that there seemed to be a preordained plan. As a small example, when I was a newly licensed driver (before the days of cell phones), my car died on the highway in my hometown of St. Louis. A dark highway after 10 pm is not a great place to have your car conk out on you. But my dad happened to be driving on the same highway at the same time and saw my car on the side of the road. Since I had already left the vehicle, he drove to the nearest gas station and there I was! Having him pull up as if we'd planned this rendezvous really blew my mind, and it taught me that synchronicity is all around us.

I'm guessing you have had a few experiences with synchronicity like that as well. If you watch old episodes of the TV show It's a Miracle, you will be blown away by some of the stories. I consider these "coincidental" moments little reminders from a greater wisdom that we are not alone. Call it God, Source, Spirit, the Universe, Higher Self, whatever you want. The name doesn't matter so much as the openness to being guided by it. If you'd like to play more with the concept of synchronicity, I suggest you "put it out there" and see what happens. When something that is statistically improbable happens, instead of writing it off as a strange coincidence, make note of it. Write the details of what took place in your journal and keep track of these little "hellos" from the Universe. And if this doesn't strike a chord with you, that's fine too. Spiritual practices will still assist you in your self-care journey.

Start Your Spiritual Practice

Many people launch their spiritual practices because of some sort of challenge or trauma in their lives. You don't need to wait until then. In fact, by launching a few spiritual practices when life is coasting along smoothly, you'll be stronger and more capable of handling those challenges when they they arise – those boulders especially. And they *will* arise! There are many options for spiritual practice. The key is to do those things that support the well-being of your mind, body, and spirit. Choose those activities that help you center your mind and find meaning and purpose in life. Below is a simple chart that outlines some of the many spiritual practices available to all:

MIND	**BODY**	**SPIRIT**
Silence	Yoga	Prayer
Meditation	T'ai Chi	Church services
Reflection	Walks in nature	Charity work
Reading inspirational material	Qi Gong	Listening to music
Journaling	Grounding/Earthing	Singing
Affirmations	Dancing	Inspirational videos

Notice the Interconnectedness

According to the late, great cellular biologist, Barry Commoner, there are four "laws of ecology," the first of which is *Everything is connected to everything else*. Similarly, we've all likely heard about the "six degrees of separation" theory, made even more popular when three college students came up with a "Six Degrees of Kevin Bacon" game while watching the movie *Footloose*. Basically, six degrees of separation is the idea that all people, on average, are six or fewer social connections away from each other. So, hey, if we're all basically interconnected anyway, wouldn't it make sense that the most universal spiritual practice would be giving and receiving unconditional love? Just imagine the impact on the world if this practice really took off! (More on this subject later.)

On a more micro-level, let's look at the interconnectedness of body, mind, and spirit. Given the interconnected nature of these three elements of our existence, it stands to reason that we can't impact one area without impacting the others. For example, dealing with a mentally stressful job, day after day, year after year (think: air traffic controller or surgeon) can take a real toll on the mind, which then also impacts the body and spirit. In contrast, sitting in meditation will calm the mind, yet doing so will also have a positive impact on the body in the form of increased physical wellness. Thus, including spiritual practices into your self-care routine is a great way to improve all three core elements of the self – body, mind, *and* spirit – even if a particular practice is targeting only one of those areas.

You may have noticed by now that many of the self-care habits I've presented so far require us to examine what thoughts we're feeding our minds. This is because the *subconscious* mind, where our beliefs, attitudes, feelings, emotions, and memories reside, is the driving force behind the thinking patterns of our *conscious* mind. Again – interconnections! Thus, by being aware of any limiting or harmful beliefs and changing them to more supportive and healthy beliefs, we can improve our ability to reason and think more clearly, resulting in more positive results. Truly, one of the most holistic approaches to improving every aspect of our lives lies in our ability to surrender to spiritual practices. To do this, we need only experiment with a few of the many practices available to us and determine which ones intuitively feel like the best match for our unique selves. And the interconnectedness of body, mind and spirit gives us a great reason to do so.

Incorporating spiritual practices isn't just about making us feel good. Some mental health professionals believe that spiritual practices also feed our human need for *hope* in a world that sometimes feels hopeless. Cultivating a "this too shall pass" mindset can help us cope with and overcome life's challenges. When one of my clients was undergoing five total joint replacements within a three-year period, she hung signs on her walls that read *This Is Temporary!* She swears that on days when the post-op pain was through the roof, those signs were the one thing that offered her a gentle reminder that things would improve. Increasing hope, being grounded, or feeling calm are some of the best results of spiritual practices. Feeling good could be just around the corner – if you stay the course instead of giving up. Where some religious beliefs might trigger a sense of guilt over our life choices, spirituality, in contrast, *always* encourages self-compassion and compassion for others.

It is my sincere belief that a holistic view of spirituality and the interconnectedness of life can change the world one person at a time, one spiritual practice at a time. By choosing to surrender to spiritual practices, you will be better equipped to keep your metaphorical car steady on the road through life. More importantly, they'll also help you enjoy the ride!

Suri, Revisited

Given what we've covered in this chapter, let's revisit Suri's situation and how spiritual practices might have fortified her to better face and survive the horrific experience she's encountered – the death of her fiancé and her cancer diagnosis. Let's assume Suri had a consistent spiritual practice already in place, as well as a strong faith in "something more" than what she can see, hear, and touch in the physical world. Would that make the sudden and tragic loss of her beloved any less heartbreaking? Absolutely not. Yet it would likely offer the spiritual fortitude she needs to survive and move through the process of grief that is essential following such devastating events.

A week after the news about her fiancé, Suri finds the inner strength to pick up her journal and write out her anger at whatever forces in the Universe exist. *Why?* is, understandably, her most pressing question. After journaling her anger, she lights a candle at her meditation table, closes her eyes, and begins to slow her breathing. In...out. In...out. Even in this meditative state, the tears continue to spill from her closed eyes. Fifteen, twenty minutes into this practice, Suri's shoulders drop a bit, her nervous system begins to calm itself. She thinks about the love she felt for her fiancé and the gratitude she feels for others in her life.

Suri sits in this peaceful, loving state with her beloved for well over an hour. When she brings her meditation to a close, she showers before her mother picks her up for a trip to their family chapel. Once inside, Suri lights a candle for her fiancé and sits in a pew staring at the candle. *Why?* she asks again of the universal presence she refers to as God. Tears fill her eyes and fall onto her lap, yet she begins to feel as if she's wrapped in a blanket of all-encompassing, unconditional love. When she is ready, her mother drives Suri back to her parents' home for a warm meal. Just being in the presence of people who've loved and cared for her is comforting. She spends the night in her childhood bedroom before returning to her apartment the next day to repeat her routine. For now, she knows that her only job is to sit with and process her grief. Her spiritual practices, in addition to the weekly sessions with a grief counselor and the support of her friends, give her the strength to continue taking things one day at a time.

Two months later, Suri realizes she's just laughed for the first time since her fiancé's death. Not a hearty or lengthy laugh, but a laugh, nonetheless. She starts incorporating long walks in the woods into her daily routine, sometimes with a friend who remains mostly silent, sometimes alone. Slowly, Suri notices that her grief has begun to diminish. It's still there, but it softens with each week. In its place is a sense that her fiancé would want her to live her life to the fullest – when she is ready. Suri sets up a little altar to memorialize him. Initially, it makes her cry whenever she walks past it, but eventually, it becomes a source of happy memories and a reminder of how fortunate she is to have had such deep love in her life. She knows that the grief of such a devastating loss will never completely vanish, but she believes that eventually it will be integrated into her life experience in a way that allows her to move forward. She has faith in this.

We are spiritual beings having a human experience.

— Wayne Dyer

❀

Intention:

I develop my spirituality and create more meaning in my life.

Now, how about digging deeper? As a warm-up to this time for reflection, I suggest listening to "Pocket Full of Sunshine" by Natasha Bedingfield.

Invitation to Reflect:

How do you use religion or spirituality to enhance your life?

_____

_____

_____

_____

_____

_____

_____

What would it take for you to incorporate more spiritual practices into your lifestyle?

_____

_____

_____

_____

_____

_____

List 3-4 of the spiritual practice ideas from this chapter that you're willing to try.

_____

_____

_____

_____

_____

Here are some actions you could take now for your self-care:

○ Develop and write down (realistic) spiritual practices to add to your morning and nighttime routine.
○ Take the time to analyze what you need to do to better understand your spiritual beliefs. Journaling is a great tool for this.
○ Read a section or chapter in your favorite spiritual guide.

Commit to doing at least one thing differently based on what you learned in this chapter. Write out an actionable goal – with a specific deadline – to satisfy this commitment.

_____

_____

_____

_____

_____

How will you celebrate or reward yourself if you reach the goal?

_____

_____

Other thoughts and reflections:

_____

_____

_____

_____

_____

_____

_____

_____

For additional resources related to this topic, please check out my website: www.abcsofselfcare.com

T

TAME ANXIETY

Anxiety's like a rocking chair. It gives you something to do, but it doesn't get you very far.

— Jodi Picoult

❧

Anxiety, which is defined as *a feeling of worry, nervousness, or unease, typically about an imminent event or something with an uncertain outcome*, is on the rise, according to research studies. Surprisingly, it is more predominant in high-income countries in the West – and that was *before* the global pandemic that hit in 2020. With the ongoing isolation brought on by Covid-19, nearly 75% of psychologists who provide treatment for anxiety disorders in the U.S. saw an increased demand for their services, per the American Psychological Association. I am not a licensed psychologist, nor do I want to offer psychological advice. For that, I encourage you to seek help from a licensed professional. What I do want to address is the issue of everyday "manageable" anxiety that will likely impact most of us at some point in our lives.

Over the years I have been coaching individuals, many of my clients have confessed that anxiety can, at times, be debilitating. This is precisely why we must tame anxiety before it controls us. Anxiety can make us feel less joyful and more out of control of our life circumstances. Left unchecked, it can morph into an anxiety disorder or depression that requires professional help to resolve. There is no shame if this happens. What is most important is to recognize when it gets to a point of being unmanageable. However, employing some basic strategies and techniques early on, and consistently, can help soothe the occasional bout of anxiety, which is natural for everyone. If those don't seem to be working, medication, therapy, or a combination of both may be necessary, but again – that is something to be taken up with licensed professionals. For the purposes of manageable anxiety as it relates to self-care, I will share some of the ways anxiety disrupts our self-care routines, as well as some of the techniques that can help us minimize, tame or cope with it.

Tia and Taming Anxiety

Tia agreed to deliver a presentation to hundreds of scientists at an upcoming industry conference eight months ago. She did it despite knowing that she dislikes drawing attention to herself and prefers to focus on her research work in the lab. Quietly. By herself. No fanfare. But the folks in the communications department of her firm were insistent that they needed one of the scientists to present at the conference and they wanted the best one. At least that's what they told her when recruiting her to do it. Sure, she was flattered, but now it's two days before her presentation and Tia has nothing in the way of presentation slides or even an outline for her talk. Each time she told herself she'd focus on the presentation, some other project took priority. And each time she blew off her promise to get it done, Tia would berate herself for being so irresponsible. She promises herself that she'll pull together her slides on the flight to the conference. Instead, she gets on the plane and feels the need to nap, despite having slept well the night before.

As her cab pulls up to the hotel where she'll be staying, Tia feels on edge and a bit dizzy, so she orders room service and watches some television. She still has a full day tomorrow; she could skip the opening sessions and get her slides and outline completed then. Tia tosses and turns all night, getting little sleep. Instead of starting the day with her usual run, she vows to get to work. With ample coffee in her system to overcome her lack of sleep, she sits at the desk in her room and stares at her laptop screen. *Where to begin, where to begin,* she wonders. Tia knows this information inside out, as she's been the lead scientist on this project. Yet she can't seem to find the right words as she chews her fingernails to the quick, staring at the computer screen. After an hour with still no words on the screen, Tia opts for a quick lunch at the conference buffet. She closes her laptop and heads downstairs, where she runs into her supervisor, Jerry.

"Hey, Tia," he says pleasantly, "I never got a copy of your presentation for tomorrow. I'd love to give it a quick once-over. Can you email it to me after lunch?" Tia puts on her best look of confidence and replies, "Sure!" Then she hightails it back to her room in lieu of eating. She feels a bit faint and dehydrated, realizing she hasn't had any water whatsoever today. She reaches for one of the overpriced bottles in the room and notices that her hand is shaking as she picks it up. She's unable to screw off the cap because her other hand is shaking as well. *What the hell?* she thinks. She tries to take a deep breath to calm the shaking yet finds she can't do that either. A series of short, gasping breaths is all she can manage. She forgets the water and crawls onto the bed in the fetal position as tears fill her eyes. Her talk is less than 19 hours away and she has nothing, nadda! *Why did I agree to do this!* she shouts, as she pounds her fists against her temples. *I should just call Jerry and tell him I quit right now.* She sees no way to complete her presentation in time, no way to get out of doing the presentation. *Loser!* she tells herself, as she falls asleep crying. When she wakes up at 8 pm, she stays up through the night, pulling together a mediocre presentation with typos and bad formatting. She'll deliver her talk with the enthusiasm of roadkill, making no eye contact with her audience. Afterward, the two folks from the communications department who are in the audience will look at one another and shake their heads in disbelief. "She's the best we've got?" one will ask the other. They'll never approach Tia again about representing the firm at a conference.

Quick Check - Select all that apply:

- ☐ I like to have control over processes and outcomes in life.
- ☐ I must have order and organization in my life.
- ☐ I would say that my coping strategies for anxiety need improvement.

Be Aware

Being aware of the presence of anxiety in your life and uncovering the root of that anxiety can start the process of taming it overall. For some, we know anxiety is creeping in when our hearts race or we feel dizzy, or we find ourselves unconsciously trembling – all physical manifestations of anxiety. For others, we experience obsessive negative thoughts that we feel incapable of stopping, or a sense of foreboding that won't go away – mental manifestations of anxiety. Being aware of any of these indicators will allow us to address the situation before it spirals beyond our control. For example, the minute we recognize that a negative thought is repeatedly running through our minds, we can slow our breath, close our eyes, and repeat an affirmative thought to counteract the negative one. "*Everything is working out for my highest good and all is well in my world,*" works for me. What would be a good "go-to" thought for you?

Next, we will want to assess the cause of our anxious thoughts. Were they triggered by something out of our control? If that's the case, then it's time to shift our focus to what *is* within our control. If it's something within our control, then writing out the challenge, the desired solution, and the steps in-between can help us tame those anxious feelings. Breaking down a seemingly insurmountable challenge into bite-sized, doable tasks often does the trick. Another helpful technique is to accept that we are experiencing anxious feelings and have compassion for ourselves for being in this emotional place. And finally, we can offer ourselves a gentle reminder that anxiety and worry will not change our circumstances, so we must stay focused on what we *can* control. In this case, that would be your ability to calm the anxiety you're feeling through deep breathing exercises, meditation, a walk to clear your head, or whatever technique works for you.

Recognize That Anxiety is Normal...To a Point

By employing some simple self-care techniques to tame the occasional bout of manageable anxiety, we can minimize its impact in our lives and prevent it from morphing into a full-blown disorder. For me, I've found that my overall level of anxiety decreases when I'm maintaining a consistent meditation practice or when I'm working with a hypnotherapist – both great tools to help tame anxiety. Other tools include cognitive behavioral therapy, acupuncture, yoga, medication (prescribed and taken only under the care of your doctor), and mindfulness.

Let's take a closer look at two simple, free, and effective tools: mindfulness and meditation. Developing a mindfulness practice involves experiencing only what is happening in the present – *this very moment* – which is all we are really guaranteed anyway. As anxiety often stems from over-focusing on the past or excessively worrying about the future, mindfulness is especially helpful for taming anxiety. Similarly, the goal of meditation practice is, "To be aware, observe and notice thoughts, feelings, and body states without becoming reactive or fused with them (i.e., believing them to be true states of the person or the world)," states Dr. Lynne Siqueland of the Children's and Adult Center for OCD and Anxiety. "It takes practice, but it gives the person both pause and freedom to make choices that are more effective." If you've never meditated before and aren't sure how to begin, here's a super simple approach to try it out:

1. Sit or lie comfortably, in a chair or on the floor, and close your eyes or focus your gaze on one object/wall.
2. Breathe naturally; make no effort to control the breath. (There are other forms of meditation that involve specific breathing techniques, but for beginners, I recommend this approach.)
3. Focus your attention on each breath and on how your body moves with each inhalation and exhalation.
4. Do this for 5 minutes, twice a day, slowly building up to 10, 20, and then 30 minutes for each session.

That's it! Pretty simple, huh? Almost too simple, right? How can something so easy be so powerful? The answer is: try it. Every day – morning and evening. You will see the results for yourself within a month's time.

Remember, occasional episodes of feeling anxious are normal; consistent or non-stop anxiety is not. It may be helpful to make a note in your calendar or journal when you've experienced an anxious episode. This will allow you to track the frequency of anxiety in your life and determine when and if it's time to seek professional support.

Know When to Get Help

While anxiety is uncomfortable, it can be helpful in terms of signaling a threat, uncertainty, trouble, or lack of preparedness. For example, if we're experiencing severe financial challenges and are feeling anxious, this is a normal response to the threat of bankruptcy. Addressing the financial challenges by creating a plan and taking steps to alleviate the challenges could help tame this anxiety. However, anxiety becomes a problem (and perhaps the start of an anxiety disorder) when, out of the blue, we feel anxious even in the absence of any threat or stressor that warrants an anxious response. It is also problematic if it interferes with our ability to function on a consistent basis. We will likely be able to intuitively discern if our anxiety is a manageable issue we can handle ourselves or if it is a bigger issue to be addressed with a professional. And if we can't discern this, then it's highly likely that seeing a professional would be a good choice.

Anxiety disorders are considered a mental illness, and in the U.S., they are quite common. Sadly, anxiety disorders can claim the lives of individuals who, outwardly, are phenomenally successful and appear to have it all together. In many cases, those with an anxiety disorder prefer to stay busy and in control and are often high-achieving perfectionists. According to Brené Brown, PhD, LMSW, those with anxiety disorders tend to either over-function or under-function as a means of coping. She has shared that, sometimes, even her own response to anxiety is to under-function, though she normally operates in high-functioning mode. So, you see, even those who are highly educated and have studied the research and literature about anxiety aren't immune to it. At some point in our lives, it's likely that we'll all have to deal with anxiety to some degree. The silver lining here is that by having experienced anxiety, we are more equipped to have empathy for others as they face their own struggles with it.

People like me and Brené, who over-function when anxious, tend to set unachievable goals and then stress out even more trying to reach them. Predictably, what comes next is shame for not achieving those goals. Because we feel bad about ourselves, we often treat ourselves in an unloving manner – all because we failed to tame the anxiety when we had the chance.

As for those whose response to anxiety is to under-function, this can play out in declining invitations, procrastinating on commitments, or not following through on even the simplest of tasks. This, of course, leads to the same cycle of shame, feeling bad, and treating ourselves in unloving ways. So basically, whether we respond to anxiety by over-functioning or under-functioning, we all end up in the same place – an emotionally bad one.

There are professional remedies that can help with severe cases of anxiety caused by trauma (something that was physically or emotionally harmful). A licensed therapist can assist with techniques such as EMDR, Eye Movement Desensitization and Reprocessing, and CBT, Cognitive-Behavioral Therapy (often called talk therapy). Please research what is best for you.

Focus on Prevention

In addition to the other self-care practices already covered that can prevent anxiety, let's look at a few other techniques to prevent or tame anxiety. Caffeine. Ah, you knew I wouldn't let you slide on this one, didn't you? Those of us who've been or still are consistent coffee or tea drinkers know how any highly-caffeinated beverage can give us the jitters – in other words, make us anxious. If, like me, you're an individual who is overly sensitive to caffeine, too much can trigger a full-blown panic attack. I recommend reducing caffeine, perhaps dramatically. Decaf coffee and green tea are great alternatives. Though they have trace amounts of caffeine, it's generally not enough to give you that caffeine buzz that coffee, black tea, energy drinks and caffeinated soda do. Additionally, teas, especially chai, matcha, yerba mate, and green tea have health benefits like reducing your risk of stroke or heart attack, preventing tooth loss, and boosting the immune system. Fun fact, the antioxidants in one cup of matcha is the equivalent of ten cups of green tea. The powered delivery system makes it better to consume than large amounts of green tea leaves. Some teas have both health benefits and side effects; therefore, I recommend you do a little research to figure out the best option for you.

Either coffee or tea counts toward fluid consumption so consider adding it to your diet to support your overall health. The best for fluid intake is – you guessed it – water. Drink more of it! Caffeine is a diuretic, so in addition to fluid loss from perspiration and urination, you'll need to replenish those fluids for better health. Plus, there are so many benefits to water consumption – it can aid in weight loss, prevent wrinkles, flush body waste, prevent kidney disease, help lower blood pressure, lubricate joints and so many more. If you're not willing to curb your caffeine habit, alternate cups of water with your caffeinated drink of choice to dilute the negative impact of caffeine. Herbal teas are a great way to calm the nervous system and the mind as well. Over time, the habit of having that cup of caffeinated coffee or tea can be transformed into having a cup of calming herbal tea. Hot water with lemon and honey and warm milk would work too. The custom of having a warm beverage remains intact, while the beverage itself is a much healthier choice.

Another way to prevent anxiety before it becomes a regular part of your existence is to know your family history. Anxiety is hereditary, so understanding your biological parents' experience with anxiety and anxiety disorders is important. If there is a history of anxiety disorders within your family, I'd suggest being proactive in implementing self-care practices that prevent anxiety and eliminating habits that can trigger it before any hereditary imprint can be activated. Best to avoid it altogether than to have to get it under control after it's already manifested in our lives.

Additionally, by understanding and working with any hereditary predispositions to anxiety, we're in a better position to prevent passing that predisposition on to our children.

The language we use is another way to prevent anxiety before it takes root. I suggest that we avoid using words that take us to "Victim-ville" and make us feel out of control. For example:

- *I can't handle this!*
- *I should be able to calm down.*
- *Ugh! I am so stressed out!*
- *This is all too much for me!*

If you find yourself unconsciously making statements like these, catch yourself in the act and quickly change to a more positive reframing of the situation, such as:

- *I can and will handle this.*
- *I am at peace.*
- *I am calm and in control.*
- *I got this! One step at a time.*

See the difference? The tasks at hand (or whatever the source of anxiety is) are still in need of your attention yet using more positive expressions will go a long way in keeping anxiety in check.

Increasing your tolerance for ambiguity can also prevent anxiety from taking over your life. Being able to go with the flow, deal with uncertainty and not have everything planned out, are hallmarks of those who can tolerate more ambiguity. This is an excellent leadership trait because it allows you to manage unpredictability or to work with someone that has a different style. Spontaneity and the unknown can be fun! It all depends on how you perceive it. One way to get more comfortable with ambiguity is to change your mindset to embrace uncertainty as a fact of life and have faith that you can handle what it brings. And see what happens when you let things naturally happen, instead of needing to have every detail mapped out. You might be surprised at the outcome. This is a great mindset to take on vacation.

And finally, we can avoid anxiety by minimizing time spent around anxious people or learning to not allow their anxiety to impact you. Anxiety breeds more anxiety, so it's helpful to surround yourself with calm, supportive people. Being in the presence of an anxious person can make us feel more anxious and uncomfortable. Unfortunately, anxiety can not only control us, but can also make us want to control others. And who likes others trying to control them? No one! Let's do our best to not only avoid spending too much time with anxious people, but to also avoid being that anxious person that others want to avoid. In the spirit of controlling what you can – you – plan ahead. Use calming techniques before being in the company of others who are anxious.

Affirmations to Address Anxiety

Below are affirmations you may wish to work with to prevent or tame anxiety in your life. Speak the affirmation consistently with conviction, as if it is already true. Then take appropriate action to curb anxiety inducing habits. Consider the ones at the end of this chapter.

- *I am calm.*
- *I have released the anxiety I'm feeling right now.*
- *I have peace.*
- *I am safe.*
- *I have happy, grateful thoughts.*
- *My anxious thoughts are released.*
- *I am strong.*
- *I am in control of my thoughts.*
- *I have this!*
- *I can do this!*
- *I keep my power.*
- *I did my best.*
- *I win or I learn.*

Tame anxiety or it will be the one in charge. Is that really how you want to live? I'm guessing it isn't. I urge you to not accept anxiety into your life like it is a family member you are stuck with. Use the suggestions in this chapter or seek professional help. Do whatever it takes to lessen the presence of anxiety in your life and the misery it brings with it.

Tia, Revisited

Now that we've covered all these tools and techniques for taming anxiety – or better yet, preventing it altogether, let's revisit Tia's situation. It's a month before the conference and Tia still hasn't started working on her presentation. She is aware that she gets incredibly nervous about public speaking, being the introvert that she is. She knows she's blown off her self-imposed deadlines for preparing, repeatedly. When her boss asks her how her talk is coming along, she takes a deep breath and tells him the truth. "Honestly? I haven't started yet. I seem to have a mental block." Jerry chuckles and says, "You know what, Tia? That sounds like a classic case of public speaking anxiety creeping up on you. I remember that feeling when I did my first conference presentation.

It was awful...and guess what? I bombed! How about we sit down together and lay out a plan to get this done?" Tia agrees and together they sit down and list the overall goals of the presentation, the key points Tia needs to make, and how many slides will likely be necessary for each key point.

Tia leaves his office feeling better already, more in control. Jerry has asked her to bring him the four slides for the first key point by tomorrow. *Totally doable!* she tells herself. Before leaving work that day, she emails the slides to Jerry and then leaves for her spin class. The next day, she tackles the next four slides and shoots them over to her boss. He sends her some positive feedback and a few minor changes, which she promptly incorporates. Tia continues to work her way through the plan for completing her presentation and within the week, it's done. Jerry suggests she practice it in the conference room for a couple of the junior scientists, so she does. They offer a few more suggestions, which she considers before making edits to her slides. Knowing how nervous she gets in front of large audiences; Tia continues to study and practice her presentation with note cards as she takes her morning walk each day. She even does what her best friend – the yin to her yang – has been encouraging her to do for years now: try meditating.

A week before Tia is to leave for the conference, she sits on the floor cross-legged and tries meditating for the first time ever. She fidgets and wonders what the point is for the first five minutes, but she sticks with it for a full fifteen minutes. She's surprised at how relaxed and calm she now feels about the upcoming conference. She schedules meditation into her day, every day, until the conference. She even starts to add what her best friend called "visualization" – seeing the outcome she wants from her presentation in her imagination. She pictures herself surrounded by colleagues after her talk, all of them congratulating her and asking questions about the research she's been conducting. She imagines herself smiling, laughing even, and enjoying all the accolades. And by the time the real presentation takes place, Tia is surprisingly calm as she takes the stage. She nails the presentation! Later, when the Communications department head suggests that she take her presentation on the road to their satellite offices, Tia wholeheartedly agrees. This is fun! she thinks to herself, surprised. Tia continues her meditation practice, even when there's no public speaking on her calendar. She has tamed her anxiety in general and feels more at peace.

Fear and anxiety many times indicate that we are moving in a positive direction, out of the safe confines of our comfort zone, and in the direction of our true purpose.

— Charles F. Glassman

Intention:

I have faith that I can remain calm during uncertainty.

Now, how about digging deeper? As a warm-up to this time for reflection, I suggest listening to "Don't Worry, Be Happy" by Bobby McFerrin.

Invitation to Reflect:

When do you become most anxious? What are your anxiety triggers?

_____

_____

_____

_____

_____

_____

_____

What healthy coping mechanisms do you have to help you manage anxiety? What support systems can you build?

_____

_____

_____

_____

What affirmations will you use when you feel yourself getting anxious?

_____

_____

_____

_____

_____

Here are some actions you could take now for your self-care:

○ Create an inventory of stressors that make you anxious. Write them in a journal. Avoid them, if possible.

○ Research coping strategies in advance and plan which ones to implement. Use the free information available at the National Institute of Anxiety and Stress.

○ Try Navy Seals deep breathing techniques when you feel anxious (aka Box Breathing and Four-Square Breathing) – Breathe in for a count of 4, hold it in your stomach and feel your belly rise. Hold the breath for a count of 4. Release your breath through your mouth counting to 8, you should hear a *swooshing* sound as it comes out. Repeat the breathing pattern 4 times in a row without a break. If it works for someone in such a high-pressure job, it can work for you!

Commit to doing at least one thing differently based on what you learned in this chapter. Write out an actionable goal – with a specific deadline – to satisfy this commitment.

_____

_____

_____

_____

_____

How will you celebrate or reward yourself if you reach the goal?

_____

_____

Other thoughts and reflections:

_____

_____

_____

_____

_____

For additional resources related to this topic, please check out my website: www.abcsofselfcare.com

$\mathcal{U}$

UNCONDITIONALLY LOVE

If we could read the secret history of our enemies, we should find in each man's life sorrow and suffering enough to disarm all hostility.

— Henry Wadsworth Longfellow

❧

At its core, unconditional love is, of course, *love without conditions*. Sounds simple right? And yet, consciously, or subconsciously, so many of us *do* put conditions on our love for others. Can you only love (platonically or otherwise) those who share your political affiliation, race, religion, or cultural background? Or someone who shares similar habits, traits, and interests? On the contrary, are you able to feel love for others if they are different? Or have a habit that rubs you the wrong way? Or that they pray to a different god than you do? Unconditional love isn't about letting others off the hook for crimes, bad attitudes, disgusting habits, or anything else that goes against your sense of decency and what is right or wrong. Those who commit crimes or acts of cruelty against others need to be held accountable. Children who misbehave need a course correction before their bad behaviors turn into habits. But being held accountable and being loved unconditionally are two different things – and they are not mutually exclusive.

As with most of the self-care habits in this book, we must each learn to love *ourselves* unconditionally too. So many of us only support ourselves if we've "earned" it, for example, got that promotion at work, lost the 15 pounds we've nagged ourselves about for years, did well on a test, etc. As part of self-care, it's important to really monitor how we talk to ourselves – and others – to make sure we're consistently coming from a place of unconditional love.

Additionally, the power of unconditional love is in the *doing*, not just the thinking or feeling. It's great to feel a sense of unconditional love for others, but what happens when that love is tested? Are we able to send an encouraging letter to a prisoner who's been convicted of murder? Can we lovingly correct a child's bad behavior without judgment? Love is actively "done" or demonstrated by being in service to others and ourselves. Acts of self-care done not as a "reward" for accomplishing something, but simply "because," demonstrate unconditional love for ourselves. Acts of kindness done for others, be they strangers, acquaintances, or close friends, demonstrate unconditional love for others. "Doing" love can also include shifting our judgments and perceptions of others so that we're able to interact with them from a place of love and kindness.

Uma and Unconditional Love

Uma has been dreading the upcoming family holiday gathering. Her sister "always" gets hammered and insists upon driving back to her condo rather than spending the night. Her brother sucks the air out of the room with all his "larger-than-life" tales of his Wall Street job and his NYC lifestyle. Her father will, no doubt, give her his best disappointed look about her latest tattoo while getting in a few judgmental jabs about her propensity to dress in black. And Uncle Will – oh, Lord – he'll no doubt come barreling in halfway through dinner and start spouting his usual conspiracy theories. As the day draws near, Uma gets more and more agitated about the group about to assemble, supposedly for a day of gratitude. *Ha! What's to be grateful for?* she asks herself. *That Sis might not kill someone while driving drunk? That Dad might not notice my new tat? That Mom might actually show some backbone and tell Dad to leave me alone about how I choose to dress and adorn my body?*

Two days before Uma is to make the two-hour drive to her childhood home, she is all but seething about the upcoming gathering of relatives under one roof. She calls her mother and lies to her. "Mom, I'm not feeling great. I think I may be coming down with something." Physically, Uma feels fine, but she's not so sure she wants to deal with all the annoyances of her family. On the morning of the family gathering, Uma texts her mom and lies about having a fever and nausea. Her mother responds by telling her to take good care of herself and even offers to drive down the next day to bring her leftovers and a fresh pot of chicken noodle soup. Uma declines her offer and mumbles about her need to get back to sleep, "so I won't be checking my phone anymore." *There, that does it,* Uma thinks. She then proceeds to go about her day, ordering Chinese food and watching a movie at home alone in lieu of seeing her large extended family. Halfway through the movie, she is in tears. She feels left out and berates herself for having blown off her relatives. *God, I can be such a jerk sometimes!* she tells herself repeatedly. *What is wrong with me?! I suck!* Uma goes to sleep feeling like the world's worst daughter, sister, niece – everything!

Quick Check - Select all that apply:

- ☐ I am often critical of others.
- ☐ I often end a relationship if they do a few minor things that rub me the wrong way.
- ☐ My love for others is sometimes tied to how they behave.

Start With Yourself

We've all heard the saying "you can't give away what you don't have." Nowhere is this more evident than in loving others. It is impossible to unconditionally love others – again, platonically, or intimately – if we don't first unconditionally love ourselves. Sure, we may each have things about ourselves we'd like to change – perhaps improving our health or drinking less or being less of a know-it-all or being more outgoing. The key is to love ourselves unconditionally while also accepting that we wish to make a few positive changes in our behavior, outlook, or lifestyle. Unconditionally loving ourselves isn't about ignoring traits or habits we want to change. It's about loving ourselves *despite* having these things, despite working on areas of our lives that we'd like to improve. If we have something about us that we dislike which cannot be changed – our height, body shape, or hair type – we must make the commitment to come to terms with and accept these features that set us apart from others. If there is no realistic way to change something about ourselves, we must learn to wholeheartedly accept and love that element of our unique selves. Accepting our physical traits or personality/behavioral flaws is the starting point to unconditionally loving ourselves, which frees us up to accept the flaws of others and love them without conditions. It really comes down to accepting our "perfect imperfections," which then allows us to accept the perfect imperfections of others.

Unconditionally loving ourselves means we love ourselves on those days when we're at our very best (Had a great workout! Helped an elderly person at a crosswalk! Shined on the job! Stuck to my meal plan!), as well as on the days when we miss the mark (Blew off the gym. Couldn't shake the blues. Called in sick to work. Crawled back in bed and devoured a pint of ice cream while watching mindless TV.). The key is to learn to love *all* of ourselves even if we'd prefer being more perfect – for those with perfectionism still running amuck in their psyche.

Behavioral research suggests that perfectionists tend to avoid their own human imperfections by projecting the perfection they want for themselves onto others. We wish we were the perfect employee, so we want our boss to be perfect. We want to be the perfect girlfriend, so we expect our partner to be perfect. We want to be the perfect artist, so we criticize the art of others. We worry that we're not the perfect parent, so we take issue with and gossip about the parenting style of others. See how this works? Others become our mirror. It's a tough cycle to break, but if we examine our criticisms and judgments of others, we might just find clues to aspects of our own lives that we'd like to improve or, perhaps more importantly, we need to accept.

Accept Others' Imperfections

What would the world look like if we could all accept the imperfections of others and, instead, offer them the compassion we want for ourselves and our own imperfections? What if we could stay calm and loving even when someone cuts us off on the highway? Perhaps we could give them the benefit of the doubt instead of jumping to the conclusion that they're just jerks. What if we viewed them as a fellow traveler on this Earth who may be having a tough day or an emergency or perhaps simply made a human error? What if we silently sent them the same sort of compassion and forgiveness we'd like for ourselves when we're the ones who inadvertently cut someone off in traffic? This means even if the offender cuts us off then flips us off – a clear indication that they are knowingly behaving like a jerk – compassion is in order.

What made them behave like a jerk? Are they having mental health issues? Did they have an abusive childhood that hardened them to the world? Are they so broken by life's hardships that they've lost their way? We'll never know for sure, but in sending compassion instead of matching their disrespectful behavior, we will better serve not only ourselves, but everyone we encounter. Remember Michelle Obama's famous catchphrase: *When they go low, we go high*. What a perfect summation of the ability to foster unconditional love for all our fellow humans. And once you've integrated the concept of unconditional love into your thoughts and beliefs, it's a lot easier to incorporate that same concept into your *actions*, which is really where it matters. Acting with unconditional love means you don't respond to being flipped off on the highway by tailing the offender, flashing your high beams at them, and flipping them off in return. It means sending compassion, perhaps even a little prayer that the circumstances triggering that sort of behavior improve, then backing off. It means accepting their flawed, imperfect behavior, forgiving them, and moving on.

What about situations that involve those we're deeply connected with – friends, family, lovers? Relationships – romantic or otherwise – work best if they are based on unconditional love. This doesn't mean we don't get angry, hurt, concerned, or annoyed by those we love. It doesn't mean we let those we care for run all over us with no boundaries. It means we commit to loving them despite their imperfect behaviors, attitudes, or perspectives. The willingness to work through any differences, as well as to forgive, are the foundation for building unconditional love within our important relationships.

Do you ever find yourself saying or thinking things about your significant other, family member or – in a low moment – a child, such as:

- *If only he would bring me flowers more often, then I could take him seriously.*
- *I wish she'd stop chewing with her mouth open all the time!*
- *I hate that my husband won't be more affectionate with me in public.*
- *My daughter had better get straight A's this semester, or else.*
- *If my grandkid's ADHD didn't make her such a Tasmanian devil, I'd spend more time with her.*
- *If my sister doesn't stop drinking so much, I'll stop going over there for Sunday dinner.*

- *How could anyone love an ex-convict?*
- *I could never love a smoker.*
- *If she would just apply herself a bit more, she could lose weight and get a man.*

Do you see the conditions placed upon others in the statements above? Pretty easy to spot.

A good self-reflection practice is to pay attention every time we find ourselves making a conditional judgment about someone we love. Then ask ourselves: *Is there something about my judgment of that person that could reflect something I don't like about myself?* If we play with this concept, maybe even journal about it a bit to see what comes up, we might just find the root cause of the conditional love we impose upon the people in our lives. This knowledge, in turn, allows us to reframe our judgments and to eliminate the conditions we put on those we love. Using one of the examples above, one's perspective could change from *I could never love a smoker* to *I care about the health of those I love, and while I wish my friend didn't smoke, I know that's her choice. I just ask that she not do it while she's with me because I don't want to breathe in secondhand smoke.*

Now, does this mean we're supposed to accept and unconditionally love people who intentionally mistreat us? Absolutely not! Loving unconditionally doesn't eliminate the need for personal boundaries. Toxic, harmful behaviors and purposely hurtful words have no place in a mutually loving relationship. If we consistently find ourselves in one of these situations, it is an act of unconditional love toward ourselves to bow out of that relationship, even if it means cutting ties with a blood relation, marital partner, or lifelong friend. Unconditional love does *not* mean unconditionally allowing others to hurt, abuse, manipulate or otherwise cause damage to us. Remember, we can't give away what we don't possess, so we must unconditionally love ourselves by only accepting healthy relationships in our lives. And for those we cut ties with, we can still send unconditional love to them in our prayers, meditations, or thoughts without allowing them into our orbit.

Respect Different Love Languages

We each have our go-to styles of expressing our love for others. These styles are known as "love languages" – a term coined by pastor and author, Gary Chapman. The basic five love languages, according to Chapman, include: (1) words of affirmation, (2) quality time, (3) receiving gifts, (4) acts of service and (5) physical touch. It's okay for our loved ones to have a different go-to love language than we do. And it's important to accept that they may express their love for us differently as well. For example, our partner may use quality time as their primary love language, while ours is to give spontaneous gifts. We may find ourselves annoyed that we don't receive little gifts frequently from our mate in return. To help the relationship thrive, we must consciously accept that they speak a different love language than we do. If we can't, we may find ourselves having ongoing problems in the relationship. If we can accept that our close relationships may involve opposing love languages, then we're better equipped to nurture a foundation of unconditional love.

Embrace Unconditional Love for All

Giving to others without expectation is perhaps the truest act of unconditional love, especially where strangers are concerned. We can develop this trait more consistently with practice, starting off with small, conscious acts of kindness. These might include allowing someone to merge on the highway when we see their turn signal flashing; letting the person with two grocery items go ahead of us and our full shopping cart in the check-out line (bonus points if that person appears impatient and anxious, behaviors that tend to discourage us from helping another). You could offer your seat on the bus or subway to a passenger who appears a bit frail or exhausted. How about practicing smiling at or greeting strangers we pass on the street, just because, or responding kindly and supportively to those we interact with. It counts when sharing our abundance with others, be it a few dollars for a homeless person on the street or some fresh-baked cookies with a neighbor. All these little acts of kindness are great ways to express unconditional love toward others. Maybe they will encourage more people to do the same (though that shouldn't be the goal), multiplying the growth of unconditional love exponentially!

Dr. Elisabeth Kubler-Ross's research focused on those near death concluded that the ultimate life lesson we are each here to learn is that of unconditional love. How beautiful and spot on is that? Kubler-Ross also states that while this is the hardest lesson we will learn, it is what we all most want and need in life. So, to anyone who feels they have no overarching purpose in life, I encourage you to adopt unconditional love as that mission.

Uma, Revisited

Let's return to Uma's situation: a large family gathering that will most assuredly involve comments and behaviors that annoy her. As the day approaches, Uma feels tense about the family get-together. She finds herself turning thoughts over and over in her mind, thoughts like *Why can't Sis just get help for her drinking problem? Why can't my brother quit bragging about how much money he makes and how cool he is to live in NYC? Why does Uncle Will have to be such an extremist? Why can't Dad just love me the way I am?*

Uma decides to spend some time examining why she's so wound up over the imperfections of those she loves. Uma realizes how devastated she'd be if she lost her sister in a drunk-driving accident. She decides to call her sister and offer to pick her up on the way to Mom and Dad's so they can "have some time alone together" before joining the larger group. This way, she'll be able to safely drive her sister back home afterward without fear for her, or others' safety. It also means she won't be tempted to drink too much.

She searches for compassion for her brother, who was, not that long ago, flat broke and living in their parent's basement. Uma realizes he is likely so relieved to finally be self-supporting that he worries about losing it all. His constant need to talk about how much money he makes is probably a reflection of a deep-seated fear of being broke again. Secretly, Uma has felt the same way at times.

Uncle Will is unlikely to change his warped views of others at his age, but that doesn't mean Uma has to sit quietly and listen to him spout his conspiracy theories. She decides to view him as a sad clown in her mind, which helps her feel compassion for – but not agreement with – his sincere belief in the half-baked opinions he feels compelled to share. She accepts that he'll likely say some ugly things at dinner, so she practices a few firm but loving responses to use when this occurs. These will allow her to establish some boundaries with him and to not be completely flustered when the inevitable "toads" pop out of his mouth.

And her father? Uma decides she's going to pull him aside, one on one, when she arrives and lovingly explain to him how his past comments about her clothing choices and tattoos hurt her feelings. She knows her father loves her deeply, so she suspects he doesn't realize how much his comments cut her to the core.

On the day of the family gathering, Uma drives to her sister's condo an hour and a half away to pick her up. They laugh and talk the whole way and her sister even thanks her for doing the driving! Once at her parents' home, Uma finds a way to talk to her father alone and she is happily surprised at how he listens to her heartfelt appeal. A tear slides down his cheek as he apologizes and pulls Uma in for a hug. While munching appetizers in the living room, her brother starts bragging about the gourmet meals he eats regularly back home. Uma just smiles and allows him to talk, while sending a silent wish that one day he will feel more emotionally and financially secure in life. None of his proclamations about his stellar NYC lifestyle bother her this time, so she's able to listen to him without being triggered. *Underneath all that bravado*, she tells herself, *is the same sweet little boy I grew up with.* And Uncle Will? Well, Uma knows she won't change his perspective over one dinner gathering. But when he makes a derogatory statement about all the homeless people trashing the neighborhood, Uma speaks up. Keeping her voice steady, she says, "Uncle Will, I love you, but there is no place here for that sort of hateful talk. Perhaps you don't realize how heartless and hurtful your words are, but now is not the appropriate time nor place." Everyone is stunned into silence. The elephant in the room has finally been addressed.

Uncle Will turns to his sister, Uma's mother, and spits, "You gonna let your hoity toity daughter talk to me that way?" Her mother replies, "Actually, Will, I feel the same as Uma and I've been extremely uncomfortable with many of your comments for years now. In fact, I'm ashamed I let you get away with it under my roof for so long. I, too, love you, but you will refrain from bringing that ugliness into our home or you will no longer be welcome here." Everyone turns to Uncle Will as he considers what has just been said. Then he tosses his napkin on his half-eaten plate of food, pushes back from the table, and grunts another rambling insult about crazy homeless drug addicts, before storming out of the house.

"Kids," Uma's father says, "we won't be inviting Uncle Will to our home again." Everyone at the table lets out a collective sigh of relief. "And Uma?" he continues, "I'm proud of you for saying what your mother and I should've said years ago to that old fool. We love Will, but we swept his nastiness under the rug for far too long, and for that I apologize to you all."

God is love and all the love there is, is mine. I shall endeavor to see something lovable in everyone I meet, and every situation in which I find myself, and as I do this, I shall accumulate a great degree of Love to be deposited in my bank account. And then when some experience comes along which seems unkind or unlovable, I shall be able to write a check on my Bank of Life which will cover every liability of hate or of unkindness.

— Ernest Holmes

❀

Intention:

I practice unconditional love.

Now, how about digging deeper? As a warm-up to this time for reflection, I suggest listening to "The Greatest Love of All" by Whitney Houston.

Invitation to Reflect:

What parts of yourself do you have to accept and love unconditionally?

_____

_____

_____

_____

_____

_____

Who in your life could use unconditional love right now?

_____

_____

_____

_____

Who can you give to right now without expecting anything in return?

_____

_____

_____

_____

Here are some actions you could take now for your self-care:

- ○ Ask someone close to you how you could demonstrate unconditional love for them.
- ○ Find at least one quality you admire in someone you dislike.
- ○ Take the online assessment created by Gary Chapman, author of the *The Five Love Languages*, to determine your love language and send it to a loved one (friend or romantic partner).

Commit to doing at least one thing differently based on what you learned in this chapter. Write out an actionable goal – with a specific deadline – to satisfy this commitment.

_____

_____

_____

_____

How will you celebrate or reward yourself if you reach the goal?

_____

_____

Other thoughts and reflections:

_____

_____

_____

_____

For additional resources related to this topic, please check out my website: www.abcsofselfcare.com

$\mathcal{V}$

VOICE YOUR NEEDS

The most courageous act is still to think for yourself. Aloud.

— Coco Chanel

❁

Many who struggle with self-care may not realize they have needs or understand the extent to which those needs have gone unmet over the years. Why is this? Because so many of us, women especially, are culturally socialized to care for others, to put the needs – and often, *wants* – of others ahead of our own. This can play out as being the People Pleaser, often focused on making sure everyone else is happy or satisfied without concern for our own well-being. Or it can play out as the Eternal Optimist, often believing we can do more than we can, in less time than it requires. Both modes of going through life can result in being annoyed or angry when our bodies actually signal us to slow down through fatigue or illness. And needs? Specifically, *our* needs? Too often, there's never enough time or attention put toward satisfying those needs, let alone even understanding what they are.

Understanding and voicing your needs is essential to a good self-care practice. Based on my work with many clients over the years, I discovered many women prioritized others' needs over their own. I remember hiring my first life coach decades ago and being shocked to learn how many unmet needs I had. My life was far too busy to include any consistent commitment to self-care, never mind time spent discovering my needs. Working with that coach was a wake-up call that propelled me to reflect more on how I was living my life and, more importantly, how I could get my needs met. And, honestly, working through that process was life-changing for me. I finally realized – and you can too – that most of the people in our lives whose needs we've put above our own have somebody else who can also care for them, even if that someone is themselves. Obviously, I'm not referring to babies, young children, people with disabilities, and others, such as the elderly, who are often dependent on others to meet their basic needs. I'm referring to people who can meet their own needs, but who *prefer* to have others meet them instead. In the end, the person we can count on the most to meet our needs is – you got it! – *ourselves.*

Vanessa and Voicing Her Needs

Vanessa has been dating her boyfriend, Vance, for over five years. In her mid-30s, she is acutely aware that her child-bearing years are slipping away. Vanessa has always wanted to have a family of her own and Vance seems to, based on how wonderfully he interacts with Vanessa's three nieces and nephews. It makes her smile just to think of how he willingly jumps into leaf piles with them, plays with their wooden blocks and Hot Wheels and often accompanies Vanessa when she takes them on an outing. Vanessa, however, has never explicitly broached the topic of children with Vance, always opting for the easier route of not making waves. She assumes that he knows she plans to have children. She assumes he wants that too, since he's so good with kids. She assumes he'll pop the question soon so they can move forward with their – correction, *her* – plans to start a family.

But deep down inside, Vanessa has her doubts. Vance knows how old she is and understands that Vanessa's ability to conceive a child is decreasing with each passing birthday. Each time she musters up the courage to have a direct conversation about her desire – no, *need* – to have children, she chickens out and changes the subject. This pattern continues for three more years, at which point Vance casually mentions that he was never that interested in having his own children, that he likes the freedom his childless lifestyle allows. Vanessa is shocked...and hurt. Why didn't he tell her this a long time ago, like, maybe the minute they were obviously a serious couple?! The disconnect between Vance's need to retain his childless freedom and Vanessa's need to have children soon morphs into fights and passive aggression and a general sense of disharmony between them. Within months, Vance suggests they "take a break," to which Vanessa declares, "forget the break; we're through."

Determined to have the children she's always dreamed of – even if it means going it alone – Vanessa arranges appointments with both an OB/GYN and a sperm bank. Unfortunately, her new OB/GYN informs her that the tests they ran indicate that Vanessa's child-bearing window has closed. Vanessa is already perimenopausal and carrying a child to term would be unlikely, even if she could conceive. Vanessa is heartbroken. She has lost both Vance and her long-imaged dream of bearing children. *Why didn't I ask him about having children years ago?* she asks herself over and over in a tone that is more accusatory than inquisitive. She will never forgive herself for not speaking up. *Never!*

Quick Check - Select all that apply:

☐ I don't believe I have a lot of needs.

☐ I am not entirely sure what my needs are.

☐ I prefer to avoid conflict in relationships even if it means I go without something that is important to me.

Accept Your Humanness

As humans, our needs, whether expressed or repressed, are something we will assess and reassess our entire lives. Needs are not something that are met at one phase of life, never to be dealt with again. As we move through the various seasons of our lives, our needs will shift and evolve as we shift and evolve. But we'll always have needs. And we'll always have to address those needs if we are committed to self-care.

What motivates us to satisfy our needs and make decisions based on these needs is widely debated by psychologists and researchers. They've created lists of human needs in various categories to help make sense of the most common ones. I prefer the list created by sisters Miki, Inbal, and Arnina Kashtan, experts in the field of Nonviolent Communication (NVC). Their list emphasizes expressing our real feelings and needs openly and honestly, yet without blame or criticism. Their list clusters our needs into 4 main categories: (1) Subsistence and Security, (2) Freedom, (3) Connection, and (4) Meaning. Self-care falls into the category of Meaning. (See a Partial List of the Kashtans' *Universal Needs* in Appendix B.)

Sociologist and co-founder of Bay Area Nonviolent Communication (BayNVC) Miki Kashtan, Ph.D. says, "The tragedy of life is that while our needs are so all-important, most of us go through life without cultivating the awareness of our needs nor the capacity to distinguish between our needs and our strategies. We rarely ask and answer why we want something, what the meaning of our pain is, or any of the many questions that would lead us to connect with our own and others' needs. Why tragic? Because when we do, so much more becomes possible." Reflecting on those needs that make us do the things we do or feel a certain way may require the help of a therapist, coach, or trusted advisor. If you're the type of person who prefers to do things on your own, the Root Cause Analysis or the 5 Whys (Chapter A) is a great tool to help figure out why we feel we need something in any particular moment. However, our responses when using these tools are subject to change based on the situation, people involved, or the timing.

At times, our striving to fulfill some of our needs gets out of hand and morphs into our being needy. This neediness can be a short-term situation or a lifelong bad habit. Remember: *needs* are healthy; *neediness* is not. Let me illustrate how this neediness can get out of hand with a few common scenarios. For example, some people can take their "need" for love to an extreme, believing they must have the love of another *specific* person to be happy. This is also called an obsession, and it rarely ends well. Can you think of a time when you felt your world would end if you didn't "make" someone else fall in love with you? Hopefully, your situation occurred in high school or college, as this classic case of a needy compulsion is most often associated with a lack of maturity.

Or let's take the example of the need for security. Taken to an extreme, this can manifest in our inability to take any risks whatsoever or to be extremely frugal with money even when our financial circumstances don't warrant it. A risk-free life can be not only dull but also lonely. If someone doesn't have the courage to change careers or partners or even something as simple as a hairstyle, then they are likely in for a miserable, unfulfilling existence.

Where the need for competence is concerned, the unhealthy extreme might involve earning degree after degree and sometimes never applying them in our careers. Sometimes our feeling of not enough-ness can motivate us to pursue more education and certifications to build confidence or achieve status because of a longing to feel respected or credible. It could also manifest in spending much of our time outside of work focused on perfecting a non-work competency, such as golf or woodworking, to the detriment of time spent with our families.

And finally, let's look at the need for positive emotions. Taken to the extreme, the needy version of this reveals itself in Pollyanna-type behavior that serves to mask any not-so-positive emotions we are fearful of expressing or acknowledging. Prolonged Pollyannaism – or "positivity bias" – can lead to accumulating deep-seated anger and resentment. The needy version of positive emotions can set us up to ignore or deny what is happening for us in real life, be it grief, sadness, disappointment, or other negative emotions. These stifled emotions can lead to anger and resentment or, worse, illness. Remember, the mind-body connection is proven and can wreak havoc under the right circumstances.

With all these human needs, the key is to strive for moderation over excess. And when our needs do get a bit out of hand, our best bet is to accept our humanness and the inevitable missteps that come with it, and then course correct.

The opposite of obsessing over our basic human needs is ignoring them, which is equally detrimental to our well-being. As world-renowned complementary-medicine expert Dr. Deepak Chopra states, "all emotions derive from needs." And our emotional needs are less likely to be expressed if we can't accept our humanness – beings that are flawed and have needs. Tal Ben-Sharar, Ph.D., a Harvard-educated expert in the field of positive psychology and founder of the Happiness Studies Academy, takes this notion a step further. Ben-Sharar states that painful emotions intensify if they aren't expressed. Alternatively, they will diminish if we recognize and accept that we have them; this is the first step. The next step is to express them in constructive ways, such as crying in a safe environment, writing about them, or talking them through with someone who can help you address them, be that a good friend or a trained therapist. By embracing our need to express painful emotions, we can positively impact our peace of mind, and therefore our overall well-being. It's all about accepting our humanness.

Be Aware of Your Needs and Wants

So how do we know if something is a need or a want? It's complicated. One way to look at it is that a *need* is typically something *essential* to our well-being, while a *want* is a preference, something that's not quite as important as a need. For example, food is a *need*, pizza is a *want* (no matter how much my pizza-loving pal Lauren would argue to the contrary). See the difference? Conflict in relationships arises when each person needs or wants different things. If each has a conflicting *need*, it's unlikely the relationship will last long, unless one of the parties is willing to suppress their own need for the other's. (I do not suggest this path, as unmet needs lead to bigger issues down the road.) For example, let's say you need to live in a mild, dry climate due to asthma, and the person you've recently met online – and with whom you share a mutual interest in pursuing – needs to live in (hot and muggy) Florida to care for his aging parents. Hmmm, I'm going to go out on a limb here and say this one likely won't work out. However, if each person in a relationship has a conflicting *want*, then healthy win-win negotiation skills and a balance of give-and-take can result in both parties getting their wants fulfilled at alternating times, or simultaneously, if an acceptable solution is found. For example, you want Chinese for dinner and your partner wants Thai. Obviously, this isn't a conflict worth breaking up over. Instead, you can decide to eat Thai food tonight and Chinese the next time you two decide to dine out. Alternatively, you could get take-out or delivery of both Chinese *and* Thai food, and each enjoy what you want, together, at home. The key when bumping up against conflicting wants in a relationship is to value ourselves enough to see our wants as being just as important as our partner's or friend's wants, and then to seek a solution that honors both people's desires.

Now, obviously, not all needs are life-or-death types of scenarios like needing a moderate, dry climate to manage asthma. Our wants and needs will vary at different times in our life. That's why some of the other self-care habits can be helpful as we grow and develop, such as Act on Awareness & Acceptance (AAA), Build Boundaries, and Keep your Power, to name a few. Taking time to reflect on whether something is a want, a strong want, a minor need, or a critical need will help in determining the best course of action.

Ask for Help

Are you the type of person who's much more comfortable giving than receiving? Do you have a tough time asking for help? Both could be signs of low self-worth. I promise you that asking for help isn't a sign of weakness, nor is it a crime. And it gets easier the more you practice. Graciously receiving help from another is a gift to the person you've allowed to help you. Just consider how good it feels when we help another person in need. Now turn the tables and realize that your accepting help from another is making that person feel good. And it can even be seen as a sign of strength because you have the self-awareness to realize when assistance from someone else could be valuable. Fun fact – Ari Weinzweig, Founder of Zingerman's, a famous Ann Arbor deli, states that one of his company's beliefs is that asking for help is a sign of strength. He *wants* and commends employees who ask for help.

When asking for help, it's best if we don't wait until it's mission-critical and time is of the essence. Instead, it's best to anticipate if we might need help and give whoever could help us a heads up. Then, we'll want to circle back and let them know if help is needed or not. My general rule of thumb, especially for technical issues, is to work on resolving something for 30 minutes on my own and if it's still unresolved, ask for help. There's no point in spending my whole day trying to figure out something that one call to the IT department or the Apple Genius Bar or my highly technical friend can resolve in five minutes. When our sense of self-worth is intact, we're naturally more comfortable asking for help when it's needed. The key is to ask before things spiral out of control. A good friend of mine jokes about how she once got incredibly flustered with computer issues and instead of asking her husband (who works in the technology field) for help, she kept going down rat holes trying to fix it herself until she finally yelled out in frustration, "I'm going to throw this @$!!# laptop out the @$!!# window!" This prompted her husband to come into her home office and jokingly say, "You know you could just say 'Hey Hon, could you give me a hand?' and I'd come in and help you, right?" They both had a good laugh about how silly she'd been, and after that, she went to him with her laptop issues *before* frustration got the best of her.

So how do we learn to ask for help in getting our needs met if it doesn't come easily to us? We practice! Talking our request out in our minds before approaching the person whose help we need will make the words come out much more smoothly. So will detaching our sense of self-worth from any negative reaction we might receive when we ask. Another trick is to step away from a situation in which our needs aren't being met and take a brief walk to clear our minds and figure out how best to broach the subject in a way that is comfortable and kind for both parties. If a walk isn't possible, even a few minutes alone in the bathroom or your car or the garage (or wherever you can have some quiet alone time to sort things out) will help.

Communicate to be Heard

We can usually tell when a need (or want) isn't getting met if we simply pay attention. We tend to feel uncomfortable and are likely experiencing social or interpersonal problems. Common signals are irritability, annoyance, or becoming argumentative. To ease this discomfort, it is imperative that we learn to voice our needs. Yet most of us don't know how to effectively communicate our needs to others so they can be heard. Because addressing these unmet needs can be difficult, many of us may opt for the path of least resistance – namely, not speaking up and just accepting that our needs aren't being met. Unfortunately, this can create more problems over time in the form of anxiety and depression. Too often, we dishonor ourselves by not seeking to get our needs met. Instead, our lives become, quite predictably, more unhappy, unhealthy, and less peaceful. Our relationships suffer as well.

We have the power to influence the outcome of our desires by fueling them with faith and belief. Faith is bigger than religion, it is unique to us all. Maintaining these mindsets also takes practice, and that practice begins with quiet reflection time to determine what needs and wants are going unfulfilled, as well as what needs and wants may have shifted. Some may have fallen by the wayside, while others may be entirely new to you. Practice checking in on what you need and want in life without asking for input from others. No one knows your genuine needs and wants like that small still voice within, though many people will happily offer their two cents. And their view will never be as accurate as your own. This approach goes hand in hand with the self-care habit of internal validation, so there's no need to have others approve of or bless your personal needs and wants.

Once you're clear on your needs and wants, communicating them in a purposeful way to the appropriate people is essential. Because communication is a developed skill, not an innate ability, it takes practice to refine our communication competency. This is an important skill to hone, especially for use in the workplace, where we must be careful about voicing our needs in a way that they can be heard, yet not create any political backlash. Dr. Lois Frankel offers some excellent techniques for this sort of purposeful communication in her book, *Nice Girls Don't Speak up or Stand Out*. Two of my favorites include:

- Speaking in Headlines: Give 1 main idea and 2-3 supporting points followed by a tagline.
- DESCript:
  - ✓ D = Describe the Purpose of the Conversation
  - ✓ E = Explain Your Position and Elicit Feedback from the Other Person
  - ✓ S = Specify Desired Outcomes
  - ✓ C = Clarify Consequences (Positive or Negative)

Another helpful communication technique revolves around speaking from our hearts. If you can T.H.I.N.K. before speaking, you'll likely increase the chances of communicating effectively and with heart. When using the T.H.I.N.K. technique, we ask ourselves: Is it **T**rue, **H**elpful, **I**nspiring, **N**ecessary, and **K**ind? T.H.I.N.K. is an excellent filter that allows us to quickly run communications through our hearts before the words leave our mouths. Using the T.H.I.N.K technique can mean the difference between communicating in a productive manner and just plain old nagging. Not every thought needs to be expressed, and the T.H.I.N.K. technique will help us prevent unnecessary conflict or thoughtlessness.

While speaking is an important element of effective communication, listening is equally – if not more – important. *Active listening* is especially helpful when it comes to voicing our needs. In a nutshell, active listening is a technique that is often used in coaching and counseling for clarification. It's also a useful tool to resolve disputes or conflicts. It requires the listener to work through four steps: (1) fully concentrate, (2) understand, (3) respond and (4) remember what was said. You can demonstrate that you were actively listening by repeating back what you thought you heard in your own words. Active listening is especially helpful if both parties in the discussion are versed in it to some degree. It's extremely valuable for addressing difficult or uncomfortable topics, such as our needs! Many of us would rather suffer than speak up about an unmet need we have, especially in our closest relationships. But remember, it goes both ways: a close friend or lover may also have unmet needs that they'll want to discuss. And if that's the case, we need to actively listen to them as well. A wise friend once told me that it's important to listen with the intention of hearing what you don't want to hear. And to that I say, "Hear, hear!"

Listening is definitely a two-way street. One important need you may have is to be heard. If you are in a relationship where someone else is doing all the talking and you are doing all the listening, it isn't a mutually beneficial conversation. Sure, there are times when one person may have more to say. If this is a regular pattern with someone, you may have to ask politely for a chance to speak or remind that person of the importance of giving you an opportunity to be heard. Hopefully, they are just as interested in hearing from you as they are in sharing their stories. Be sure to use the T.N.K or T.H.I.N.K filter for this conversation.

Voicing your needs in a manner that is clear, kind, and effective won't guarantee that all your needs will be met. However, it does increase your chances. Because, come on, how do unmet needs have a chance of being addressed if you're not even willing to voice them? Getting our needs and some of our wants met is vital to our mental health and to self-care. It can mean the difference between happiness and unhappiness, health or lack of health, peace of mind and chaos. We each have the choice to make, and I'm trusting that you'll make the right one.

Vanessa, Revisited

Let's revisit Vanessa's situation to see how she might have handled things differently. Vanessa and Vance have been dating for six months and they seem to be a great match. They love one another's company, enjoy a lot of the same activities, share similar values, and even attend the same church (which is where they met). One thing Vanessa is unclear about is how Vance feels about having children one day. For her, it's a deal-breaker. She wants to be a mother, wants to experience pregnancy and childbirth. Now that this relationship is clearly more than a few dates, Vanessa wants to honor herself by speaking her truth about this essential need in her life – namely, her lifelong desire to have a family.

She thinks through how she will express this need to Vance, even writing out her thoughts in advance so she doesn't forget anything. She also wants to make sure she communicates in a way that isn't demanding, but rather, kindly speaking her truth. She then tells Vance that she would like to speak to him about something that's extremely important to her, so they set a special date just for this purpose. After their discussion, it is clear that Vance and Vanessa have conflicting needs: she plans to have children, he plans to remain childless. Through many tears, they agree that it's best not to continue the relationship, knowing there is such a significant mismatch of needs. They part ways, heartbroken, but confident that they made the right decision. In time, Vanessa begins dating again. In no time at all, she finds herself in another committed relationship that feels as solid as she and Vance once had. Only this time, she lets her boyfriend know that she plans on starting a family one day and if children aren't in his plan, she will understand, and they can part ways amicably. She tells him she'd rather hear a painful truth than an agreeable lie. Her boyfriend laughs and lets her know that he too wants a family one day but was too afraid to scare her off by saying it earlier in their relationship. They both share a good laugh, as well as a sigh of relief. They continue dating, growing even closer over the following year, at which point they decide to get married. Today, Vanessa and her husband are the delighted parents of three children. What a difference voicing her needs made in Vanessa's life!

When we speak we are afraid our words will not be heard or welcomed. But when we are silent, we are still afraid. So it is better to speak.

— Audre Lorde

✿

Intention:

I communicate my needs in a thoughtful way.

Now, how about digging deeper? As a warm-up to this time for reflection, I suggest listening to "Brave" by Sarah Bareilles.

Invitation to Reflect:

What is one unmet need that you have not yet expressed in an important (romantic or platonic) relationship?

_____

_____

_____

_____

What is your concern about voicing that need?

_____

_____

_____

_____

Write out how you could ask for the need to be met using the T.H.I.N.K. filter.

_____

_____

_____

_____

Here are some actions you can take now for your self-care:

○ Use the _Universal Human Needs-Partial List_ in Appendix B to discover at least one unmet need.
○ Write out another message to someone about an unmet need using the T.H.I.N.K. filter.
○ Ask someone to help on at least one project that would allow them to use their unique expertise.

Commit to doing at least one thing differently based on what you've learned in this chapter. Write out an actionable goal – with a specific deadline – to satisfy this commitment.

_____

_____

_____

_____

How will you celebrate or reward yourself if you reach the goal?

_____

_____

Other thoughts and reflections:

_____

_____

_____

_____

_____

_____

_____

_____

For additional resources related to this topic, please check out my website: www.abcsofselfcare.com

W

WATCH YOUR WALLET

Too many people spend money they earned to buy things they don't want to impress people that they don't like.

— Will Rogers

❦

I don't often mention that I am a former CPA. It doesn't usually come up in conversation. The comment that inspired me to change careers was "You have too much personality to be an accountant." No truer words were spoken (with apologies to the many accountants out there with personality). It takes a lot of attention to detail and stellar spreadsheet skills to be a successful accountant, and I learned that I prefer to deal with people and their challenges rather than the challenge of numbers. Yet I'm still so grateful that I learned the language of business by studying accounting. While being an accountant ultimately wasn't my calling, I learned some valuable skills that have helped me to minimize financial stress.

Because it's hard to focus on connection, communication, and love when you are struggling to make ends meet, watching your wallet – and your overall financial health – is an important aspect of self-care. In addition to creating personal stress, financial hardships can also result in relationship stress. In fact, one study revealed that 41% of divorced GenXers and 29% of divorced Boomers say their marriages ended due to disagreements about money. Across all generations, another study showed that money fights are the second leading cause of divorce behind infidelity. Wow, right? Maybe money can't buy love, but it might just prevent the deterioration of an important long-term relationship! And maintaining healthy finances can also help keep the relationship you have with yourself on even ground. So again, if we're committed to self-care then we must also be committed to watching our wallets. This includes living within your means, monitoring your credit card balances, saving – especially for retirement and large purchases and even asking for help.

Wanda and Watching Her Wallet

Wanda is thrilled when she lands a new role on a sitcom picked up for 12 episodes with the possibility of a back 9. It's her first regular acting gig! She celebrates by buying a new car with all the upgrades – leather seats, sunroof, high-end sound system – even though it costs six times what she paid for her current car, which she'd bought used. She makes this purchase with an auto loan because she hasn't received her first paycheck yet, but no worries. She'll be rolling in the dough soon enough! Wanda then gives her old car to a friend who always claimed to have a soft spot for it. Who needs trade in value anyway when her career is taking off? Wanda lives a 45-minute drive, with traffic, from the CBS lot where the series will be filmed. She decides she'd like to be much closer. After all, there is almost always traffic in LA, she reasons. So, she starts investigating rental properties and finds an awesome place that's only ten minutes away! Plus, it's a *townhouse*, not some small apartment in a crowded complex. And it's twice the square footage, so she'll finally be able to set up that in-home gym she's always wanted.

She signs a new lease and orders both a NordicTrack treadmill and a Peloton stationary bike to be delivered the week she moves in. She writes a check for her first month's rent and security deposit, while putting the two pieces of pricey exercise equipment on a credit card. Wanda is in a rush on moving day, so she blows off cleaning the apartment she just vacated, also leaving behind several things in need of repair. She shrugs off the fact that she'll likely lose her $2500 security deposit because of this. But who cares? She's making more than she ever dreamed possible now! Next up: a new wardrobe. Sure, she has plenty of clothes, but Wanda is certain she will need cool, more fashionable styles to hang with her new Hollywood friends. If she's going to be a successful actress, she needs to look the part, she tells herself, plopping another credit card down at Nordstrom, spending $1400 in less than 2 hours. She is also in need of additional furniture to fill the townhouse, so she shops online, applying for store credit cards as she goes, easily approved because of her new income.

Wanda's new role keeps her busy, often working late on the set. So, of course, grocery shopping and cooking at home fall by the wayside. She could eat more at craft services; however, the food isn't healthy or filling. Instead, Wanda typically orders take-out on her drive home from work. Her favorites are sushi and, well, more sushi. Sure, it's pricier than making soup or a salad at home, but hey – she's earned it. And the best accompaniment to sushi? A nice high-end sake, of course.

The credit card bills start rolling in and Wanda realizes she can't cover the full balances, so she pays the minimum amount due. When she applies for yet another credit card, she is declined for carrying too much credit card debt. This motivates Wanda to sit down one weekend and review her regular monthly expenses, as well as all of her "one-time" charges. She is sincerely shocked when she realizes she has been spending more than her new income can possibly cover. Gulp! That 10% fee to her agent was not part of the plan. As interest charges on her credit cards start spiraling out of control, Wanda calls both NordicTrack and Peloton to return the pricey items, but she learns that both are past their return date. She calls the car dealership to see about swapping her high-end vehicle for a more affordable model, only to learn how much her new car's value dropped the minute she drove it off the lot. Pretty soon, she must choose between buying food or paying the minimum amounts on her credit cards, so she chooses food. Phone calls from the creditors start coming in and Wanda is so stressed she stops answering her phone altogether. Despite doubling her income, Wanda did not watch her wallet at all...and now she finds herself with a negative net worth and a credit score that continues to drop each month. The shame of it all keeps her from seeking help from those with greater financial management skills, so this downward cycle continues. At the rate she's going, if Wanda doesn't change her ways drastically, she'll be barreling toward bankruptcy in no time.

Quick Check - Select all that apply:

- ☐ I often feel I can't afford the things I want.
- ☐ I have no idea how much money I have left over each month after my bills are paid.
- ☐ If my car, or another major asset, needs unexpected repairs or if I incur an unexpected major medical bill, I would be financially devastated.

Know Your Relationship with Money

Before we can change behaviors and develop new habits with money, or anything else, we may have to examine our mindset (emotions, beliefs, and values) about it. The way we think about money could impact many areas of our lives. For example, if we have an abundance mentality, we likely believe there is enough money for ourselves and everyone else in general; we can have more if we choose; we can readily accept gifts of money and easily spend it or give it away. A scarcity mentality, on the other hand, leaves us thinking we need more money, no matter what our bank account balance may be. Also, if others have more money than us, we're doing something wrong; there is not enough money to go around. These two opposing mindsets apply to a lot more than simply money. They also apply to other "resources" we have at our disposal, such as time, information, expertise, kindness, food, etc. Take a minute to read through the chart below and see which mindset is more in line with how you view your own resources. Which mindset do you suppose is more helpful in creating even more in the way of financial health?

Scarcity Mindset	Abundance Mindset
There is never enough money for these bills.	There is more money where that came from.
I am entitled to everything I have.	I am grateful for everything I have.
I can't afford (fill in the blank).	I am capable of saving for (fill in the blank).
I need to withhold this info because someone else might benefit from it.	I share this information so my colleagues and clients can also benefit from it.
I must promote myself and my accomplishments to stand out.	I can promote myself and others because we all make unique contributions.
I don't think I can do that; it's too risky.	I can accomplish what I set my mind to.
I am afraid of (fill in the blank).	I have faith that (fill in the blank).
I must hoard my money; after all, it doesn't grow on trees.	I can be generous and share my money because I can always attract more.

How we were raised has an impact on our views about money. Yes, we get emotionally "wounded" in childhood in many ways, even though our parents likely did the best they could. If we were repeatedly told we couldn't do something when we were younger – for example, play sports well or comprehend math – we may feel inadequate in that area as adults. If we couldn't afford certain things as children – for example, a trip to the candy store after school or the senior class trip – as adults, we could feel like what we want is out of the realm of possibility.

I didn't realize that I came from a low-income household until I was a senior in high school, and the yearbook, class ring and graduation gear were beyond my family's budget. Thankfully, my mom was a good fundraiser and found relatives more than willing to help pay for them. However, I still remember the shame I felt from her not being able to simply write a check like most of the other parents. I am so proud of her, though, for stepping up and working outside the home, which was unusual for women of her generation, when my dad was unable to consistently support the family with his many business ventures. She chose to separate from him and make it on her own – with occasional help from my grandparents. I so admired her bravery and perseverance in taking care of four girls alone, on minimum wage, and with no help from social services. At the same time, she accomplished all of this without ever making us feel poor.

Many of our beliefs about money, helpful or unhelpful, come to us because of observing how our parents or other primary caregivers handled finances when we were young. Were they stressed and tight-fisted? Comfortable and generous? Always late paying the rent? Able to support charitable causes? Look back at your own childhood. Did financial stresses within your family get passed down to you? Stress, angst, and fears about money in our adult lives are likely the result of our early experiences with the financial aspects of life. Regardless, if we want to beef up our financial abundance, we must consciously change our mindset about money to attract more of it into our lives.

Like it or not, money is a reality of this physical life on earth. We all need it to secure our basic needs: food, shelter, utilities, clothing, etc. In other words, we need money to survive. If we don't feel deserving enough or smart enough or capable enough to generate the financial resources to cover our needs, that mindset will absolutely affect our ability to achieve what we need and want in life. Part of "watching our wallets" is watching what we say to ourselves regarding money and our worthiness regarding money. Some of the most common things we tell ourselves that set us up for financial hardship are:

- *I'll never be able to start a retirement account.*
- *This mortgage is killing me!*
- *Where does my paycheck go? It seems to have evaporated into thin air...again!*
- *These credit card charges are killing me.*
- *I can't ever seem to catch a break.*

Learning to replace these sorts of self-defeating statements with more supportive ones will go a long way in helping us break the scarcity mindset we may have inherited from childhood or adopted over the years. It's helpful to state these in the present tense, as if they're already true, for our minds to believe them – which, in turn, increases the likelihood that they *will* become true.

- *I now have a growing retirement account.*
- *My mortgage is manageable and allows me to live in this house that I love.*
- *My paychecks continue to increase over time and always cover my needs.*
- *It's nice to have these credit cards; I don't need them though.*
- *My financial resources are always expanding, and I have more than enough.*

Speaking to ourselves in ways that promote an abundance mindset does not mean behaving impulsively and purchasing things that are currently beyond our means. It means filling our minds with the types of beliefs that support and influence our ability to create more income. Remember, the more we have, the more we can share with others.

Track Your Net Worth

Please don't let your eyes glaze over at the words "net worth" because this will not be an extensive lesson in accounting. Promise. The idea here is to make our lives easier and reduce stress by understanding a few key concepts and keeping a closer eye on our finances. One of the most basic accounting formulas is: Assets – Liabilities = Net Worth.

When you have more assets (homes, cars, cash in the bank, things you can liquidate for cash) than liabilities (credit card debt, mortgages, loans, other money you owe) you have a *positive net worth* or *positive financial position*. This is good. On the contrary, if you have more liabilities than assets, you have a negative net worth. Meaning, you *owe* more than you *own*. Not good. By tracking your net worth, you know if you can handle an unforeseen financial crisis – with savings or by selling assets to stay afloat. Some outwardly wealthy people are underwater financially because they have more liabilities than assets. This is not a good situation for anyone to be in. Imagine the stress of trying to "keep up appearances" within one's social circles while, inside, feeling like a failure and knowing the truth about our net worth. It's no fun to be drowning in debt, as some of us know personally, having been there at some point in our lives. Wealth, in its most honest form, comes down to having a positive net worth.

We can make our money work for us by investing in assets that create wealth and financial freedom. (I recommend Robert Kiyosaki's *Rich Dad Poor Dad* book series and CASHFLOW ® games for understanding these concepts more in-depth.) Ideally you want to invest in assets that appreciate and/or produce income. So, if most of your assets are clothes and shoes, you may need to diversify your "portfolio" a bit, as clothing cannot be liquidated for cash in an emergency as easily as, say, stocks or real estate.

Your home is a good asset if the appreciation value is greater than the cost of ownership. That is why the famous phrase "location, location, location" is so important. Using the formula above, if your house is worth $500,000 and you owe $450,000 and the cost to operate it (with taxes, repairs, etc.) is $60,000, then it is technically *not* an *asset*. It's a *liability* due to its negative net worth. A rental property, on the other hand, could be an asset if the rental produces income that exceeds the cost of financing and operating it. Bottomline: you want to invest more in assets that provide income and increase your "assets column". At the same time, you want to reduce your liabilities and expenses, to decrease that side of the equation. Basic stuff, right? Yet as of 2017, one in five U.S. households had a negative net worth. Ouch!

Increase Cash Flow

Another basic formula for all of us to understand and embrace is this: Income – Expenses = Net Income. Income may include paychecks, pension benefits, child support, royalties, and interest on savings. Expenses include rent or mortgage payments, utilities, groceries, insurance, and other bills. And net income, or *cash flow*, is money we could be saving or investing. It's natural to want to increase income and reduce expenses, right? So, let's get to it!

Here are some ways we can increase income:

- Get a side job.
- Work overtime.
- Request a raise or promotion.
- Put working-age children to work.
- Require rent payments from adult children who still live with you.

And here are some ways to decrease expenses:

- Avoid loans of any kind.
- Put off big purchases until you can pay cash.
- Avoid using credit cards; stick with a debit card.
- Eat at home more often.
- Shop at thrift stores or online sites like Craigslist.
- Use coupons and comparison shop to find deals.
- Negotiate credit card interest rates.

Save for a Rainy Day

Many people get themselves into a financial pickle because they don't have enough savings to cover unexpected costs associated with emergencies. Increasing net income will give us more opportunities to save. Some financial experts say we need to reserve between 3 and 12 months of our regular operating expenses in savings for an inevitable emergency. It's especially important to create this sort of financial cushion with our savings if we have fewer income sources, our income fluctuates, or our income is not secure or consistent. Perhaps it's called a "cushion" because it allows us to sleep better at night.

Making savings a priority can decrease stress levels, both personally and within our key relationships. Particularly, when the car breaks down or an unexpected medical situation occurs. Other ways you can protect yourself from financial ruin and enhance your ability to save include:

- Working on the communication, love, and connection in your marriage...because divorce is costly. (Note to self.)

- Get and maintain health insurance coverage, as medical bills are a major source of financial debt.
- Get and maintain other forms of insurance such as auto, rental/homeowners, and long-term care, as the challenges associated with these can be costly if not covered.
- Turn to our greater communities and allow others to help us financially, through devastating emergencies, such as the death or serious illness of a loved one. Online fundraising campaigns can be an effective means of doing this, while also giving others the gift of helping someone they care about – you.
- Don't seek personal loans from (or provide them to) friends and family for anything less than an unforeseen cost tied to an emergency. Can't afford groceries this month because you got laid off during the pandemic? Yes. New PlayStation 5 because you love gaming, and you want the latest console? No! Absolutely not, in fact. And if you can help someone you love who has a genuine emergency need for a loan, I recommend just giving them the money. A financial gift will generate much less stress in that relationship than the unspoken angst of an unpaid loan.

Monitor Your Accounts

Staying on top of what goes into both our asset column (banking and investments) as well as liability column (credit cards and loans) is important for our credit score *and* our sanity. I once saw my credit score dip dangerously low because of an unpaid $5 transaction! I had charged business expenses on a seldom-used personal credit card and paid the bill in full after receiving the reimbursement check from my company. Or so I thought. Apparently, the hotel later charged my credit card $5 for a bottle of water (yes, *one* stinking bottle!) without me realizing it. I was then charged late fees by the bank until I had a balance of $43 on a card that I rarely monitored due to lack of use. The bank eventually closed that account, but not before reporting it as being three-months past due to the credit-scoring bureaus. I didn't learn of this unpaid balance and account closure until my credit score went down. And although all my other cards were paid on time via automatic withdrawals, it didn't prevent my credit score from dropping, which led to some of my active credit accounts having their limits lowered or closed. Lesson learned! I now monitor all my accounts regularly, by receiving text and email notifications of payments and activity on each of my credit cards. I also downloaded apps to stay on top of my credit score, as well as my asset and liability accounts. Finally, and perhaps most importantly, I forgave myself for not being on top of my accounts earlier. The peace of mind I have now about my finances is invaluable.

Get Help

I can't recommend enough that everyone enlist the aid of a financial advisor that you respect and trust to help protect and grow your assets. The best financial advice I've ever received has come from two folks in particular: a longtime friend, and Suze Orman, a well-known financial expert (who I don't know personally). Suze's *5-Step Financial Action Plan* may be challenging and take years to accomplish (I'm still working on a couple of the steps myself), but it will take us far in preventing the stress associated with a negative net worth.

Suze Orman's 5-Step Financial Action Plan:

- Step 1: Pay Off Your Credit Card Debt. Suze says the number one thing people lie about is how much credit card debt they have.
- Step 2: Raise Your FICO Score.
- Step 3: Create a Spending Action Plan.
- Step 4: Create a Savings Action Plan.
- Step 5: Create a Retirement Action Plan.

One of the best self-care steps we can take is getting our financial house in order. We will automatically reduce our stress and avoid unnecessary anxiety. We may also have more fun because we can save for and fund *experiences* that offer lifelong memories, such as traveling to interesting places or to visit with old friends. (And while we're talking about traveling, did you know you can use a vacation planner, who puts together trips for groups, and allows you to pay for the future trip in monthly installments?) Regardless of how each of us chooses to use our newfound financial freedom, watching our wallets is a sure-fire way to greater peace and happiness overall.

Wanda, Revisited

One of the biggest mistakes people make with their money is spending it before they actually have it. Wanda is a classic example of spending based on potentiality vs. reality. Let's see how watching her wallet may've helped Wanda avoid the financial predicament she put herself in. Wanda receives and accepts the new acting role, which thrills her. She celebrates by buying a decent bottle of wine and inviting a friend to her apartment for dinner. Having grown up in a family that struggled to pay its bills, Wanda has vowed never to put herself in that situation as an adult. She will do whatever it takes to live within her means. She would prefer a shorter commute to work, but, after surveying the available housing options closer to the CBS lot, Wanda decides to stay put. After all, her landlord has always been fair and kept rental increases minimal. Why move just to save 35 minutes a day? She does, however, need more reliable transportation. So, she comparison-shops with three different car dealerships to trade-in her vehicle and use the payout as a down payment toward a newer used car — nothing too fancy, just something safe and reliable. By using good negotiation skills, Wanda gets a great trade-in value and a low-interest-rate monthly payment on her new car that she can easily cover.

Wanda tracks her expenses each month and is happy to see that she has money left over each pay period that she can tuck away towards buying a house one day. She maxes out her contribution to the union's 401k program (maximizing the match by her employer) and puts the rest of her cash flow into a high-yield savings account. Even though she's tempted to eat out more now that she's making a nice living, Wanda chooses instead to make saving money more enjoyable! She tries new approaches, like cooking meals for the entire week on Sunday, leaving her weeknights free, or challenging herself to cook and eat more vegetables for a month. She is giddy when she sees how much more she's able to save this way! After all, the show may not be renewed for a third season. Still, within two years, Wanda had amassed enough savings to buy her first condo. She is even ok with not being able to afford a single-family home yet, even though her family in Iowa keeps reminding her of this fact. She has learned all she can about mortgages and found a trustworthy broker to assist her in locking in a great deal — with the help of her stellar credit history, of course! Wanda has clearly learned the value of watching her wallet and is in a good position to weather any financial storms that come her way. Well done, Wanda!

I had to make my own living and my own opportunity. But I made it! Don't sit down and wait for the opportunities to come. Get up and make them.

— Madam CJ Walker

❧

Intention:

I deserve abundance and am a good custodian of my wealth.

Now, how about digging deeper? As a warm-up to this time for reflection, I suggest listening to "Money is Coming to Me" by Eddie Watkins, Jr.

Invitation to Reflect:

What limiting beliefs do you have about money that keep you from attracting more abundance?

_____

_____

_____

_____

What is the source of these limiting beliefs?

_____

_____

_____

_____

What can you do differently to achieve the material success and personal fulfillment you've always wanted? Think of things that could increase net worth, cash flow or savings.

_____

_____

_____

Here are some actions you could take now for your self-care:

- ○ Track all your expenses for one full week. Write them in your calendar or in an online note. Or cancel a monthly subscription you currently use infrequently.
- ○ Set at least one specific financial goal for the next month/year/five years.
- ○ Call your financial advisor (or find one if you don't already have one) for an appointment today or add it to your calendar.

Commit to doing at least one thing differently based on what you learned in this chapter. Write out an actionable goal – with a specific deadline – to satisfy this commitment.

_____

_____

_____

_____

How will you celebrate or reward yourself if you reach the goal?

_____

_____

Other thoughts and reflections:

_____

_____

_____

_____

_____

For additional resources related to this topic, please check out my website: www.abcsofselfcare.com

X

XOXO - KISS (X) AND HUG (O) OFTEN

I have learned that there is more power in a good strong hug than in a thousand meaningful words.

— Ann Hood

❁

Like being without food, water, sleep, and oxygen, lack of affection can also have an adverse impact on our health, both physically and emotionally. Sometimes referred to as "skin hunger," the lack of affection often goes hand in hand with people who are less happy, more lonely, more likely to experience mood or anxiety disorders, and less physically healthy overall. A researcher in this area, Dr. Kory Floyd, focused her research on the communication of affection in personal relationships. And while her study doesn't definitively point to a lack of affection as the *cause* of these ailments, the correlation is undeniable. Affection is good for the soul and is therefore an important aspect of any self-care lifestyle. Hugs and kisses are not only good for our relationships, but they can also relieve stress, anxiety, and pain, while also lowering blood pressure. They are calming when we've just heard bad news. They can even help us lose weight. (Sold!) The science is clear: affection, physical intimacy and authentic emotional connections provide tremendous health and psychological benefits. So, illness and pandemics aside, we should all ramp up our level of consensual hugging and kissing!

Xena and XOXOs

Xena grew up in the foster-care system, living in three different homes during her childhood. One of her former foster parents was very affectionate. The others all seemed to be too busy or stressed to pay attention to things such as a bedtime hug or a hello kiss when she returned from school each day. Xena often found herself retreating into books and stories to cope with the loneliness of being a foster child. At 18, she went away to school, earned her degree, and began her professional life. At 26 years old, Xena entered her first serious relationship.

At first, everything about it felt wonderful and exciting. But soon after moving in together, after a year of dating, Xena found herself pulling back a bit, even ducking away from situations that would usually elicit a hug or a kiss from her boyfriend. She also found herself losing interest in their sex life and began blaming headaches or fatigue for her lack of desire. She wasn't sure why she had lost all interest in sex and affection with her boyfriend, but she assumed it was normal. After all, she'd never been in a serious relationship before, and she'd heard from other couples that the "thrill" decreased over time. She knew that she loved her boyfriend, although found herself unable to express it physically. When her beloved asks her what's up, she pretends not to understand what he's talking about. After a few unsuccessful attempts to gently engage her in a conversation about their physical relationship, he gives up. Ultimately, the lack of affection, and likely sex as well, led to the breakup. Xena was crushed. She swore off dating to avoid ever having to feel this level of heartbreak again.

Ten years after the decline of her first and only serious relationship, Xena still looks up her ex on social media and thinks of him with tears in her eyes. When photos of his wedding are posted, she feels the same level of heartache she felt when they broke up a decade earlier. Xena has no idea how to shift her predicament. She assumes she is just another broken person, unable to love and, more tragically, unlovable.

Quick Check - Select all that apply:

☐ I find myself often withdrawing affection when I'm angry.
☐ I often find myself emotionally closing off from people.
☐ I am not used to exhibiting affection in my family.

Feed the Need

Hugs, kisses, and affection in general aren't simply good for us, they're necessary to our well-being. Hugging and kissing make us feel more loving and more likely to smile. And guess what? Smiling has healing properties as well! It is a simple mood-enhancing activity that helps our bodies emit more cortisol and endorphins, which are also known to create increased feelings of joy, euphoria, and general well-being. Smiling and affection are two free and simple ways to strengthen our immune systems. Do we really need more reasons than that to include a healthy dose of smiling and affection in our daily lives?

If we aren't getting enough kisses and hugs at home, or in our primary relationships, it might be time to figure out what we need to do to fix this (without accosting strangers – that's just creepy and wrong). Could we simply initiate more hugs? Ask for them? Have a heart to heart with our partner or love interest about our needs? Sometimes it's a matter of differing needs that aren't necessarily mutually exclusive. For example, some people may need greater levels of physical intimacy. Being rejected hurts deeply, which in turn strains the emotional connection they feel to their partner. Others may be just the opposite, needing a greater emotional connection before their physical desires kick in. It's a conversation worth having with your partner to reap the overall physical and psychological benefits of human touch.

Some psychological research indicates that physical or emotional withdrawal can be a way we cope with past hurts or offenses, either from within our current relationship or from previous ones. Left unaddressed, resentment can fester and create a chasm between us and our partners. And that's not healthy for anyone involved. One way to address this sort of distancing behavior when we recognize it is to implement the power of AAA (No, not an auto service that comes to your home to jumpstart your affection). Be Aware that there is low affection or physical distancing in your relationship, Accept the way things are, and then Act to change it – even if that means seeking out professional help through couple's counseling. If infidelity is the reason affection is being withheld, then I strongly recommend professional intervention, as that is a much larger issue that is beyond the scope of this book. The need for affection is undeniable, so we must do what is necessary to maintain a healthy level of kissing (X) and hugging (O).

A lack of affection in childhood can have long term detrimental effects, including developmental and social relatability issues. Research from numerous universities, such as UCLA and Notre Dame, shows the innate need children have to receive warmth and affection from their parents or primary caregivers. Children who did not have affectionate parents tend to develop lower self-esteem and behave in ways that reflect alienation, hostility, or aggression. On the contrary, children who grew up with healthy doses of affection at home tend to have higher self-esteem, strong academic performance, strong communication with their parents, and fewer psychological and behavioral issues. So, while kids need an abundance of affection, giving it to them is a mutually beneficial endeavor. And there's nothing quite as lovely as getting a big hug from a child, so it's a win-win!

What do we do when we don't have a child or partner at home to offer us affection on a regular basis? We offer it to ourselves! I've been known to walk around my home giving myself a good hug while proclaiming, "I love myself; I love myself; I love myself." Okay, so I wouldn't want a neighbor to walk in on me while I do this but trust me – it works! Not only does it reinforce the self-love we should each be feeling for ourselves, but it also feels really good. Hugging is so important to our overall well-being that there are actually professional cuddlers out there. Imagine earning money to offer platonic hugs and cuddles to clients! And if self-hugs or professional cuddlers aren't your thing, you can at least do yourself a favor and buy a body pillow or weighted blanket to feel hugged.

Know What No Means

Of course, all touching is not good touching. There are often employee guidelines to protect us from sexual harassment and misconduct in the workplace. It's important to understand what these guidelines are so we do not fall victim to unwanted advances, and also so we keep our own behaviors in check. Schools have strict protocols as well, which serve to protect kids from inappropriate touching. "Side hugs" are one such protocol. Different cultures have different norms regarding affection. For example, in many European cultures it is not only acceptable, but expected, to kiss others, strangers included. In other cultures, this could be perceived as inappropriately invading someone's personal space. Given these cultural differences, it's always best to ask or observe what is appropriate before initiating affection.

The important thing to keep in mind with all affection is that there are boundaries, both personal and organizational, that must be respected. Hug and kiss often, but do so with consent, respect, and propriety in mind. But if you get the green light, move in for a big ole bear hug!

Xena, Revisited

Let's return to the situation of Xena in her first serious, intimate relationship. How might she have addressed her withdrawal from affection with her partner? Here's how: Xena realizes she is losing interest in having sex with her boyfriend and finds herself frequently ducking away from his attempts to give her a hug or even a quick kiss on the cheek. When he asks her, for the third time, why she seems to have lost interest in him, she bursts into tears. "I don't know," she confesses. "It's not that I love you any less. I just feel like I've lost all physical desire and I don't understand why. Am I just broken?" When her boyfriend pulls her in for a comforting hug, she allows him to. And when he gently suggests that they see a professional counselor together, she reluctantly agrees. At their first counseling session, Xena learns that children who lacked affection in childhood are likely to exhibit this sort of withdrawing behavior as adults. She had no idea! She probes the counselor for more information, and by the end of their session, Xena has a referral to a respected psychologist who specializes in working with adults who grew up without a strong or loving parental relationship. Bolstered by the understanding that she is not "broken" or unloving, Xena begins a journey to repair the missing elements of her childhood. As she does so, her ability to reconnect physically with her boyfriend increases. Ultimately, Xena can fully reengage in both her sex life and day to day affection. Whether or not her current relationship will go the distance remains to be seen, but Xena no longer feels the need to withdraw from her boyfriend. She is emotionally and physically *in*...and it shows.

A kiss without a hug is like a flower without the fragrance.

— Proverb

221

Intention:

I make real connections and get my kisses and hugs often.

Now, how about digging deeper? As a warm-up to this time for reflection, I suggest listening to "XOXOXO" by Black Eyed Peas.

Invitation to Reflect:

How could you get more physical touch, especially kisses and hugs, in your life?

_____

_____

_____

_____

Who in your life could use more kisses and hugs? What can you do about it?

_____

_____

_____

If applicable, what makes you withdraw physically from someone important in your life? Can you identify your triggers?

_____

_____

_____

Here are some actions you could take now for your self-care:

○ Hug yourself right now and say, "I love me" 3 times and/or ask for a hug and kiss from a loved one.
○ Go to a church or group event of compassionate people, where hugging is encouraged.
○ Think of someone who could use a hug and provide one in the near future.

Commit to doing at least one thing differently based on what you learned in this chapter. Write out an actionable goal – with a specific deadline – to satisfy this commitment.

_____

_____

_____

_____

How will you celebrate or reward yourself if you reach the goal?

_____

_____

Other thoughts and reflections:

_____

_____

_____

_____

_____

For additional resources related to this topic, please check out my website: www.abcsofselfcare.com

𝒴

YIELD TO POSITIVE PERSPECTIVES

A positive attitude is a person's best weapon to survive in today's increasingly complex world.

— Elwood Chapman

❧

Okay, all you self-proclaimed "realists" out there – this one's for you. By definition, a realist is someone who accepts a situation as it is and is prepared to deal with it accordingly. Sounds good, right? But how many of us who say we're "just being realistic" are actually leaning toward a negative perspective before it's even close to being clear what the outcome of a particular situation will be? Or is it possible that we're so afraid of being labeled a Pollyanna that we err in the opposite direction? Seeking and yielding to the most positive perspective of anything in our lives isn't about losing touch with reality. It's about knowing that most situations contain both positive and negative aspects, and consciously choosing the more positive view. Even the most awful circumstances often contain a silver lining.

Let's be clear – this isn't about ignoring or denying the deep grief of life's truly heartbreaking experiences. Nor is it about condoning the horrific or criminal actions of others. It's about a nuance of how we choose to interpret various experiences, situations, and circumstances in our everyday lives. When faced with the choice to take a negative perspective or positive perspective in life, we should yield to the positive one as much as possible. We all know a Grumpy Gus when we encounter them, and we also know when we ourselves have been that person. It's no fun for either, is it?

Yolanda and Yielding to Positive Perspectives

Yolanda has been saving for years to buy her own home and finally has enough for a down payment. When she launches her home-buying effort, she learns that the area she's looking in is extremely competitive. Homes that go on the market often have multiple offers on the first day. Discouraged, Yolanda is certain she'll never be able to compete with other home buyers. When her realtor finds several listings that meet Yolanda's requirements, she is thrilled. After visiting all three properties, she chooses to put in an offer on one of them. "The market's so tight, I'll bet I don't get it," she confesses to her realtor. "Let's not get ahead of ourselves," her realtor replies. "If it's meant to be, I'm sure it'll all work out. And if it doesn't, that just means there's something better out there for you!" *Oh great,* Yolanda thinks to herself. *I've got one of those kooky "new agey" folks for a realtor.*

Despite offering close to full price, two days later Yolanda learns that she was slightly outbid by another buyer and the seller took the higher offer. *Of course, they did!* she thinks, bitterly. *Everyone's only about the money these days.* The following week, Yolanda's realtor calls her, bubbling with excitement. Another home came on the market, and it seems to fit Yolanda's requirements even more than the previous home. Yolanda doubts that yet agrees to see the home anyway. She is delightfully surprised when she walks through the property and realizes it *is* better for her than the other one. When Yolanda says she'd like to make an offer, her realtor suggests that Yolanda write a letter to the seller, sharing the reasons she loves this house. Yolanda declines. "It's just a money game, nothing more," she tells the realtor. Her offer is submitted without a letter.

Again, Yolanda learns that the seller chose to accept someone else's offer. When she learns that the accepted offer was lower than hers, Yolanda loses her cool. "How could you mess this up for me?" she barks at her realtor. "No one is stupid enough to agree to less money!" "Actually," her realtor sheepishly replies, "sellers do that more often than you'd think. In this case, the other offer came from a family, who apparently wrote a sweet letter about how much their children would love living in this home. Sellers often respond to that sort of personal touch." *Bull!* Yolanda thinks. *This realtor is just not good.* Yolanda ends her professional relationship with the realtor and begins searching for homes on her own. Obviously, realtors are just not competent enough to get the job done. A year later, Yolanda is still unable to close on a home. She finally gives up, telling herself that people are idiots and home buying is a bigger hassle than it's worth. The whole experience has left her with a bad taste in her mouth and it will be years before she attempts to become a homeowner again.

Quick Check - Select all that apply:

- ☐ I consider myself a realist.
- ☐ I often shame, blame, or criticize myself and/or others.
- ☐ I often imagine the worst possible thing happening.

Commit to Positive Thinking

As you might imagine, the more positive thinking and positive self-talk we incorporate into our lives, the greater our chances of maintaining positive perspectives. Negative thinking and negative self-talk, on the other hand, lead to an increase in negative perspectives. It's fine to be a realist, so long as we're not using that characterization as a mask for being a "glass half empty" type of person. There *is* a difference. If we find ourselves caught in a loop of viewing the small everyday inconveniences or undesired outcomes negatively, we might want to ask ourselves the question Dr. Phil often asks those on his show who are stuck in a bad habit: *How's that working for you?* If we're honest with ourselves, most of us would admit that we dislike viewing our lives so negatively, dragging all that worry around with us, and having people avoid us because our pessimism is discouraging. On top of the icky feeling it gives us, going through life with a negative perspective as our default mode also tends to create more negative outcomes. It may even draw more pessimistic people into our lives. Like attracts like. What you *expect* to get is often what you end up getting. So why on earth wouldn't we all want to develop the habit of cultivating the most positive outlook possible?

As we discussed earlier in this book, we're only capable of holding *one* thought in our minds at any given moment. So, one of the tricks to developing a more positive perspective is to really monitor our thoughts; and the minute we feel a pessimistic one creeping in, change it. Retrain your brain! For example, when you got to this chapter, you might have thought, *this hippy-dippy positive thinking stuff isn't for me.* Instead, perhaps you could replace that thought with, *I'm open to a different perspective and will consider incorporating this idea into my life.* Sounds a bit more optimistic, no?

Trading negative perspectives for positive ones is an effective strategy for building a consistently good attitude. And a good attitude tends to attract people to us rather than repel them. Elwood Chapman, an expert on the subject of positive attitude, defines "attitude" *as the way we mentally look at things.* We've likely all seen the difference in our own lives when we go through our days with a positive attitude vs. a negative one. Our successes and desired outcomes seem to fall into place more easily, we feel a sense of flow in our lives, people respond to us more favorably, and we tend to be happier and more at peace.

Hypnotherapist and success coach, Ted Moreno, often reminds his clients that "we are six inches away from our success, so we have to change our mindset and where we are placing our attention." You may have heard the legend of the Two Wolves, which likely originated in Native American culture. In this story, a grandfather uses the metaphor of two wolves fighting within him to explain his inner conflict to his grandson. The grandson then asks, "Which one wins?" His grandfather replies, "Whichever one I feed." The same is true for our perspective on life – we've got our inner pessimist wolf and our inner optimist wolf. It's important to be aware of which one we're always feeding. Because, whether we're aware of it or not, we *are* feeding one of them at any given moment, with every thought we tell ourselves. Another way to view these two opposing inner voices is to view them as a positive versus a negative inner critic. Your positive inner critic acts as a helpful, rational guide. It's your intuition if you will. Your negative inner critic is likely parroting unhelpful feedback you received in life that you've internalized with repetition. This critic is, weirdly, trying to keep you safe by preventing you from taking risks. But this is a classic case of good intentions gone awry. *You shouldn't try rollerblading; you're too clumsy, you'll look foolish.* Or...*The men you date always leave, so why put your heart out there only to be broken?* Or...*You never seem to catch a break, so don't even bother going for that promotion.* If you have an inner critic that feeds you this sort of negative stuff, you need to shift your focus to feeding that other "wolf" asap!

So, how do we feed the positive wolf? One way is through affirmations, which give us a simple way to feed our optimism and positive outlook. Speak the affirmation with conviction, as if it is already true. Then take appropriate action to curb negative thinking. Consider the ones at the end of this chapter. It's better to come up with your own, but here are some powerful ones to get you started:

- I have the power to control my thoughts.
- I am optimistic.
- I give others the benefit of the doubt.
- I assume positive intent in others.
- I have released all negativity from my life.
- I welcome positivity.
- I let go of doubt and fear.
- I am the best version of myself.
- I choose to be happy.
- I have positive people and situations in my life.
- I am a magnet for positivity, abundance, and joy.
- I see the good in others.
- I have success into my life.
- Everything happens for my highest good.

One of my favorite singers, Karen Drucker, sings her affirmations. She believes that if we say our affirmations, they speak to our heads, and if we *sing* our them, they speak to our hearts. I put her songs on repeat to use as my own affirmations. Works like a charm!

Resist the Negativity Bias

The *negativity bias*, also known as the negativity effect, is the innate human tendency to give more importance to negative experiences in our lives than to positive or neutral experiences.

It means we have a built-in proclivity to respond more to negative information than to positive information. If that weren't challenging enough, some research reveals that negative emotions have three times the impact of positive ones. Yikes!

The origin of the negativity bias is thought to be an adaptive element of our human evolution that came about thousands of years ago when our ancestors were subject to numerous environmental threats, like, say, being eaten by a giant hyena or a cave bear. It's unlikely that we'll encounter this sort of predator, outside of Alaska, but the bias remains as part of our internal wiring. Allowing the negativity bias to run rampant in our lives sets us up for all sorts of psychological challenges, so it's extremely important to be on the lookout for this tendency and to squash it like a bug!

One of the most common forms of allowing our negativity bias to run the show is in the simple language many of us use daily. If you often say things like *I have to interface with clients all day.* Or...*I have to go to the gym and workout.* Or...*I have to take my kid to the park;* may I suggest one small verbal change – from "have to" to "get to." *I get to interface with clients all day. I get to go to the gym and workout. I get to take my kid to the park.* Notice the attitude of gratitude? See the difference that makes? Small changes, made consistently, will keep the negativity bias in check.

Another technique for shifting away from negativity bias comes to us from author Gabby Bernstein, who recommends the Choose Again Method. Here's how it works:

1. Notice a fearful or negative thought and how that thought makes you feel.
2. Forgive yourself for having that thought.
3. Choose again by reaching for the next best thought, one that you can believe.

Sound simple? Well guess what? It's also a powerful tool for positively impacting our nervous system, while breaking a bad habit *and* feeding the positive perspective within us. An example that comes to mind in my own life has to do with business travel. Here's how I'd apply the Choose Again Method:

1. Grrr, I always lose things when I travel! This makes me feel like a scatterbrain.
2. I forgive myself for thinking I'm a scatterbrain. Besides, they're just *things*.
3. I am perfectly capable of keeping track of my things when I travel. Besides, I should treat myself to a new toothbrush anyway!

Someone who used this method for much more distant travel is astronaut Christina Koch. She spent 11 months cooped up in a small compartment in space, sometimes thinking to herself, *I wish I could have a latte right now.* Rather than obsess over her lack of fancy coffee access, Christina said she learned to immediately replace that sort of unproductive thought with one such as, *I'm experiencing an opportunity you can only have when you're in space.* That was a surefire way to shift her perspective from the negativity of dwelling on unattainable things to the positive perspective of enjoying the unique opportunity of space flight.

Shift Your Perspective

Now that we're (hopefully) convinced that a positive perspective is far better than a negative one, it's time to figure out which methods are most effective for shifting to a positive perspective when it seems to elude us. Here are a few techniques to practice:

- **Mindfulness**. We already covered this topic earlier, so you know what to do. Sometimes, just spending five minutes being mindful can refocus our thoughts away from worry about the future, to all the goodness in our lives in the here and now. Incorporating mindfulness into our daily lives will take us far in maintaining a positive perspective by alleviating worry and fear, two of the biggest buzzkills when it comes to our personal outlook.
- **Joy Inventory**. Make a list of things that bring you joy. Now, pick one and do it! Even a five-minute break to dance or sing or call an old friend is enough to shift from a negative perspective to a positive perspective. Joy is a great foundation for positivity!
- **Silver Lining Search**. Every situation, event, or circumstance in our lives offers a silver lining, some element of goodness, even if it's the tiniest of bright spots in an otherwise dreary experience. You may have to dig for it, but it's there. Practice finding the blessing or silver lining in every crisis, emergency, or unpleasant situation.
- **Attitude Accountability Partner**. Holding ourselves accountable for our attitude and outlook can be done by teaming up with someone we trust (and see or speak with frequently) to gently point out when we're off base. We can even do the same for them, assuming they're interested.

If we commit to yielding to positive perspectives by practicing the techniques in this chapter, we're likely to discover that in no time at all we've developed a habit of positivity. We start expecting good things. We figure out the best way to have a good day. And more days with a consistently positive perspective is essential to the ultimate goal of creating more happiness, health and peace of mind.

Yolanda, Revisited

What if Yolanda had been able to adopt a more positive perspective toward her home-buying effort? Let's see what the outcome could've been had she leaned toward taking a "glass half full" approach. Yolanda knows she's in a competitive housing market and believes that the right home is waiting for her, if she follows the advice of real estate experts and practices patience. She views this endeavor – the largest purchase she's ever made in her life – as a fun game, one in which she knows she'll eventually win. Her realtor takes her to see three homes, one of which is appealing enough to warrant making an offer. Yolanda is nervous, so her realtor says, "If it's meant to be, I'm sure it'll all work out. And if it doesn't, that just means there's something better out there for you!" Yolanda laughs and admits that she's never thought of it that way.

A few days later, Yolanda learns that another offer came in higher than hers and she lost the house. "Okay," she tells her realtor, "I'm disappointed, but I'm going to trust in what you suggested: that there's a better home out there for me." A week later, when her realtor shows her a new listing, Yolanda is over the moon. "I love this one even more than the other one! What can I do to increase my odds of getting it?" she asks. When her realtor suggests that she include a personal letter to the owners with her offer, Yolanda immediately agrees. "Great idea!" she says. She sits down and shares stories of the fond memories she had in her childhood home and how similar this home feels to her. She names the specific details that are especially appealing to her – the deep windowsills just like the ones she used to sit in reading as a child, the long front porch, big enough to hold several rocking chairs like the ones she grew up rocking in with her grandmother. She tells the current owners that she hopes to raise her own children in this home one day, and to create the kind of happy memories she herself has of her own childhood home. Before handing the letter off the realtor, Yolanda gives it a little silent blessing.

Once the paperwork is submitted, she goes for a run, smiling at the thought that she might soon be moving into her new home. *And if not that one, then I'll know there's something even better out there for me,* she reminds herself. A few days later, her realtor calls with an update, "Well, apparently you weren't the only one who loved that home. The sellers got two additional offers, one for less, and one for more," the realtor tells her. "But guess what? They said they loved the thoughtfulness of your letter and the idea of passing along their old home to someone who would appreciate it as they had. You got the house, Yolanda!" Yolanda screams in excitement. "Awesome! I can't thank you enough!" she says with genuine gratitude. As she moves into her new home two months later, she imagines herself as an old woman, her children all grown and living lives of their own. And Yolanda vows that when the time comes for her to sell this house to its next owner, she will sell it to the person who seems most connected to it rather than to the highest bidder. She wants to offer someone else the same kindness that the previous owners offered her. That night she takes her realtor, now a friend, to dinner to thank her for helping her keep an open mind and a positive perspective.

Everything can be taken from a man but one thing: the last of the human freedoms – to choose one's attitude in any given set of circumstances, to choose one's own way.

— Viktor Frankl

❧

Intention:

I passionately and purposefully replace negative thoughts with positive ones.

Now, how about digging deeper? As a warm-up to this time for reflection, I suggest listening to "You Gotta Be" by Des'ree.

Invitation to Reflect:

How could certain situations in your life be improved with an infusion of positivity?

_____

_____

_____

_____

_____

Think about a situation that is grim, like a loss or a traumatic event. How could you put a positive spin on it, that you can buy into? Take your time with this one.

_____

_____

_____

_____

When negative thoughts arise, what is one phrase you can automatically replace it with? (Hint: mine is "Everything will work out for my highest good." Or "I am grateful for…")

_____

_____

_____

_____

_____

Here are some actions you could take now for your self-care:

○ Create a list of "go to" positive affirmations in the voice recorder or in a note on your phone. Speak the affirmation with conviction, as if it is already true. Then choose to shift your perspective.
○ Try one of the perspective-shifting techniques in this chapter and share it with a friend.
○ Think of a silver lining in a "bad" situation, event, or circumstance in your life.

Commit to doing at least one thing differently based on what you learned in this chapter. Write out an actionable goal – with a specific deadline – to satisfy this commitment.

_____

_____

_____

_____

_____

How will you celebrate or reward yourself if you reach the goal?

_____

_____

Other thoughts and reflections:

_____

_____

_____

_____

_____

_____

_____

For additional resources related to this topic, please check out my website: www.abcsofselfcare.com

𝒵

ZEALFULLY PLAY

When you can laugh, life is worth living.

— Carl Reiner

❧

To be "zealful" is to be filled with enthusiasm and energy. So, playing zealfully involves a lot of laughter. Fun and playfulness allow us to relax more and chill out! And guess what this all leads to? Being more focused, productive, and engaged overall in this thing called life. Basically, playing zealfully can lead to a much richer life, in every way.

We've likely all heard the phrase "laughter is the best medicine," which was popularized by Norman Cousins long before the mind-body connection was accepted by mainstream western medicine. Cousins was diagnosed with heart disease and later with a crippling connective tissue disease and the equally crippling ankylosing spondylitis, which came with a 1 in 500 chance of recovery. As treatments were limited, Cousins developed his own treatment plan that involved mega doses of Vitamin C and laughter through immersing himself in humorous films. Despite his doctors' prognosis, Cousins lived far longer than expected – 36 years beyond the initial discovery of his heart disease! Since Cousins' death in 1990, even more research now supports his theory that laughter could improve our immune function, mood, oxygen intake and stress resistance. It can also reduce pain and high blood pressure. It can relax us, burn calories, diffuse anger, and speed up forgiveness. Laughter has even been linked to longevity! Look no further than the queen of comedy, Betty White, who is still yucking it up at the ripe old age of 99 (as of the writing of this manuscript). And if all that weren't enough, laughter could also improve your dating prospects, as being happy and in a good mood are extremely attractive traits. Talk about a super-power! And the best news of all? Laughter is free and comes with only good side effects!

Zendaya and Zealful Play

Zendaya is gearing up for her finals in nursing school. She's always had an interest in helping others, and after caring for her mother during her time in hospice until her death, Zendaya was more motivated than ever to return to school and become a nurse. She feels this calling in her bones and has taken her courses and classwork very seriously. She's a bit stressed about her upcoming exams, so when some friends from school invite her out to blow off steam and have a few beers before they buckle down to study through the weekend, Zendaya declines. "Sorry," she tells them, "I really want to ace these finals to honor my mom." None of her friends want to argue with her about the reasons for not taking a break. Even though most of them understand that a bit of fun before they dive back into the books would be good for all of them.

They go to a local karaoke bar that's also hosting a Trivia Night, while Zendaya stays at home. By 8 pm, she's exhausted and goes to bed, chiding herself for not being able to stay awake longer. The next day when another friend invites her to take a study break and go for a quick run with her, Zendaya again declines. Her friend pushes a bit, reminding her that a bit of movement would do her well during this stressful end to her semester. Zendaya doesn't change her mind. When her sister calls that afternoon and says, "Omigod! I know you're studying, but your goofy little nephew just did something so hilarious I just had to call and share it with you!" Instead of welcoming the brief call, Zendaya snaps at her sister for not respecting her need to take these finals seriously. "Jeez, lighten up!" says her sister before hanging up the phone without sharing her anecdote.

That evening – and the next two evenings as well – Zendaya forces herself to stay awake with plenty of coffee. She blows off her regular dance class and stops answering her phone. On Tuesday morning, she is fatigued and grumpy, her mind a bit foggy from all the non-stop studying and excessive caffeine. She stares at the exam that's put before her...and her mind. goes. blank. She struggles to remember the answers to questions she knows she studied. *Dammit, Zendaya! You should know this!* she repeats to herself several times. When her professor informs the class that time is up, Zendaya looks around to see that she is one of only three students left in the classroom. And she still has a few questions she hasn't even gotten to yet. She leaves the room and goes straight to the library, forgoing a lunch break, to study more before her next final in a few hours.

Don't mess up this one! she warns herself, as she walks into the next classroom. But again, when she looks at the test, her mind turns to mush. Fearful of running out of time, she rushes through her answers, not checking her work. When she finishes the last test of her nursing program, instead of feeling joy and relief, Zendaya feels nothing but disappointment in herself. A few classmates are gathered in the hallway, all making plans to go celebrate at a local restaurant. Zendaya declines the invitation, feeling like she betrayed the memory of her mother by stumbling her way through her finals. Instead, she heads home and sits alone, hungry and upset. It is no surprise that when her test scores come back at the end of the week, Zendaya has gotten Ds on both exams.

Quick Check - Select all that apply:

☐ I have difficulty laughing at myself, especially if I make a mistake.
☐ I would be described as serious minded.
☐ I tend to frown a lot.

Look for Opportunities to Laugh and Play

Sure, life is serious and, yes, we have responsibilities. Given this, wouldn't it be more fun if we attended to our responsibilities with a little more zeal, a touch of silliness, a playful attitude?

Play + Laughter = A Better Life!

Play and laughter make dealing with the good, the bad and the just plain ugly much easier. I especially rely on humor whenever I make a mistake – I laugh it off. I also share my missteps with family or friends to share another laugh, while also subtly encouraging them to lighten up about their own mistakes. I also stay in contact with those people in my life who know how to make me laugh, as I too need reminders. We're human – never apologize for that! We mess up sometime. Laughter and play also helped me manage my own anxiety by not taking every little aspect of life so darn seriously. Even if I still get tense from time to time, playing zealfully makes all the difference in how quickly I return to my center, my equilibrium.

Dancing is how I zealfully play. Dancing can make even the most rhythmically challenged among us smile and laugh. The beauty of dancing is that we can do it just about anywhere, with others or solo, to music that's loud and fast or slow and smooth. Think of the last time you witnessed someone dancing by themselves to music you couldn't hear. You smiled, didn't you? See that? In addition to helping ourselves, dancing has an infectious way of raising the vibration and mood of others as well. Personally, I can't sit still when good dance music comes on, so I'm grateful that music isn't played in my work meetings, or I'd be reprimanded for boogying around the office! I recommend creating a good dance playlist to have on hand for those days when you're feeling low or stressed and need a fun pick-me-up. Or choose one of the songs from the playlist in this book and listen to one, or two or three on a break. Works like a charm!

Play Like a Kid

At times, it's helpful to reach back into our past and recall the many ways we played as children. What did we do for fun? What were our favorite books, movies, games? If we have kids, can we share some of those past favorites with them? If we don't have kids, we can borrow from a friend! While living in Maryland, I often borrowed my godson to engage in fun "laugh fests" on a regular basis. He is also on my "makes me laugh" list. Hanging out with children has a way of reconnecting us with our instinctual need for play. Have you ever watched young children play? They have an amazing ability to convert anything – an empty cardboard box, string, random objects – into a game. But it's not just about children's games and modes of play; it's also helpful to play adult games. A friend of mine recalls a time when her 17-year-old daughter wanted to host a game night and asked her and her husband to participate. They begrudgingly agreed (they would've preferred to read). Although, once they got into the game, they went all in! She told me she literally almost wet herself laughing, it was so fun being silly. She and her husband ended up being the ones to suggest another game night after all the fun they'd both had! Zealfully playing is not only good for our own sense of well-being, but it can also improve our connection to others, as was the case with my friend and her daughter – not to mention her daughter's friends. If you don't have friends nearby to play with, join a Meetup group with others who enjoy the types of games you do: Dominoes, Scrabble, Chess, Monopoly, Charades, Pictionary, Clue. Or maybe you are lucky enough to have something similar to Gamehaus in Glendale, CA, where you can play hundreds of board games with friends. The possibilities are endless! If you do have friends nearby, host your own game night. Sometimes, it's just the break we need from the seriousness of the world.

Think about how much fun you had as a child. Free from the responsibilities of adulthood, many of us were more curious, spontaneous, and enthusiastic back then. We smiled, giggled or flat-out belly laughed at just about anything. What happened to those silly open-hearted kids we once were? Invite them back! Research shows that the average 4-year-old laughs about 300 times a day, compared to the average 40-year-old, who only laughs about 4 times a day. What the...?! It seems that once we grow up, get a "real" job, become "important," we somehow manage to lose touch with that inner child who wants only to explore and giggle and play. We trade laughter and silliness for paychecks and business suits. But guess what? It's not a mutually exclusive choice! We can – and *should* – have both in our lives if our goal is to be well-rounded, happy, whole human beings.

I urge you, please don't trade laughter and play for anything! If we absolutely can't find something to laugh about or anything to be playful with, it may be time to reevaluate how we are spending our time and who we are spending it with. Life is too short to forgo the joys of play. Figure out a way to inject more fun into your workday, study time or chores. A client of mine was notorious for spicing up her company's annual sales meetings by writing silly product-marketing skits, dressing in costume, recruiting her CEO and other executive-team members to participate in the skits. She even snuck her dog into a fancy "pet-free" hotel to use as a prop in one of her comedic presentations. Just because it's work doesn't mean it can't be fun, silly, or playful. In fact, in the right situation, this sort of infusion of zealful play might just reap greater results. Infusing the workplace with a greater degree of laughter, fun and playfulness is a fantastic way to help improve the culture of your team or company. Be that person. Be the fun one who knows how to lighten the mood for others. Play more – with zeal!

Zendaya, Revisited

What could the outcome have been had Zendaya incorporated a bit more play into her life during finals week? Let's assume Zendaya's mother had taught her the value of incorporating laughter and play into her life, *especially* when things are stressful. When Zendaya's nursing school friends invite her to go out Friday night to blow off a bit of steam, she agrees. "But only for a few hours," she says, to which they all agree. At the karaoke bar, Zendaya is invited to get on stage and belt out a round of Gloria Gaynor's "I Will Survive" with her friends. They sing-shout at the top of their lungs, laughing themselves silly on stage. Next up, the Trivia Contest! Zendaya pulls a team together and they attempt to compete with the clearly stronger trivia teams in the room. When Zendaya shouts out several obviously wrong answers in a row, she and her friends nearly fall on the floor laughing. The nerdy (read: much better) team doesn't see the humor in Zendaya's responses – which only makes her laugh harder. Her face hurting from laughing so hard, Zendaya goes home and straight to bed.

The next morning, she awakes, puts on some old school disco at top volume and begins dancing around her apartment as she sets up her textbooks and laptop on the kitchen counter. She sets her phone alarm for two hours and gets down to the business of studying. During her study break, she takes a quick walk around the block, listening to a comedy podcast as she goes. Two more hours of studying lay ahead before her next break, during which she dances again. Her weekend continues like this, with study sessions and breaks, which also include longer breaks to go to her favorite dance class. When Zendaya wraps up her last exam on Tuesday, she is the first one to suggest they all go out to celebrate. At a local restaurant, they toast one another and cheer the end of the nursing program. And guess what? When Zendaya receives her test scores on Friday, they're both A's. *Mom would be proud*, she thinks to herself. And she would.

And the next time Zendaya and her fellow nurses return to the karaoke bar, Zendaya is just as terrible at the trivia game as she was previously. But she still laughs just as much!

The body heals with play, the mind heals with laughter and the spirit heals with joy.

– Proverb

❀

238

Intention:

I give myself permission to zealfully play.

Now, how about digging deeper? As a warm-up to this time for reflection, I suggest listening to "Happy" by Pharrell Williams.

Invitation to Reflect:

Think of a time someone made a difficult situation more fun. How did they do it?

_____

_____

_____

_____

_____

_____

_____

_____

Are there ways you could take care of the serious stuff in a more carefree manner?

_____

_____

_____

_____

_____

_____

_____

What fun activities could you add to your life right now?

_____

_____

_____

_____

_____

_____

Here are some actions you could take now for your self-care: _____

- ○ Strive to make daily chores more fun by playing music or talking with friends at the same time.
- ○ Smile more – even at strangers.
- ○ Take at least a 5 min break during your workday to dance, be silly or listen to your favorite songs.

Commit to doing at least one thing differently based on what you learned in this chapter. Write out an actionable goal – with a specific deadline – to satisfy this commitment.

_____

_____

_____

_____

_____

How will you celebrate or reward yourself if you reach the goal?

_____

_____

Other thoughts and reflections:

_____

_____

_____

_____

_____

_____

_____

_____

_____

For additional resources related to this topic, please check out my website: www.abcsofselfcare.com

WRAP UP

It is my sincere wish that the insights and stories in this book have given you, dear reader, the encouragement, and tools to integrate self-care habits more consistently and permanently into your everyday life. I hope that the material I've shared has strengthened your resolve to expect more out of life and to anticipate greater outcomes for and from yourself.

We all possess the freedom of choice, and that requires us to continuously make choices around what we want to do, need to do, and should do. It allows us to choose love over fear, courage over fear, faith over fear, action over fear – basically *anything* over fear! Former editor of *Essence*, Susan Taylor, says, "Fear is the root of insecurity that creates greed and insensitivity, it fuels racism, sexism, homophobia (all the social injustices actually), and senseless violence. It makes people disempower others to empower themselves. Nothing good comes from fear."

So please, please do not allow fear of failure – or even fear of success – to prevent you from incorporating greater levels of self-care into your lifestyle. Even baby steps in support of this goal will ultimately get you there. Self-care is like bathing: it's not a one-and-done endeavor, but rather a lifelong commitment, a marathon vs. a sprint. One choice at a time, we can choose the activities, actions and behaviors that add up to a better life. We can choose positive thoughts over negative thoughts, happiness over suffering, ourselves over other people, win-win over win-lose, gentle words over harsh words, real connection over disingenuous connections (like some social media ones). You get my drift. We get to make those choices, moment to moment, that can tip the scale toward happiness, health, and peace. We must get comfortable with going through life on *our* terms, tuning into our intuition and our bodies to see what they may be telling us, and then making choices we can be content with. We must be willing to protect our precious selves by saying *no* to someone else's idea of what we ought to be doing, to boldly say *yes* to our own needs. This is what self-care (and self-love) looks like: to keep your highest good at the heart of your many choices and actions in life.

The ancient Chinese philosopher, Lao Tzu, said it best: *Watch your thoughts, they become your words; watch your words, they become your actions; watch your actions, they become your habits; watch your habits, they become your character; watch your character, it becomes your destiny.*

I said it at the beginning of this book, but it bears repeating as we wrap up our time together: Action cures fear. American poet and activist, Amanda Gorman, put it best when she stated, "There is always light. If only we're brave enough to see it. If only we're brave enough to be it." I encourage you to *be brave*. Keep moving forward and create the life you want. Take one small action – any action – toward creating a happier, healthier, and more peaceful version of you. Do it today.

I believe in you.

I would sincerely appreciate it if you would share with me what actions you took (or are taking) after reading *The ABCs of Self-Care*. Website www.abcsofselfcare.com

I also invite you to stay in touch by joining my mailing list at (www.abcsofselfcare.com) or connecting with me on Instagram @abcsofselfcare. As a token of my appreciation, I will periodically send you information to support you on your self-care journey.

With love,

Sheri

ACKNOWLEDGEMENTS

Like any major project, this book required a village to complete, and I am forever grateful to all the villagers who made it possible! I love you all, unconditionally, and am grateful that you are always there when I need you the most.

First and foremost, I want to thank all my coaching clients and friends who were willing to be vulnerable with me, trusting me with your stories as we discussed self-care challenges. Thank you for helping me see the value in writing a book to help others develop the habits and mindsets to create a self-care lifestyle.

To my friend and book consultant extraordinaire, Lauren Ward Larsen, founder of THIA Strategic Storytelling – I am extremely grateful for your help in shaping and editing the manuscript, offering creative ideas and extensive resources, as well as putting your storytelling ability to work in creating fictional stories for each chapter. You made my vision for the book come to life! Thanks for doubling as a motivational coach, helping me stay focused as the many details of writing a book threatened to overwhelm me.

To my mentor and friend, Dr. Lois Frankel – you were an integral part of this journey from the concept phase to manuscript editing and every step in between. Thank you for contributing to the birth of my "baby" by brainstorming with me, writing the foreword, reviewing the cover design, and lending valuable resource materials from your book, *Nice Girls Don't Speak Up or Stand Out*.

To my sister, Hermione Cloney, for squeezing me into your already demanding schedule and contributing your wordsmithing superpowers and thoughtful suggestions. I am eternally grateful.

To Cori Gray at ArtHouse Graphics, the greatest cover designer I could have asked for! Thank you for your creativity, artful eye and for capturing the feel of this book in your beautiful cover design.

Heartfelt thanks to my writing group members, Susanne Walker and Deidre Johnson. We finished Cynthia James' "Women Creating Our Futures" Mastermind Group together and decided to support each other's writing goals, and you two certainly came through. You were invaluable as accountability partners, reality checkers, and advice givers throughout the entire process.

For those who read early drafts and gave me feedback, I am so grateful! Your input made such a difference in the direction of this book. Jackie Reed, you were a constant cheerleader from the first time I shared the concept with you. Thank you for going through the manuscript with a fine-toothed comb and, with your artistically inclined husband, Lambert Mathieu, recommending inspirational songs for the Self-Care Playlist. Billy (Chris) Bland, you gave me invaluable feedback on the manuscript and self-care questionnaire. You were also so patient with me asking for song recommendations, no matter how many times I called on you. I learned a lot from both of you special people in my life.

To my psychologist friends who made sure I didn't confuse readers as I simplified psychological lingo and questionnaire design, I'm so grateful for your expertise: Denise Wolfe, Ph.D., Julie Jackson, PsyD, Princess Walsh, PsyD, Zariah "Tiffany" Horton, MFT, and Delecia Ellers, Ph.D. Since I have only an "armchair psychology degree" earned by reading a gazillion self-help books, attending trainings, and getting help from therapists, hypnotherapists, and coaches, your insights were particularly valuable in bringing this book to life.

I'm so grateful for other friends and family members who contributed by sharing personal experiences, reading early drafts, and giving me advice on specific elements of the manuscript. Thank you, Zayd Abdul Karim Ph.D. ("Dr. Z"), Linda Johnson, Zee Najarian, April Betts, Natashia Betts, Gracey Lee, Celeste Day Drake, and Vanestra Myers. You were all vital contributors to the rich content of this book.

Also high on my list to thank are two other sisters. Kat Wilson, you continually encouraged me to keep going and shared with me the important lessons gleaned from publishing your book, *Breaking Barriers: Empowering Relationships Between Mothers and Daughters*. Marcia Thompson, you supported me by keeping me fed with delicious, healthy food and basically doing almost whatever I needed to lighten my load so I could focus on birthing this baby.

To my friends and colleagues in The Black Women Scholars and Practitioners Collective (BWSPC): Gena Davis, Ph.D., Desiree Saddler, Donna Winfrey, Teressa Moore Griffin, Amber Mays, Argentine Craig, Ph.D., and Stephanie Shipp, Ph.D. You have all been a tremendous support, both personally and professionally, throughout this process – more than you know. Thank you.

I give to Reverend Pam McGregor and my spiritual community at the Science of Mind Spiritual Center in Los Angeles my deepest gratitude. Thank you for the practical insights, classes, moral support, and friendships that have greatly impacted my spiritual journey.

Much gratitude to Ted Moreno, Certified Hypnotherapist, who, as my success coach, transformed my life over the last six years. You made it possible for me to believe this book could come to life and helped me create a life that is happy, healthy, peaceful, and – most of all – fulfilling. I am also grateful to Emma Dietrich, Certified Hypnotherapist. Thank you for guiding me to make further shifts in my consciousness that were helpful as I attended to my own self-care while completing this book.

Many thanks to Damian Goldvarg of Goldvarg Consulting Group for helping me refine my skills as a certified coach, so that I can fulfill my mission of helping others create better lives.

Grateful for my meditation group, Better Together. Because like-minded people came together to meditate on positive messages and affirmations, we changed ourselves and the people around us. Thanks to you all for taking the 31-Day Self-Care Adventure and to Rose Catherine Pinkney for bringing us all together.

Thank you, Anisa Rashad, President of ARE Global Solutions, who gave me the coaching opportunity of a lifetime, for which I am eternally grateful.

Last but certainly not least, special thanks to the Hay House Writer's Community moderators, Reid Tracy and Kelly Notaras. Your guidance was extremely valuable during my writing process. To Michael March, the ever-patient Publishing Coordinator at Balboa Press (a division of Hay House), thank you for having the skill to pry the manuscript from my hands. Without your gentle nudging, I would likely be making improvements for years to come. The need for self-care is greater than ever, so many thanks to everyone at Balboa Press for helping me bring my message to the world.

APPENDIX A | SELF-CARE QUESTIONNAIRE

You can choose to read this book in alphabetical order or prioritize certain chapters. This questionnaire is designed to help you discover the self-care areas that would benefit from your immediate attention vs. ones that you can work on later. Read each statement and decide if it fits best in the True or False category. Pick the answer that most fits right now. Quickly decide if it is True most of the time or not and put a check mark in the corresponding box.

This is for your eyes only or to share with your Accountability Partner. The quality of your results will depend on how honest you are when answering. Do your best to answer quickly and not overanalyze the statements. Go with your first instinct.

Emotional	True	False
I often compare myself to others then feel despair.		
I often feel inadequate as a spouse, parent, friend, sibling, coach, or leader.		
I often have trouble making minor decisions without input from a trusted advisor.		
I often feel hurt by negative comments received on social media.		
I often bring up the same stories over and over, both to myself and to others, with the same amount of feeling attached, as if it occurred yesterday.		
I feel like I'm stuck in a cycle of victimhood – to people, circumstances, and outcomes.		
I review my work over and over to make sure everything is of the highest quality.		
I am often stuck and do nothing toward achieving my dreams, fearing imperfect results.		
I like to have control over processes and outcomes in life.		
I would say that my coping strategies for anxiety need improvement.		

Practical	True	False
I often stay busy and seldom take time to think about my life.		
I want a different life, but I seem to keep doing the same things I've always done.		
I often procrastinate about doing my self-care practices.		
I often avoid asking for help to handle my responsibilities.		
I often say I don't have time for self-care.		
I feel like I am constantly fighting fires.		
I have no idea how much money I have left over each month after my bills are paid.		
If my car, or another major asset, needs unexpected repairs or if I incur an unexpected major medical bill, I would be financially devastated.		

Physical	True	False
I have difficulty sticking to intentions/goals/New Year's resolutions.		
I am not sure what to do or where to start for better self-care.		
I usually don't pay much attention to minor health issues.		
I am often sick or already have a major illness.		
I often find myself emotionally closing off from people.		
I am not used to exhibiting affection in my family.		

Mental	True	False
I second guess my choices – especially if I don't like the way a situation turned out.		
I often say I *should, ought to*, or *have to* do things in a certain way.		
I am often willing to volunteer my time for a good cause, even if my life is already busy.		
I often do things for people who can do it themselves (personally and professionally) because it makes me feel good about myself; in fact, I depend on this feeling.		
I am more concerned with being nice than with being assertive in my requests.		
I say "sorry" way too much – even if I haven't done anything wrong.		
I'm often rushing to and from places.		
I often react badly if things don't go as planned.		
I often shame, blame, or criticize myself and/or others.		
I often imagine the worst possible thing happening.		

Social	True	False
I'm a people pleaser (aka, the "disease to please"), sometimes to the extreme.		
I've set aside my own challenges that require extra attention (e.g., preparing for a move, working through grief, staying focused during a busy period at work) to help others with less pressing needs.		
I often hold grudges.		
I have lingering anger, bitterness, and/or resentment over past hurts.		
I like making others happy, even if, at times, it is inconvenient.		
I often say yes to something even if I'm exhausted.		
I have difficulty maintaining healthy friendships and/or romantic relationships.		
I am estranged from one or more family members.		
I am not entirely sure what my needs are.		
I prefer to avoid conflict in relationships even if it means I go without something that is important to me.		
I have difficulty laughing at myself, especially if I make a mistake.		
I don't often make time for fun activities.		
Spiritual	True	False
I often feel as if nothing good happens to me.		
I often take things/people for granted.		
I often feel like I'm in this world alone without support.		
I believe religion is the same as spirituality.		
I am often critical of others.		
My love for others is sometimes tied to how they behave.		

Prioritize

The first self-care habit is to Act on Awareness and Acceptance. Therefore, when you have completed the entire questionnaire, become *aware* of the self-care categories that are your strengths and those that are your opportunities for improvement. First, reflect on your self-care strengths (all the False answers) and give yourself a pat on the back (literally) for making choices and taking action for your self-care. Next, reflect on your self-care opportunities (all the True answers). It is ok to have a few or many – *accept* this is as true based on where you are now. Give yourself another pat on the back (literally) for making choices and taking action to improve your self-care by reading this book. Finally, *act* – prioritize the self-care categories in the chart below based on your questionnaire responses and your gut instinct on which ones feel the most urgent. Your first priority category may or may not be the one with the most True responses. Once you've ranked the six self-care categories, write each priority number in the corresponding panel on the second chart. This will help you keep track of which chapters support a category.

I recommend reading or exploring the chapters associated with your top 3 self-care categories first. Then you can move into the chapters associated with your bottom 3 categories. Alternatively, you can simply read this book in chronological order without skipping around. Remember, the right approach is the one that works best for *you*. The key is to practice the self-care suggestions offered in each chapter. Your happiness, health and peace of mind depend on it!

Self-Care Priorities

1.	
2.	
3.	
4.	
5.	
6.	

Self-Care Categories and Related Chapters	
Emotional • **E**mbrace Enough-ness • **I**nternally Validate • **M**ake Peace with your Past • **P**revent Perfectionism • **T**ame Anxiety	**Practical** • **A**ct on Awareness and Acceptance • **J**ust Start • **Q**uestion Your Time Management • **W**atch Your Wallet
Physical • **D**iscipline Yourself • **L**isten to Your Body • **X**OXO: Kiss(O) and Hug (X) Often	**Mental** • **C**hoose Wisely • **H**ave Healthy Self-Advocacy • **K**eep your Power • **R**educe Stress • **Y**ield to Positive Perspectives
Social • **B**uild Boundaries • **F**orgive • **N**-O is Your New Y-E-S • **O**bserve Relationships • **V**oice your Needs	**Spiritual** • **G**row with Gratitude • **S**urrender to Spiritual Practices • **U**nconditionally Love • **Z**ealfully Play

APPENDIX B | SELF-CARE RESOURCES

Letter A: Act on Awareness and Acceptance

Root Cause Analysis (5 Whys System) ① Worksheet

Use one worksheet for each challenge. In the spaces below, answer the question: *Why is this a challenge?* When you get that answer, ask *Why?* again and build on the last answer given. (See example in Letter A.) By asking the question *Why?* for each of the previous answers given, you drill down to the essence of a challenge. Keep asking *Why?* until you feel you have reached the root cause of each challenge. You may need to ask the question more than 5 times. Focus on *you* and your actions and feelings – not others and their actions) – during this exercise. Consider seeking assistance from a professional therapist or coach to facilitate the exercise for several challenges.

①Root cause analysis is often used in business to solve challenges at the root level as opposed to symptoms. It is an excellent way to reflect on challenges you face in developing a self-care mindset and lifestyle.

Challenge: _____

WHY?

WHY?

WHY?

WHY?

WHY?

Action I Will Take

Letter A: Core Values List (from www.JamesClear.com and The LeaderShape Institute)

I recommend that you circle all the values that resonate with you, ones you care about. Then pick no more than 10 as your Core Values.

Authenticity	Fame	Peace
Achievement	Friendships	Pleasure
Adventure	Fun	Poise
Authority	Growth	Popularity
Autonomy	Happiness	Recognition
Balance	Honesty	Religion
Beauty	Humor	Reputation
Boldness	Influence	Respect
Compassion	Inner Harmony	Responsibility
Challenge	Justice	Security
Citizenship	Kindness	Self-Respect
Community	Knowledge	Service
Competency	Leadership	Spirituality
Contribution	Learning	Stability
Creativity	Love	Success
Curiosity	Loyalty	Status
Determination	Meaningful Work	Trustworthiness
Fairness	Openness	Wealth

Letter M: Make Peace with Your Past

Get to the Love - Letter Format

Dear_____ (Add person's name, even if it is your own)

<u>Anger and Blame</u>

I hate it when _____

I don't like it when _____

You make me mad when _____

I am fed up with _____

<u>Hurt and Sadness</u>

I feel sad when _____

I feel hurt when _____

I feel awful when _____

I feel disappointed because _____

<u>Fear</u>

I'm afraid that _____

I feel scared because _____

I feel afraid because _____

Guilt

I am guilty for _____

I am sorry that _____

Please forgive me for _____

I didn't mean to _____

Love, Gratitude, and Forgiveness

I love you because _____

I love you when _____

Thank you for _____

I understand that _____

I forgive you for _____

I appreciate you when _____

I want _____

Letter V: Voice Your Needs

Universal Human Needs – Partial List

(Without reference to specific people, time, actions, things)

Subsistence and Security	Connection	Meaning	Freedom
Physical Sustenance	*Affection*	*Sense of Self*	*Autonomy*
Air	Appreciation	Authenticity	Choice
Food	Attention	Competence	Ease
Health	Closeness	Creativity	Independence
Movement	Companionship	Dignity	Power
Physical Safety	Harmony	Growth	Self-Responsibility
Rest/Sleep	Intimacy	Healing	Space
Shelter	Love	Honesty	Spontaneity
Touch	Nurturing	Integrity	
Water	Sexual Expression	Self-acceptance	
	Support	Self-care	
	Tenderness	Self-connection	
	Warmth	Self-knowledge	
		Self-realization	
		Mattering to myself	
Security	*To Matter*	*Understanding*	*Leisure/Relaxation*
Consistency	Acceptance	Awareness	Humor
Order/Structure	Care	Clarity	Joy
Peace (external)	Compassion	Discovery	Play
Peace of Mind	Consideration	Learning	Pleasure
Protection	Empathy	Making sense of life	Rejuvenation
Safety (emotional)	Kindness	Stimulation	
Stability	Mutual Recognition		
Trusting	Respect	*Meaning*	
	To be heard, seen	Aliveness	
	To be known, understood	Challenge	
	To be trusted	Consciousness	
	Understanding others	Contribution	

Subsistence and Security	Connection	Meaning	Freedom
		Creativity	
		Effectiveness	
		Exploration	
		Integration	
		Purpose	

Community	Transcendence
Belonging	Beauty
Communication	Celebration of life
Cooperation	Communion
Equality	Faith
Inclusion	Flow
Mutuality	Hope
Participation	Inspiration
Partnership	Mourning
Self-expression	Peace (internal)
Sharing	Presence

What are your Top 10 Needs? Circle them.   Today's Date _____

This list builds on Marshall Rosenberg's original needs list with categories adapted from Manfred Max-Neef. Neither exhaustive nor definitive, it can be used for study and for discovery about each person's authentic experience.

©2014 Inbal, Miki and Arnina Kashtan • nvc@baynvc.org
• www.baynvc.org • 510-433-0700

Letter V: Voice Your Needs

Worksheets for preparing to speak in "headlines"

HEADLINE COMMUNICATION*

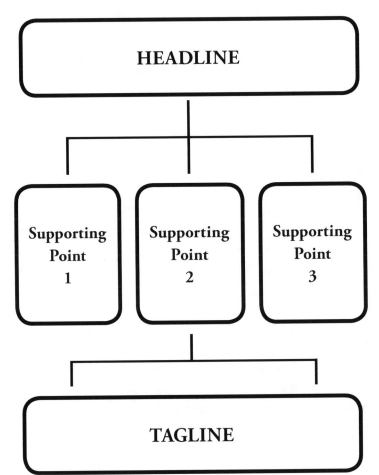

HEADLINE COMMUNICATION*

(Worksheet)

HEADLINE

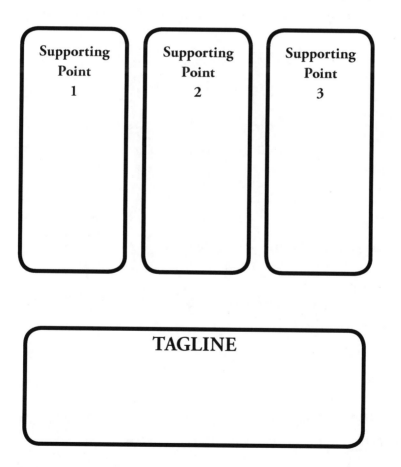

| Supporting Point 1 | Supporting Point 2 | Supporting Point 3 |

TAGLINE

---

* From Dr. Lois Frankel, *Nice Girls Don't Speak up or Stand Out.* For more information contact Lois at www.drloisfrankel.com.

Letter V: Voice Your Needs

THE DESCript*

D = Describe the Purpose of the Conversation

I'd like to talk to you about something that happened in our meeting yesterday.

E = Explain Your Position and Elicit Feedback from the Other Person

I observed that each time I took the floor to speak, you started texting and checking e-mails. It made me feel that what I had to say wasn't important enough for your full attention. I'm wondering if you understand what I'm saying and how you see the situation? (Now simply listen without agreeing or arguing.)

S = Specify Desired Outcomes

OK. I understand what you're saying. What I would really appreciate is if you would not only listen to what I'm saying, but also comment on it. You have a lot of knowledge and I have no doubt your input would be valuable to me.

C = Clarify Consequences (Positive or Negative)

Positive

I think if we can better support one another in this way, we would both get a lot out of it and the department would be better for it.

Negative

We can't seem to agree on how to move forward on this issue. I can only tell you that without mutual support, the end product won't have the same quality as if we did.

---

* Developed by Sharon and Gordon Bower

THE DESCript: YOUR TURN

(Print Copies of This Chart for Future Use)

D = Describe the Purpose of the Conversation

E = Explain Your Position and Elicit Feedback from the Other Person

S = Specify Desired Outcomes

C = Clarify Consequences (Positive or Negative)

Positive

Negative

APPENDIX C | SELF-CARE PLAYLIST

Chapter	Song	Artist
A - Act on Awareness and Acceptance	Scars to Your Beautiful	Alessia Cara
B - Build Boundaries	Me Time	Heather Headley
C - Choose Wisely	My Wish	Rascal Flatts
D - Discipline Yourself	Rise Up	Andra Day
E - Embrace Enough-ness	You Say	Lauren Daigle
F - Forgive	Forgiveness	Matthew West
G - Grow with Gratitude	Grateful: A Love Song to the World	Nimo Patel – Featuring Daniel Nahmod
H - Have Healthy Self-Advocacy	Man in the Mirror	Michael Jackson
I - Internally Validate	This is Me	Keala Settle
J - Just Start	Never Give Up	Sia
K - Keep Your Power	No Playing Small	Fearless Soul
L - Listen to Your Body	Move Your Body	Beyoncé
M - Make Peace with Your Past	Let It Go	Idina Menzel
N - N-O Is Your New Y-E-S	N-O Is My New Yes!	Karen Drucker & John Hoy
O - Observe Relationships	ROAR	Katy Perry
P – Prevent Perfectionism	Imperfect Is the New Perfect	Caitlin Crosby
Q - Question Your Time Management	Eye of the Tiger	Survivor
R - Reduce Stress	Conga	Gloria Estefan and Miami Sound Machine

S - Surrender to Spiritual Practices	Pocket Full of Sunshine	Natasha Bedingfield
T - Tame Anxiety	Don't Worry Be Happy	Bobby McFerrin
U - Unconditionally Love	The Greatest Love of All	Whitney Houston
V - Voice Your Needs	Brave	Sarah Bareilles
W - Watch Your Wallet	Money is Coming to Me	Eddie Watkins, Jr.
X - XOXO - Kiss (X) and Hug (O) Often	XOXOXO	Black Eyed Peas
Y - Yield to Positive Perspectives	You Gotta Be	Des'ree
Z - Zealfully Play	Happy	Pharrell Williams

Printed in the United States
by Baker & Taylor Publisher Services